Architecture
Space of Flows

Presenting a collection of exploratory ideas, this book offers an understanding of buildings, people and settlements through concepts of flow. Flows make buildings work; indeed flows make things in general work, including settlements, machines and people. We need there to be a flow of nourishment, of energy and water. Building materials flow from quarries into buildings – in the case of steel and glass, a flow of energy takes them into a molten stage. Eventually they erode into dust. Energy is produced from flows of material – oil, water, wind – and work is turned into liquid assets.

The metaphorical term 'the space of flows' was coined by the sociologist Manuel Castells who used it to express the instantaneous electronic flow of capital around the world markets. In recent years there has been a huge growth in interest in various aspects of fluidity in architecture and urban planning. This book addresses this rising topic and the interest in processes that flow across traditional boundaries from the person to the building, from the sense of self to the settlement, from economics to identity.

The most important thing that the book does is to re-focus our attention on the idea of flow and its pervasive importance. This is a corrective in a culture that has traditionally given a high value to the perfection of form. Form is easier to pin down and measure, easier to talk about, but flows are what makes things work, and even the most compelling of forms is redundant if it does not connect with the flows that give it a role.

Andrew Ballantyne is Professor of Architecture at Newcastle University, UK. His books include *What is Architecture?*, *Deleuze and Guattari for Architects* and *Architecture Theory*.

Chris L. Smith is an Associate Professor in Architectural Design and Techné and is an Associate Dean of the Faculty of Architecture at the University of Sydney. His research is concerned with the interdisciplinary nexus of philosophy, biology and architectural theory.

Architecture in the Space of Flows

Edited by Andrew Ballantyne and Chris L. Smith

LONDON AND NEW YORK

First published 2012
by Routledge
2 Park Square, Milton Park, Abingdon, Oxon, OX14 4RN

Simultaneously published in the USA and Canada
by Routledge
711 Third Avenue, New York, NY 10017

Routledge is an imprint of the Taylor & Francis Group, an informa business

© 2012 selection and editorial material,
Andrew Ballantyne and Chris L. Smith; individual chapters, the contributors

The right of the editor to be identified as the author of the editorial material, and of the authors for their individual chapters, has been asserted in accordance with sections 77 and 78 of the Copyright, Designs and Patents Act 1988.

All rights reserved. No part of this book may be reprinted or reproduced or utilised in any form or by any electronic, mechanical, or other means, now known or hereafter invented, including photocopying and recording, or in any information storage or retrieval system, without permission in writing from the publishers.

British Library Cataloguing in Publication Data
A catalogue record for this book is available from the British Library

Library of Congress Cataloging-in-Publication Data
Architecture in the space of flows / edited by Andrew Ballantyne and Chris Smith.
 p. cm.
 Includes bibliographical references and index.
 1. Architecture—Philosophy. 2. Architecture and society. I. Ballantyne, Andrew.
 II. Smith, Chris (Chris L.)
 NA2500.A7346 2012
 720.1—dc22
 2011009476

ISBN13: 978–0–415–58541–5 (hbk)
ISBN13: 978–0–415–58542–2 (pbk)

Typeset in Univers by Swales & Willis Ltd, Exeter, Devon

Printed and bound in Great Britain by
TJ International Ltd, Padstow, Cornwall

To Emily Apter, Brian Massumi, Erin Manning and Anthony Vidler

Contents

List of Figures	ix
Illustration Credits	xiii
Author Biographies	xv
Acknowledgements	xxi

1 Fluxions 1
Andrew Ballantyne and Chris L. Smith

Part One: Places in Flux 41

2 Theoretical, Conceptual, Ethical and Methodological Stakes to Induce a New Age: M.U.D. 43
Marc Godts and Nel Janssens

3 Oceanic Spaces of Flow 63
Amanda Yates

4 Interpretive Flow: A 1930s Trans-Cultural Architectural Nexus 81
Åsa Andersson

5 Solar Flow: The Uses of Light in Gold Coast Living 99
Patricia Wise

6 Trade Flow: Architectures of Informal Markets 117
Peter Mörtenböck and Helge Mooshammer

7 Local Flows: Rom-Hoob's Phenomena of Transition 135
Soranart Sinuraibhan

Part Two: Spaces of Flow 145

8 Controlling Flow: On the Logistics of Distributive Space 147
Craig Martin

9 Temporal Flows 161
Steve Basson

Contents

10 Navigating Flow: Architecture of the Blogosphere   179
Wael Salah Fahmi

11 The (Not So) Smooth Flow Between Architecture and Life   199
Stephen Loo

Part Three: Envoi   215

12 Limits of Fluxion   217
Michael Tawa

    Index   239

List of Figures

Chapter 1

1.1	A nautilus at home.	11
1.2	Striated plantation, Boh tea, Cameron Highlands, Malaysia.	25

Chapter 2

2.1	A pleasant moment in time: M.U.D as Ambient Information and Cognition System.	44
2.2	A pleasant moment in time: M.U.D as Ambient Information and Cognition System.	45
2.3	A pleasant moment in time: M.U.D as Ambient Information and Cognition System.	46
2.4	67km of Belgian coastline.	49
2.5	An enormous number of little things.	51
2.6	Not grouped in layers but like pixels.	51
2.7	Their signal depending on resolution.	53
2.8	Pixels redefining constantly.	54
2.9	Time/place/network related traces and a proactive memory about what you are going to be next.	56
2.10	A possible moment in time.	57
2.11	Close up of the artist's impression made as flemish tapestry of 8.40 m by 6.20 m.	59
2.12	Close up of the artist's impression made as flemish tapestry of 8.40 m by 6.20 m.	60
2.13	Close up of the artist's impression made as flemish tapestry of 8.40 m by 6.20 m.	61

Chapter 3

3.1	Early morning, Tokatea, Coromandel Peninsula: open phase.	65
3.2	Ground House: articulated concrete landscape.	72
3.3	Ground House: recessed interior.	72
3.4	Sounds House: interior–exterior field.	74
3.5	Sounds House: open phase.	74
3.6	Sounds House: open phase.	75
3.7	Tokatea: open phase with concrete landscape.	75
3.8	Tokatea: articulated landscape.	76
3.9	Tokatea: open phase, dining zone.	77
3.10	Tokatea: site and landscape.	78

List of Figures

Chapter 4

4.1 From Elsa Beskow, *Ocka, Nutte och Pillerill*. (Cropped, original in colour.) © Elsa Beskow. 82
4.2 Summer cottage by Georg Scherman. ©Åsa Andersson 2010. 83
4.3 Ground floor plan by Georg Scherman (cropped). Photographer: Matti Östling. ©Arkitekturmuseet. 83
4.4 Sliding glass door in Kyoto (Higashiyama area). ©Åsa Andersson 2003. 85
4.5 From the collection after Georg Scherman. View of the ground floor 'open-air room' (*friluftsrum*) and probably the family Hill, to whom Scherman was related. Photographer: unknown. ©Arkitekturmuseet. 86
4.6 Summer cottage by Georg Scherman. View of the ground floor 'open-air room' (*friluftsrum*) with the added sliding glass doors (a drawing for these doors is dated 1959). ©Åsa Andersson 2007. 86
4.7 The *machiai*, *tsukubai* and garden of the old Zui-Ki-Tei teahouse at Etnografiska Museet in Stockholm. ©Åsa Andersson 2007. 87
4.8 Details from the summer cottage by Georg Scherman. ©Åsa Andersson 2007–2010. 89
4.9 The pond garden at Asakura Choso Museum, Yanaka, Tokyo. ©Åsa Andersson 2007. 91
4.10 Summer cottage by Georg Scherman. Photographer: unknown. ©Arkitekturmuseet. 93
4.11 Summer cottage by Georg Scherman. Photographer: unknown. ©Arkitekturmuseet. 93
4.12 Details from the summer cottage by Georg Scherman. ©Åsa Andersson 2010. 95
4.13 Details from the summer cottage by Georg Scherman. ©Åsa Andersson 2010. 96

Chapter 5

5.1 Gold Coast City from Q1 – view to north. Image: Creative Commons (this file is licensed under the Creative Commons Attribution ShareAlike licence versions 2.5, 2.0 and 1.0). 100
5.2 One of Q1's 'enclosed' balconies. Image: used with permission of Sunland Group Ltd. 106
5.3 View to the south-east from Circle. Image and text: Circle sales brochure, used with permission of Sunland Group Ltd. 107
5.4 Circle interior. Image: Circle sales brochure, used with permission of Sunland Group Ltd. 110
5.5 Q1's 'crown'; dining facilities, observation deck and upper floors. Image: Sunland Group Annual Report, 2006, used with permission of Sunland Group Ltd. 112

List of Figures

Chapter 6

6.1 and 6.2 Arizona Market along the Arizona Corridor near Brčko,
Bosnia and Herzegovina, August 2006. 120
All images: © Peter Mörtenböck & Helge Mooshammer. 122
6.3 and 6.4 Istanbul Topkapı, informal market along the Byzantine
city walls, October 2005. 124,125
6.5 'The Russian Court' at the Vernisazh complex, Moscow Izmailovo,
June 2008. 126
6.6 Cherkizovsky Market surrounding the former Stalinets Stadium,
Moscow Izmailovo, June 2006. 129

Chapter 7

7.1 Aerial photograph of Samut Songkhram. The railway track is
transformed into a footpath, defining a corridor through the
market. Source: www.pointasia.com (accessed 8 June 2007);
photograph by Sinuraibhan. 137
7.2 Rom-Hoob Market and surrounding area. The market begins near
Mae-Klong station and stretches down along the railway track. It
terminates at the other end of the main road.
Source: www.pointasia.com (accessed 9 June 2007). 138
7.3 A sequence showing the market space in transformation
(left to right). Six times a day, the space within Rom-Hoob Market
is converted from a busy market to an empty corridor where the
train can pass through. The train is an ALSTHOM 4201-4203 model
(Width: 2.80 metres, Height: 3.88 metres, Length:
168 metres x 5–7 bogies, Maximum Operating Speed: 95 km/h).
Source: Sinuraibhan. 139
7.4 Variety of market stalls. (1) Lightweight goods are placed on small
tables or laid on the floor. (2) Portable stands assembled from a
piece of wood and metal stands. (3) Stands with wheels are more
convenient to move. (4) Heavy goods are placed on bigger tables
(wheels attached). (5) Meats and household products need a big,
strong table but must be able to move easily when the train
comes. Source: Sinuraibhan. 140
7.5 Building a sunshade. Materials: A tent sheet, a bamboo or metal
pole, ropes, or whatever is found on site and enables construction.
Performance capacity: It can be collapsed by 1–2 people and
stretched out up to 2 metres in length and lifted up to
2–3 metres high.
Important: The structure must be able to close or move quickly
when the train passes through the market, and the stand should
be able to be dismantled and slid in and out easily.
Notes: No skill or technical knowledge required.
Source: Sinuraibhan. 140

List of Figures

7.6 Supporting structure. The whole structure of the sunshade is supported by two wooden or metal sticks which are designed to sit on the column. Ropes and other equipment ensuring structural integrity are applied. Source: Sinuraibhan. 141

7.7 Rom-Hoob Market, where the everyday space is enfolded. Source: Sinuraibhan. 141

Chapter 10

10.1 Photoblogs of street demonstrations – Midan al Tahrir (Liberation Square). Source: Fahmi, 2006. 191

10.2 Video stills (vlogs) of street demonstrations – Midan al Tahrir. Source: Fahmi, 2006. 192

10.3 Photoblogs of sit-in – Unions' Street: Judges' Club. Source: Fahmi, 2006. 193

Chapter 12

12.1 untitled #1, Tawa. 217
12.2 untitled #2, Tawa. 218
12.3 untitled #3, Tawa. 219
12.4 untitled #4, Tawa. 220
12.5 untitled #5, Tawa. 221
12.6 untitled #6, Tawa. 222
12.7 untitled #7, Tawa. 223
12.8 untitled #8, Tawa. 224
12.9 untitled #9, Tawa. 225
12.10 untitled #10, Tawa. 226
12.11 untitled #11, Tawa. 227
12.12 untitled #12, Tawa. 228
12.13 untitled #13, Tawa. 229
12.14 untitled #14, Tawa. 230
12.15 untitled #15, Tawa. 231

Illustration Credits

The authors and publishers gratefully acknowledge the following for permission to reproduce material in the book. Every effort has been made to contact and acknowledge copyright owners. The publishers would be grateful to hear from any copyright holder who is not acknowledged here and will undertake to rectify any errors or omissions in future printings or editions of the book.

Arkitekturmuseet, Stockholm
Asakura Choso Museum, Yanaka, Tokyo
Elsa Beskow
Creative Commons
FLC extended
National Geographic
Matti Östling
Pointasia.com
Georg Scherman
Sunland Group Ltd.

Author Biographies

Åsa Andersson
Åsa Andersson works across images, site-related art installations and prose-poetic text projects. She holds a PhD in Fine Art and Philosophy: *Intimations of Intimacy; Phenomenological Encounters Between Contemporary Art & Philosophy*, Staffordshire University, 1999. Relating to this are interests in language, expanded photographic practices, fragile constructions, modernist/contemporary art and architecture, and Japanese aesthetics, such as intuited in Noh theatre and the tea ceremony. Recent activities include the *Nagasawa Art Park Artist-in-Residence* programme in Japanese water-based woodblock printmaking, on Awaji Island, Japan. Åsa is based in Stockholm, Sweden, where she acts as a 0.5 Research Coordinator at Kungl. Konsthögskolan (Royal Institute of Art, KKH). She also drives buses and undertakes practice-based PhD supervision at the School of Contemporary Art and Graphic Design at Leeds Metropolitan University, UK. Previously she has contributed to a children's philosophy/photography project, *Ta(l)king Pictures*.

Andrew Ballantyne
Andrew Ballantyne is Professor of Architecture at Newcastle University, UK. He has written widely on architecture and identity, and his books include *What is Architecture?* (2002), *Architecture Theory* (2005) and *Deleuze for Architects* (2007). His *Architecture: A Very Short Introduction* (2003) has been translated into 20 languages, and is now available with more illustrations as *Architecture: Brief Insight* (2010). He has chaired the Society of Architectural Historians of Great Britain and his historical studies include *Architecture, Landscape and Liberty* (1997), *Architecture as Experience* (2005), *Paliochora on Kythera: Survey and Interpretation* (2008), *Rural and Urban: Architecture Between Two Cultures* (2004), *Tudoresque: In Search of the Ideal Home* (2011) and *Key Historical Buildings* (2012).

Steve Basson
Dr Steve Basson is an Associate Professor in Architectural History and Theory in the Department of Architecture and Interior Architecture, Curtin University. His research is in the area of historical, theoretical and perceptual relationships of architectural and urban space. In particular, his research and many publications have concentrated on the philosophy and theory of architectural history; with the social, cultural, political and psychological relationships that impact upon the identity, use, perception and design of architectural and urban space; and upon those strategies and rationalities of power that impact upon the use, organization and necessity of various architectural and urban forms. He is currently the School of Built Environment's Chair and Coordinator of Research and Creative Production; Director of the Built

Environment Research Unit, Curtin University; and editor of *Reflections: Journal of Built Environment Research.*

Wael Salah Fahmi

Wael Salah Fahmi was trained as an architect at Cairo University and received his PhD in Planning and Landscape from the University of Manchester (UK). He teaches architecture and urban design as an Associate Professor of Urbanism at the Architecture Department, Helwan University in Cairo. On the one hand, through his studio Urban Design Experimental Research Studio (UDERS) Wael explores deconstructive experimentation within urban spaces, postmodern spatiality and representation of city imaging employing narratives, digital photo imaging, video stills and architectural diagrams. On the other hand, as a visiting academic at the University of Manchester, Wael has been undertaking joint research on Greater Cairo's urban growth problems and housing crisis. Further research focuses on the rehabilitation of historical Cairo, the informal cemetery settlements, and garbage collectors' community. Recent publications cover subjects such as street movements within Cairo's public spaces (*Environment and Urbanization*) and Cairo's nineteenth- and early twentieth-century contested European Quarter and architectural heritage (*International Development Planning Review*).

Marc Godts

Marc Godts has been involved in independent architectural practice since 1984. Experimental work includes *Work in Dimension Zero*, 1992 and ongoing. He is a teacher at Sint-Lucas School of Architecture, Brussels; initiator of the EXPLORATIVE architecture masters trajectory and the BY DESIGN FOR DESIGN research training session; and co-initiator of the CALIBRATING master lab. He is also the founder of the free association of designers FLC extended (FLC being short for fucklecorbusier). Marc has been working on collectivity and on spaces of limit and future conflicts. He is currently conducting artistic research in the field of architecture, as doctoral candidate at the IVOK (Instituut voor Onderzoek in de Kunsten/Institute for Artistic Research), Sint-Lucas School of Architecture, in association with K.U. Leuven, on the topic of 'KILLSPACE'.

Nel Janssens

Nel Janssens is an architect/spatial planner, teaching at the Sint-Lucas School of Architecture, Brussels and Ghent (www.sintlucas.be). She worked as an architect at T.O.P.office/Luc Deleu in Antwerp. Currently she conducts doctoral research at Chalmers University of Technology, Göteborg, and the Sint-Lucas School of Architecture. The topic of her thesis is 'Projective Research in Urbanism'. She co-edited the book *Transdisciplinary Knowledge Production in Architecture and Urbanism: Towards Hybrid Modes of Inquiry* (Springer Publishers) together with Isabelle Doucet.

Stephen Loo

Dr Stephen Loo is Professor of Architecture at the School of Architecture and Design, University of Tasmania. He has published widely on the spatiality of language, affect and the biophilosophy of the contemporary subject, which includes ethico-aesthetic models for human action, posthumanist ethics and experimental digital thinking. His current research interest is the connections between space, psychoanalysis and the entomological imagination. Stephen is a practising architect and Founding Partner of architectural, design and interpretation practice Mulloway Studio.

Craig Martin
Craig Martin is Senior Lecturer at the School of Media and Culture, University for the Creative Arts, UK, where he teaches design theory. He is also a PhD candidate in the Department of Geography at Royal Holloway, University of London. His research revolves around corporeal/non-corporeal mobilities, spatial theories and materialities. Recent and forthcoming articles include 'Legitimating Movement: The Organisational Forces of Contemporary Time-Space', in *Nonsite to Celebration Park: Essays on Art and the Politics of Space*, edited by Ed Whittaker and Alex Landrum, (Bath Spa University, 2008) and 'Turbulent Stillness: The Politics of Uncertainty and the Undocumented Migrant', in *Stillness in a Mobile World*, edited by David Bissell and Gillian Fuller (Routledge, 2010). He is also the co-editor (with Judith Rugg) of *Spatialities: Geographies of Art and Architecture* (Intellect, forthcoming 2011).

Helge Mooshammer
Helge Mooshammer is director of the Austrian Science Fund (FWF) research projects *Other Markets* (2010–13) and *Relational Architecture* (2006–9) at the School of Architecture and Urban Planning at Vienna University of Technology. In 2008 he was Research Fellow at the International Research Center for Cultural Studies (IFK), Vienna, and currently teaches at Goldsmiths, University of London. His research is concerned with new forms of urban sociality arising from processes of transnationalization, transient and informal land use, and newly emerging regimes of governance. His books include *Cruising: Architektur, Psychoanalyse und Queer Cultures* (2005) and, together with Peter Mörtenböck, *Visuelle Kultur: Körper-Räume-Medien* (co-ed., 2003), *Networked Cultures: Parallel Architectures and the Politics of Space* (co-ed., 2008) and *Netzwerk Kultur: Die Kunst der Verbindung in einer globalisierten Welt* (2010).

Peter Mörtenböck
Peter Mörtenböck is Professor of Visual Culture at the Vienna University of Technology and Visiting Fellow in the Department of Visual Cultures at Goldsmiths, University of London, where he has initiated the *Networked Cultures* project (www.networkedcultures.org), a global research platform focusing on translocally connected spatial practices. His current research explores the potential of networked ecologies and collaborative forms of knowledge production vis-à-vis the dynamics of geopolitical conflict and urban transformation. He is the author of numerous articles and books, including *Die virtuelle Dimension: Architektur, Subjektivität und Cyberspace* (2001) and, together with Helge Mooshammer, *Visuelle Kultur: Körper-Räume-Medien* (co-ed., 2003), *Networked Cultures: Parallel Architectures and the Politics of Space* (co-ed., 2008) and *Netzwerk Kultur: Die Kunst der Verbindung in einer globalisierten Welt* (2010).

Author Biographies

Soranart Sinuraibhan

Soranart Sinuraibhan is Assistant Professor of Architecture and Associate Dean for International Affairs at Khon Kaen University in Thailand. He received a PhD in Architecture from the University of Sheffield, in the UK. Supervised by Professor Jeremy Till, he completed his doctoral thesis on an alternative form of architectural drawing in 2005. He has delivered academic papers at conferences nationally and internationally. His research focuses on modern architecture and the role of representation in everyday design, with particular attention paid to the built environment. He is currently researching an Asian Design Encyclopedia, which is supported by International Institute for Advanced Study in Japan.

Chris L. Smith

Dr Chris L. Smith is an Associate Dean (Education) and Associate Professor in Architectural Design and Techné at the University of Sydney. Chris's research is concerned with the interdisciplinary nexus of philosophy, biology and architectural theory. He has published on the political philosophy of Gilles Deleuze and Félix Guattari; technologies of the body; and the influence of 'the eclipse of Darwinism' phase on contemporary architectural theory. Presently Chris is concentrating on the changing relation the discourses of philosophy, biology and architecture maintain in respect to notions of matter and materiality and the medicalization of architecture.

Michael Tawa

Dr Michael Tawa is Professor of Architecture at the University of Sydney. His recent book *Agencies of the Frame: Tectonic Strategies in Cinema and Architecture* was recently published by Cambridge Scholars Publishing. He is currently completing a second book, *Theorising the Project*, for the same publisher. He is a practising architect and has taught architectural design and theory in Sydney and Adelaide (Australia) and Newcastle (UK).

Patricia Wise

Patricia Wise has taught cultural theory across humanities, creative arts and communications at Griffith University's Gold Coast campus since 1990 (Head of School 2000–5). From a background in cultural policy research, she has become increasingly engaged in urban studies, especially in how to fashion flexible analytics for the rapid transformations typical of 'new' cities. Thinking about the complex, untidy intersections in such cities – between people, place, space, culture and milieus – has produced unexpected and/or idiosyncratic recognitions, such as the extent to which developers' discourses can be disproportionately implicated in the negotiation of identities when a city and most of its residents have limited historical continuity.

Amanda Yates

Amanda Yates is an architect and academic. She began her research-based architectural practice, Archiscape, in 1999. Amanda's research focuses upon indigenous knowledge and explores the relationship between architecture and its temporal environment – architecture is explored here as a discipline of time as well as space, where interior and exterior are temporal rather than spatial conditions and architecture becomes event rather than hermetic object. Amanda has published in various journals including IDEA and *Illusions* and recently completed a chapter for a book on indigenous knowledge and sustainable urban design. Amanda's *whakapapa* (ancestral) links include Ngati Whakaue, Ngati Rangiwewehi, Rongowhakaata and Ngati Pakeha.

Acknowledgements

The essays collected here developed in the wake of a conference at Newcastle University: *Architecture in the Space of Flows*, which brought together people from many places and disciplines. We would like to thank Karen Ritchie who coordinated that event, Sally Jane Norman who hosted it at Newcastle's Culture Lab, and everyone who contributed with their papers and participation.

Thank you also to Jacob Voorthuis and Gonçalo Furtado, at the universities of Eindhoven and Porto respectively, for the opportunities to present parts of Chapter 1.

Andrew Ballantyne and Chris L. Smith, Newcastle, Asquins and Sydney

Chapter 1

Fluxions

Andrew Ballantyne and Chris L. Smith

Shells

Herakleitos of Ephesus may have been the first to articulate the idea that the world is in a state of flux when he said that 'everything flows' (*ta panta rhei*). People before him had noticed that things change, but he made a lasting reputation by extending the reach of the idea. It was not only individual creatures that changed – by growing up and growing old – but also the mountains, the clouds and the stars in the heavens. The change could be so slow that a person's lifespan might not be long enough to notice it, and at the time (around 500 BCE) it was not exactly *reasonable* for Herakleitos to have this conviction, but in our age it is the conventional wisdom. Monumental architecture has generally set itself against change. The ancient Egyptian pyramids are a powerful emblem of the appeal of the illusion of permanence. The purity of their Euclidean geometry makes them seem surprisingly modern and therefore, given their age, timeless; but that too is an illusion. Le Corbusier defined architecture as 'the masterful, correct, and magnificent play of volumes brought together in light',[1] and it is a view that the pyramids exemplify: eternal authoritative form in brilliant light at the edge of the desert – prismatic triangles set against the cloudless sky and endless horizon.

From a Herakleitean standpoint, however, it all looks rather different. If Euclid – who came from the Greek city of Alexandria, in Egypt – or Le Corbusier saw fixed geometric volumes, by contrast they can be seen as a few moments in a process that encompasses the formation of the Earth, the extraction of stone from the ground, its assemblage by swarms of people into a geometric mound that then begins to decay – robbed of the treasures buried within and of its pale limestone surface, then eroded by wind to return eventually to the desert sand, having outlasted the original swarms of people and maybe outlasting humanity. The pyramids used up the surplus resource of a civilization that was generated largely by means of a very different flow: the Nile. It was the connections that were made possible by the Nile (as an immense thoroughfare) that constituted the civilization and enabled the concentration of resources that allowed such a stratified society to develop, and for it to accumulate such wealth. Much of its prosperity derived from the fertile ground that was irrigated by the Nile's annual flooding of a narrow strip of land, with desert to either side, hundreds of miles long.[2] The flow of water generated life, and fostered the activity of populations along the Nile. They lived for the most part in modest buildings made of sun-dried brick, which vanished long ago. Even the ultra-elite rulers dwelt magnificently in buildings of which there is now little trace. The life and activity that tapped into, produced and then directed vast resources into pyramid-building, was sustained by buildings that have all disappeared. When we read about the architecture of ancient Egypt, we are told about the pyramids and magnificent temples, but we hear little about the buildings that made life possible – the buildings that were actually known on a daily basis to the people of that society. The monumental buildings that resisted absorption into the flux have all the attention, while the productive, life-promoting buildings are edged out of the discourse.

The thing that Herakleitos most famously said is that we can never twice step into the same river.[3] The water moves on and is away by the time we return to the river, but we have developed a habit of giving the watercourse a name and a consistency. It would seem odd that we give such an active force a name, a proper noun, rather than assigning it a verb. The Nile is so-called because of the channel it runs along, not because of the particular water that is in it. We might think that we are naming the flow, but in fact in our effort to give it Euclidean stability, we name its container. The state, when it controls a commodity as precious as water, as it does in hydraulic civilizations, confines it and makes it Euclidean, quantifiable and controllable, in conduits, pipes, embankments.[4] The pyramids remotely impose their geometries on the flux, and harness the life-giving flow to state control and monument-production. The human life and settlements seem peripheral to the process, as if humanity flourished on the spillage from the great orthogonal system.

It is possible to find a narrative to make sense of architecture through this spillage, which at the moment seems peripheral, but which ought to be seen as the mainstream. There is a history of modern architecture that has lapped against the monumental, remaining aware of fluidities. One such spillage might be found in the architecture of Eileen Gray. Gray took issue with Le Corbusier. It was understandable. He had let himself into her house and painted eight large murals on her walls. He had himself photographed while doing it, and he was wearing no clothes. The sense of violation and outrage is mitigated for Le Corbusier, but not for Gray, by the fact that Le Corbusier had been encouraged by Gray's lover, Jean Badovici, a Romanian art-dealer and her collaborator on some projects. Gray had discouraged the idea of the murals and found them disruptive to the harmony she had set up. She admired Le Corbusier's work, and at first welcomed his attention, but came to find him and Badovici noisy and troublesome, and ultimately very intrusive. She moved on, ever the free spirit, leaving Badovici with the house and the neighbour.

The house overlooked the sea at Roquebrune, near Monte Carlo. The main living room was raised up and faced the clean horizon with a wall of plate glass that opened up on to a terrace. It was a remarkable design for 1934 and Le Corbusier was entranced by it. Gray's background was aristocratic, but her life was bohemian, and her lovers were more often women than men, so she lived without the clutter of her ancestors' grand Irish houses or inherited furniture, and was not inclined to be stifled by conventions that did not suit her. She always had a maid, never learning to cook, so the image of living that comes through in the house is glamorous and leisured. The service rooms are insignificant, while the focus of domestic life was the living room-boudoir that flowed into the dining space, barely defined as a room, and very much a place for sociability. There is a photograph of Badovici, Le Corbusier and his wife Yvonne at this table, but Gray is not in the picture. Perhaps she was taking it.

Le Corbusier later designed some apartments that were built just behind the house, and built himself a tiny summer studio, intrusively close – between Gray's house and the sea. He swam here daily during the summers of his later years; he had a heart attack in the water and died on the shore, making Gray's house the last building he saw. Now outside the house there is a monument to Le Corbusier on the waterfront. The house is reached by way of the Promenade Le Corbusier. His buildings collectively constitute a UNESCO World Heritage Site, and Gray's house itself was allowed to fall into dilapidation. It is now being rescued and restored, in large part because of the presence in it of Le Corbusier's murals. Gray's presence here has almost been wiped away. She was never a tenacious self-promoter, and was content to let Badovici have credit for some of her work, because he had encouraged her to do it, but even she felt angry and indignant where Le Corbusier's behaviour was concerned. She wrote:

> A house is not a *machine à habiter*. It is man's shell, his continuation, his spreading out, his spiritual emanation. Not only its sculptural harmony, but its whole organization, every aspect of the whole work combined, come together to make it human in the most profound sense.[5]

This conception of architecture is emphatically not only about the masterful, correct and magnificent play of volumes brought together in light, which could be subsumed as 'sculptural harmony'. For Gray the shell is not an element that can be isolated and admired as an object, but rather a 'continuation'. The hermit crab lives in a shell that was made for it by another creature (usually a sea snail). As the crab grows, it needs to trade-up to larger shells, and it finds them. So in this case the shell is definitely a dwelling, but it is more usual for creatures that live in shells to make their own. The 'fit' between a mollusc and its shell is so perfect that it is difficult to say whether the shell is part of the creature or is its dwelling. The process involves the mollusc depositing layers of calcium carbonate, which is found in rocks. Indeed it is rock. It oozes through the mollusc's skin in a mucous fluid that is composed of proteins and calcium carbonate, some of which crystallizes as aragonite, making a smooth, iridescent lining against the mollusc's body, while a rocky outer layer faces the world.[6] Some of the proteins dissolve and are washed away, leaving the shell almost entirely composed of rock. It is in fact masonry, directed without conscious awareness, with rock molecules rather than ashlar blocks as the components, making possible an exquisite adjustment to the housed body. In some senses it is a minimal dwelling. At human scale it is the equivalent of the *pithos* that Diogenes adopted as his abode, or Le Corbusier's little *cabanon*, at Roquebrune, or the toolboxes (6 feet long by 3 wide) that Henry Thoreau saw beside the railway tracks at

Concord, and imagined might serve as overnight accommodation for someone who was strapped for cash.[7] Such a shelter would enable a person to hang on to their independence and stop them from slipping into servility and drudgery, needing to take on regular but uncongenial employment so as to be able to spend the income paying the bank the interest on its loan. If most of us live lives of quiet desperation, as Thoreau said, then this is one of the roots of our problem. If we produced our houses as naturally as we produce our bones – and we make our bones by doing something very like the mollusc's biomineralization – then we would use up much less of our life's energy and effort in paying for them. These very small dwellings would limit the activities that could take place in the home. Thoreau did not try the toolbox as a practical experiment, but did for a while live in his not-much-larger hut by Walden Pond. This was large enough to stand up in, to read and write, and to invite someone in for a close conversation. The process by which it was formed was very different from the production of a shell or our bones, and even it is excessive by the mollusc's standards.

Our external masonry is clumsier and more self-conscious than our internal masonry, which we have to carry around with us. We ask it to accommodate not only our real needs, but also our social aspirations and the possessions accumulated through a lifetime, maybe including heirlooms that have never been useful to us but which we take on with a sense of duty and familial identity. Houses often do much more than meet our need for practical and effective shelter, and it is the excess that enables most of us to pass as respectable citizens. If we were all to produce our own shell and accumulate nothing, living like Diogenes, then no status would accrue from buildings and possessions, we would have no mortgages, and the social order that we know in the West would never have emerged. Our social order is driven by consumption and desire, and most of us live on the edge of one kind of desperation or another, so as to maximize the good things that life might offer. Some people give a higher priority to possessions, some to freedom, some to pleasure, some to social status. Somehow most of us find a balance that we can tolerate, but the newspapers are peppered with stories of people for whom things did not work out tolerably. 'Resignation,' said Thoreau, 'is confirmed desperation.'[8]

First Move

Samuel Butler describes the improvisational quality of a first move in fine-tuning an environment. His purpose here is to demonstrate how with repetition an action moves from being the focus of conscious thought to being an unconscious habit that becomes impossible to shake. His tone is facetious, but his point is serious and fundamental. He used to work in the British Library's domed reading room at the British Museum, in the days before internet search-engines gave us access to information in a manner that is so much less place-specific. The British Library has now moved away to its own building, and the room that Butler describes (designed by Sydney Smirke in 1854) now stands as a splendid but redundant monument in the museum's central courtyard. In Butler's day it was connected with the most extensive collection of documents that was available anywhere. However, it was furnished with flat tables, and Butler explained:

> I cannot write unless I have a sloping desk, and the reading-room of the British Museum, where alone I can compose freely, is unprovided with sloping desks. Like every other organism, if I cannot get exactly what I want I make shift with the next thing to it; true, there are no desks in the reading-room, but, as I once heard a visitor from the country say, 'it contains a large number of very interesting works.' I know it was not right, and hope the Museum authorities will not be severe upon me if any of them reads this confession; but I wanted a desk, and set myself to consider which of the many very interesting works which a grateful nation places at the disposal of its would-be authors was best suited for my purpose.
>
> For mere reading I suppose one book is pretty much as good as another; but the choice of a desk-book is a more serious matter. It must be neither too thick nor too thin; it must be large enough to make a substantial support; it must be strongly bound so as not to yield or give; it must not be too troublesome to carry backwards and forwards; and it must live on shelf C, D, or E, so that there need be no stooping or reaching too high.[9]

Eventually, Butler finds a book that perfectly meets all his needs (Frost's *Lives of Eminent Christians* – the *ne plus ultra* of everything that a book should be) and it becomes part of his habitual routine in writing to take this book from its shelf before starting to write.[10] 'It is to this book alone,' he said, 'that I have looked for support during many years of literary labour.'[11] However, on returning to the library to write his piece for the *Universal Review*, which is here being quoted, he finds that the book has been re-shelved and is no longer on the open shelves. By this time he is so habitually dependent on it that its absence threatens to end his literary career.

Habit is the basis of Butler's unscientific theory of evolution, outlined in his book *Life and Habit*. Here he argues that skills like playing a piece of music on the piano, are a model for the many other habits we acquire and which we subsequently perform unconsciously. Writing is a skill that was learnt with laborious effort and much concentration on the formation of letters and words, but when we write as adults we form our letters unconsciously and think about the sense we are trying to convey with our writing, not about how to shape the individual letters. When we learn a new piece at the piano, even the first time a skilled sight-reader attempts it, involves concentration and effort. If it is a difficult piece then there will be many hesitations while the groupings of notes are deciphered and then played. With many repetitions the sequence of notes is grasped unconsciously, and the conscious mind is directed to such matters as expression rather than thinking deliberately about which note to hit in the next fraction of a second and of which we therefore remain aware. With a skill like this the learning process is apparent, so we remain aware of it. Butler suggests that some of the things we have been doing unconsciously all our lives – things like seeing, growing or breathing – were once learnt with difficulty, not by any recent relatives, but by very distant pre-human ancestors.[12] Sadly, given the attractiveness of the idea, it is not scientifically plausible, as no experimental evidence has yet been found to support the idea that learned behavior can be inherited.[13]

The idea does, however, have plausibility in two senses: first, through the development of an individual through the course of a life; and, second, in respect to the manner by which externalized objects, architectures and other technical expressions relate to memory. In respect to the first sense, we 'inherit' at least some of the habits of our childhood in our adult selves, remaining recognizably the same characters, while also replacing every molecule in our body. 'The child is father of the man', as Wordsworth put it.[14] Just as the mollusc absorbs minerals, metabolizes them and turns them into its shell, so do we renew our bones with calcium – and there are problems if we do not. In the same way that we cannot twice step into the same river, so we are never at two points in our life the same person: there is a regular flow of molecules into and through the body, renewing our solid flesh. We encounter new ideas and make them our own. We establish new goals when the old ones are achieved, and in any given period of our lives we have many roles that can take on the character of fairly independent identities. And yet our habits continue with us – not only the inescapable universal habits like eating and breathing, but also little character-denoting habits, like the habit of wearing expensive shoes, or of preferring tea to coffee, yellow to orange, or the habit of arguing with received wisdom, or declining to engage with new ideas. We feel comfortable with some opportunities that come our way, but decline others, maybe because they are immoral or anti-social, but most likely, in the heat of the moment, because they do not seem like the sort of thing that 'I' would do. It would involve revising one's habitual behaviour, one's sense of oneself. The things we might do are conditioned by the things we have done; the things we avoid or embrace at small scale, become, at a larger scale, the things for which we achieve notoriety (if we succeed) or which destroy us. Or, as Herakleitos put it: 'character is destiny'.[15]

In the second sense, Butler's idea that some of the things we have been doing unconsciously all our lives were once learnt with difficulty (and not by any genetic flow) would seem feasible in respect to the manner by which the alterations we make to our context become used and useful by others in other times. Bernard Stiegler refers to this as the 'industrialization of memory', the manner by which that which we produce becomes the context or condition for a people yet to come.[16] We can, however, trace this idea back some way and engage with it prior to the human. In *On the Origin of Species*, Darwin, whose phraseology is always precise, repeatedly refers to the external context of any creature or species as the 'conditions of life'.[17] For Darwin an individual organism is both vehicle and terminal and any notion of character or identity is corrupted by the plurality of 'identities' that the theory of natural selection necessitates. The idea of context and exterior as the 'conditions of life', avoids the separation of context from organism or world from body, which Descartes had made programmatic. In a Cartesian description there is a dialectic between the world and the body, but in Darwin there is no break. He sees instead a continuation of the world into the body. The world is for Darwin the condition or precondition of body as life-former, in which the organism is to be seen as simultaneously a product of and inseparable from its environment. There is also a more subtle sense by which Darwin sees the world as an emanation from the body: a figure-ground description, making the 'figure' the focus of attention, is removed in favour of a relational understanding that exteriorizes the body.

According to Darwin, and today's orthodoxy, the body does not evolve in the course of its own life. Although the body is integral to the evolutionary process, evolution does not happen because of any process of renewal or change within an individual body, but through the (re)production of other bodies. Evolution's temporality is at a very different scale to the timings that we humans experience in an individual lifespan. Chapter 3, Amanda Yates's 'Oceanic Spaces of Flow', and Chapter 9, Steve Basson's 'Temporal Flows', remind us of the phenomenon of time to which all bodies, architectures, artefacts and molecules are subject and of the relational and experiential terms by which we must think the ceaseless flux of duration. For Darwin it is not just the (re)production of other bodies over geological time through which evolution occurs but very much the ever-altered 'condition of life' itself. This means that for Darwin the body is provisional and contingent on an externalized temporal and spatial niche and can only be described (enter discourse) in relational terms.[18] The shell that is generated by one body can be used as a home or a 'condition of life' for another, just as architecture and our cities are a condition for a people yet to come. Gottfried Semper, writing some thirty years after the publication of *On the Origin of Species,* suggests that:

> The old monuments are correctly designated as fossil shells of extinct organisms of society, but these shells did not grow into the back on the latter, like snail shells, nor did they shoot up like coral reefs according to some blind process of nature. They are free creations of man, who used intelligence, observation of nature, genius, will, knowledge and power, in their production.[19]

Semper embraces the idea of buildings as biomineralization but his positioning of 'man' remains that of the heroic protagonist of Enlightened civilization. If we displace the individual's consciousness from the centre of the story, then the important focus is the (now-extinct) 'organisms of society'. It was these larger-than-human organisms, which were vitalized by humans, and constituted through the relations between humans, that were housed in these monuments. Think, for example, of Manchester Town Hall, an imposing civic monument designed by Alfred Waterhouse and completed in 1877 – a splendid building, and (for us) a fine example of the shell of a Victorian civic organism. Its most splendid room is the Council Chamber, where the city's governing body assembled to take key decisions. The bulk of the building, though, is made up of the offices and facilities required to make those decisions take effect. There was a small corps of councillors and a significantly larger group of town-hall officers, with an army of deputies, clerks and support staff who needed accommodation suitable to their status. Some people, like the mayor, had an important ceremonial and theatrical role, which demanded an

Andrew Ballantyne and Chris L. Smith

appropriate setting. Most of the people who worked in the building, however, from the copy clerks to the cleaners, could disappear into the background. The grand vaulted circulation spaces that connect the principal entrance with the Council Chamber have a counterpart in the warren of inconspicuous little corridors connecting offices in the upper parts of the building. At times these circulation systems take people past one another while keeping them apart, as though the meeting of people of different classes would result in contamination of some sort. The building is still in use, but if it were designed today it would be different. There would be less segregation, but also perhaps fewer offices on this central site, now that so much of the business can be conducted electronically, by people who do not need to be in the same room as one another, so long as they are in contact. The social organism has evolved into something different from what the building was designed to house in the 1870s, but the shell that it unconsciously produced remains in place – in perpetuity, now that it is Grade 1 listed. Now, when Semper says that monuments 'are free creations of man, who used intelligence, observation of nature, genius, will, knowledge and power, in their production' he is writing as a representative of that class of men, with whose consciousness he is of course well attuned. The architecture-world is highly inclined to attribute creativity, intelligence and genius to architects. However, the social organism that commissioned the town hall was significantly less inclined to do so. 'Manchester' the social organism could certainly have taken the view that Waterhouse was a useful dietary supplement, whose work on the building cured the city of an indigestion that had prevented it working properly. However, the city operates without a conscious awareness that is separate from that of its citizens. Politicians and entrepreneurs who depend on connecting with the public must have awareness of the 'mood of the city' and a sense of what the social organism will do next, and they might even have some capacity to influence that mood. There is no doubt that the social organism has feelings, even if there is doubt about its having consciousness. We can be sure that no matter how great the creativity, intelligence and genius of Waterhouse, he would not have been able to build a town hall of such magnificence had he been commissioned to do the work in 2011. He would have been designing for, and would have been part of, a different social organism.

Within the architecture-world the architect is a heroic figure, whose creativity, intelligence and genius deserve recognition with esteem, medals and prizes. The rest of the world seems to exist so as to bring nourishment and opportunity to the social organism that is the architecture-world. There are alternative views. Commercial developers do not employ contemporary architects for the sake of their creativity, intelligence and genius, but because they need a plausible building design in order to enhance the value of their investment. From the point of view of the social organism, it is the activity and the flow that matters, not the architect's creativity, intelligence and genius, nor the sense of style or formal resolution, or any of the things that are usually aestheticized in our responses to buildings. In this space of flows it is algorithms all the way down: it is the bottom line on the balance sheet that determines the decision, not a personal appreciation of creativity, intelligence and genius. The developer is not even to be characterized as personally greedy, because she or he is likely to be managing the investment on behalf of an institution, such as a pension fund, that benefits ordinary people. The personal feeling for greed need not be there, but its performance is an institutional requirement. 'Greed is good', said Gordon Gekko in *Wall Street*, conflating the personal with the institutional morality.[20] The social organism that is constituted through these algorithms, global capitalism, has its internal logic that is not human and that does nothing in itself to nurture humane creativity, intelligence and genius except where there is a profit to be turned from them.

The logic of Wall Street is profoundly different from the person-centred logic of Diogenes and Epicurus. It is the logic of the markets that generates the desperation that Thoreau saw as endemic among his compatriots, who were making themselves too busy in order to pay for assets that they did not need. In *Desperate Housewives* the desperation is not only acknowledged, it seems to have become aspirational.[21] The stories are about keeping up appearances in a high-maintenance neighbourhood, and the comedy is in the gap between the picture-perfect appearances and the backstage bickering, embarrassments and murders that maintain the images of serenity and perfection. As a social phenomenon it connects strongly with the images that fill the news-stands – celebrities looking lovely and living enviable lives, or going to pieces in public. Diogenes' *pithos*, Epicurus' garden and Thoreau's hut would not be suitable settings for these personalities – but nor would they engender the conditions that led them to their desperate state. It is not news. It is old wisdom. We (as a society – as a social organism) know about the desperation, and we take the steps we know we need to take so as to get it. Our houses and our workplaces are part of that process, and we try to keep ourselves busy enough to pay the bills and keep the big questions in the unconcious. We know that a big, showy house and an expensive lifestyle will bring desperation to those who have them on borrowed money, but spurred on by envy with surprising frequency we choose bling and desperation over the little shell, freedom and contentment.

Bartleby

Herman Melville's story 'Bartleby' is about a scrivener – a clerk, working in a lawyer's office on Wall Street, whose job is to make accurate copies of legal documents in good copperplate handwriting.[22] Before the invention of, first, carbon paper and then the photocopier, every office that needed multiple copies of documents employed such people; now no one does so, and the photocopier has taken over the duties, which it performs with amazing rapidity and accuracy. Melville's Bartleby is a character who personifies the qualities and world-view one would project on to the scrivener-world: modest, without a troublesome independence of mind, but self-effacing to a degree that becomes quietly fascinating. In the scrivener-world Bartleby is a genius and a hero of renunciation. He has intelligence – he might not be called on to exercise judgement, and in the story he avoids taking on extraneous responsibilities, but making accurate copies of legal documents in good handwriting is a skilled task. Were he a less idealized character he would in reality have had a home life with family, recreation, food and sleep. He would have participated in the activities of consumption and reproduction that bind the social organism together and perpetuate it. However, in the world of the social organism for which he works, Bartleby is very little, and he seems to have taken this on as his own estimate of his worth, so his supervisor has more worries about Bartleby's needs than does Bartleby himself. He effaces himself to the point of invisibility, asserting his will only in acts of renunciation.

Part of what makes Melville's story compelling now is the fact that this whole profession has quietly disappeared without complaint. From the social organism's point of view the replacement by the photocopier is unproblematic. From the point of view of an individual losing a livelihood, it would have been traumatic, but the process was gradual and the clerks were intelligent enough to be able to adapt to other possibilities. From the perspective of a social organism that commissions buildings, the architect can be as invisible. The architect's creativity, intelligence and genius are part of the conscious awareness of others in the architecture-world, but might pass unnoticed in the unconscious workings of a great social organism.

Darwin, however, tries to overcome Victorian anthropomorphism by restricting his direct references to 'man' in the very early chapters of *On the Origin of Species* to descriptions of man as the organizer of husbandry and 'artificial selection'.[23] This approach to the human emphasizes a principle of emergence and the idea that the organism (human or otherwise) is at once a passive, receptive space in the gradual motion of evolution and very much able to influence other organisms, their contexts or *milieux*. In this sense the productions of the body – the habits, the husbandry, the buildings, the cities – operate as a 'condition of life'.

The Point

The shell is an exquisite thing, but that is not the point of it. It is produced as an adjunct to the mollusc's life, and it helps to make that life possible. The life is the point, not the shell. The nautilus produces a particularly beautiful shell that has been analysed in connection with proportion. The shell's logarithmic spiral is generated by the nautilus outgrowing the original shell and forming a new chamber attached to the old one; so the coils of the spiral are a history of personal growth. The additive progression makes a classic Fibonacci series, where the size of the chambers escalates with each iteration, corresponding to the current size of the creature's body. And what a creature it is. Between its eyes, around its mouth, there is a mass of tentacles – up to 90 of them (figure 1.1). Two of the tentacles are broad and leathery, and can be used defensively to close the end of the shell when the creature has retreated inside. The old chambers are used to trap air, giving the creature some buoyancy, which is useful when it is moving about. In order to move it squirts a jet of water from its mouth, which propels it along backwards, so it can never see where it is going. The shell by itself certainly looks masterful, correct and magnificent, and its example may lie behind the volutes in Ionic capitals, but it is the 'spiritual emanation' of a weird, primitive creature that dates back to the time of the dinosaurs and keeps bumping into things. If we are mesmerized by the shell's perfect proportions, the mathematical precision of which can be exaggerated, we can lose sight of the life that produced the shell, and which the shell protected.

Figure 1.1 A
nautilus at home

'Nautilus' means 'sailor', and the creature was so-named because, once upon a time, people thought that it used its broad, leathery tentacles to catch the wind, and sail about on the sea. That was a misapprehension, but it captures the way in which people are inclined to project quasi-human ways of understanding on to creatures that think very differently, if indeed they think at all. We can be reasonably sure that the nautilus does not think about perfect proportion and has never heard of the golden section or the Fibonacci series. In building its masonry, all its thinking is dispersed and incorporated in the body, and if it had a conscious preoccupation, it would be felt as cravings for foods rich in calcium carbonate, such as crabs' legs.

Another survival from the Jurassic era, perfectly attuned to the world of flow, is the sea squirt, which is seen as a primitive relative of backboned creatures because in its immature tadpole-like phase it does have a backbone, and something like a brain. When it is in this phase it experiments and plays, but then it finds a place where there is a flow of nutrients – the underside of a rock, or sometimes a boat – and it settles down. Once in place it ingests its brain and never moves again, letting the currents bring to it as much stimulation as it will ever need. Its 'intelligent' phase lasts for only a few hours, but it might be an indication of where intelligence began, and certainly makes the sea squirt a closer relative to mammals than are any of the molluscs. It is also becoming proverbial, as the creature that eats its brain, as if its mode of life might offer a lesson to humans.[24] We seem to be at our most playful and inventive in the earlier stages of life, and learn to substitute knowledge and experience for creative play and receptivity to new ideas. It is a tendency that we must educate ourselves to resist, developing a way of recognizing when it is good to put our established ways of doing things into abeyance, so that we can think experimentally. The sea squirt is a warning – a model of what one might become as one finds a congenial role and settles into an habitual performance of

11

unchallenging duties. It might be what we are genetically programmed to do, but it does not feel like being alive. It seems more like an embodied development of the internalized desperation noted by Thoreau. It is transformed first into resignation, then into habit and the very fibre of our being. It is admirable in its way, but how much more stimulating to be able to move on, to leave it all behind and drift away to a new set of experiences. The sea squirt is brilliantly adapted to its passive existence, the flows of nutrients coming its way without effort, and nothing wants to eat it, so it is proliferating unchallenged along the United States' Eastern Seaboard, excluding some of the species that have traditionally flourished there. As an individual species it is undoubtedly a success, but as part of the *milieu* it is a problem.

A flow establishes a line – a *thalweg* – along which one can move in either direction, upstream or downstream. Conceptually the important thing is to notice the line, and then it is a secondary detail to notice the direction of travel. Becoming smaller is conceptually the same thing as becoming larger – they both involve the idea that size can change.[25] Similarly any change has its vector: becoming paler or darker, becoming wetter or drier. In Stephen Loo's 'The (Not So) Smooth Flow Between Architecture and Life', Chapter 11, it becomes clear that such movements are effectively defined less by geometric coordinates than by defining vectors and field relations. Such movements respond to and cause continuous variations, whose constantly changing directionality and proliferation depend upon the actions of participants negotiating the field themselves, resulting in an emergent simultaneity between cause and effect. This is not to say that the opposite poles of a vector are the same thing as one another, but that if there is a line to be drawn between them then they have something in common: they are at the ends of the same path. Wall Street has Gordon Gekko at one end of it and Bartleby at the other. It is possible, at least in the imagination, to move from one end to the other: from glamour and desperation to renunciation and contentment. To live beyond one's shell, beyond one's real needs, is to embrace becoming desperate. Eileen Gray, who knew when to move on, said that 'There is a road which leads upward and there is a road which leads downward. Both are one and the same.' Peter Adam made it the concluding sentence of his biography of her, standing as a gnomic epitaph.[26] She did not mention, and he did not notice, that she was quoting Herakleitos.[27]

Multitudes

An individual drop of water can move through air, but we would not say that it is flowing. In a crowd – a thousand million drops – it becomes an infinitesimal part of a flow. Flow is a phenomenon of multitudes, not individuals. The 'individual' here is a fairly arbitrary idea, as the single drop is composed of a huge number of molecules, and the large body of water has no memory of the drops of which it was composed. At the molecular scale, the body of water is a crowd or a species. At human scale is it experienced as a substance with well-recognized properties: wet, splashy, transparent, drinkable, etc.

Human scale is of course a fairly arbitrary measure – as random as the molecular, the mineral, the regional, the global, the cosmological. Shifts in scale from the individual to the multitude have a history of challenging and upsetting understandings of self and world. In the fourth century BCE, when Epicurus of Samos imagined the origins of the universe, he described a stream of atoms falling through space. A swerve (*clinamen*) in the path of one of these atoms caused it to collide with others and set a train of events in motion that resulted in the formation of the world. It is a compelling vision that did not depend on the interventions of gods, so some people saw it as a threat to piety, not only in the ancient world where the idea was conceived, but also during the Middle Ages. It was only in the seventeenth century that Epicurus' atoms were firmly reintroduced into science.[28]

The shift from the individual to the multitude was a key cause of concern in the reception of Darwin's theory of natural selection. The shift in attention from individual organisms to species over many generations seemed to erode the hard distinctions between species. In this respect the multitude of species was a direct challenge to the habits and resignations of polite society; as when John Ruskin spoke of 'the filthy heraldries which record the relation of humanity to the ascidian and the crocodile'.[29] Indeed many Victorian rejections of Darwinian theory rested upon notions of miscegeny and bestiality manifest either as 'the frog in the bed' or, as with Ruskin, a fearful *descent of man* where the flow of heredity could run between all species, including the human.[30] The appeal to temporal and relational understandings that were appropriate for considering the 'species' as opposed to the 'individual' is often manifest as the too-painful total loss of the human body. The biological narrative of Darwin, following the geological history of Lyell, demonstrated that it is possible for humans to describe a world that has no human protagonists: a world before the existence of the human and a contemporary world that pays no regard to the human.[31] The discreet absence of the human body from much of the narrative of *On the Origin of Species* was not an anaesthetic exclusion but rather a shifting in concentration to the multitude. Despite the decision to exclude any subjectified 'human' from the discourse, the tendency of the argument from the outset is to range the human alongside all other forms of life, as husbander.[32] Consciousness, however, plays no part in natural selection and in the early chapter of *On the Origin of Species* dedicated to 'artificial selection', any reference to the conscious is delicately omitted in favour of a model of multitudes in order to address the motions of evolution. Darwin's world is a world of instincts and impulsions and Darwin's thought can be located between the 'freeplay' and 'history' defined by Jacques Derrida:[33]

> Freeplay tries to pass beyond man and humanism, the name man being the name of that being who [. . .] through the history of all of his history – has dreamed of full presence, the reassuring foundation, the origin and the end of the game.[34]

A feature common to both Derrida's discourse and Darwin's pragmatism is a shift from notions of innate consciousness to a strategy locating bodies in, and indeed as, a system of external relations, that is, a relocation of subjectivity to the flows of an exterior world. Consciousness as a notion serves Darwin no useful purpose since in his world meaning inheres exclusively in the impassive body and its exteriors (irrespective of what a body may have thought). Likewise in Derrida's account, consciousness serves little useful purpose since meaning inheres exclusively in textual objects incapable of the stability and coherence that anthropomorphic consciousness presupposes. Darwin's position in *On the Origin of Species* is less determined than Derrida's post-Freudian readings (and both positions are less determined than that of the sea quirt which entirely ingests its brain). It is not as though the brain and consciousness do not matter; it is that they are less operable at the scale of the multitude; where the *nonconscious* (to use Brian Massumi's term) transient condition provides perhaps a better model for thinking the various emergences and becomings of the multitude.[35]

Nonconscious Thinking

Most of the thinking that goes on in our bodies is nonconscious. It is impossible for us to give a direct account of it, and we do not notice it happening. Some of it is going on in the brain, but much of it is devolved to places elsewhere in the body. If the temperature drops, then the pores in my skin contract. I can notice it happening, but it is not something that my brain controls: it is a response to sensors in the skin, which take *decisions* based on local conditions. Consciously I can take a decision to move closer to a source of heat, or put on some warmer clothing, which will make the pores relax, but I cannot through any act of will get my pores to relax. Normally I would not notice the pores at all. I might consciously think about feeling comfortable, but comfort is a very self-effacing feeling, and it would be discomfort that I would be more likely to notice. There are many comparable things going on in the body. My heart was working for years before I was taught what it did, and even after that I did not learn to control it directly. I can make it beat faster if I exercise, but not by direct willpower.

One has a similar sense of being 'out of control' in 'affairs of the heart'. A high proportion of literature concerns itself with moments when our emotions take us by surprise – when we fall in love or behave with a heroism that we did not expect we could find. Somehow in the heat of the moment, things happen and something other than conscious reasoning seems to step in and decide. A great author can lead us along the way, step by step, so that we can understand how we too could, in particular circumstances, fall into another's arms with the expectation of perpetual bliss, or could, in the grip of other passions become a murderer, an adulterer or a martyr for a principle. La Mettrie in *L'Homme Machine* describes how there is a mechanical aspect to the passions and he gives the particularly memorable example of the Wild Girl of Chalons. We do not know the details of what went on when she murdered her sister, or quite what escalation of passion and panic kicked in to inform what the girl did. La Mettrie believed the girl, however, when she said that she had no intention of eating her sister, though that was what she ended up doing.[36] If we are going to understand her at all then we need imaginatively to reconstruct circumstances where emotions are intensified to the point where they derail the conscious mind's illusion that it is in charge, and unleash the instincts of the wild beasts that also live in us and through us, but which we normally keep comfortable, contented and asleep, so that we can manage with the routines of civilized discourse. The lives of quiet desperation acknowledge the presence of these wild beasts and the need to house them. In a genuinely resigned life they might as well be dead, but it is perhaps from an apparently resigned life that they are most likely to reassert their continuing vitality, as they did in the Wild Girl of Chalons or in the random massacres that are the rumbling passacaglia of our times.

Desire

There is a long ascetic tradition of trying to conquer desire, most strongly associated with the Stoics, but also important in Epicurus' ethics. He sought to keep desire under control not by eliminating it, but by managing it. The way to be happy, he taught, is to have a very limited appetite, so that one can satisfy it and still live within one's means. This meant that he developed a reputation as a hedonist, but the point of the teaching was really about leading a quiet life that reduces the demands of appetite, so that contentment is easy to attain. The philosophically rigorous part is in reducing the appetite. Spinoza similarly taught us to pay attention to our desires. We know about our desires and feel free when can act upon them; but where do our desires come from? What makes us feel these things? Deleuze and Guattari's attempt to address this question produced the 'desiring machines' of their first collaborative text, *Anti-Oedipus*, as a way of giving an account of the nonconscious production of conscious desire. Concepts, physical circumstances and previous experiences act on one another to produce the current state of mind and the volition one feels in the present. The machines that produce desire are assembled from components as disparate as blood, milk, dancing snowflakes and an idea of redemption. Lenz, the 'schizo going for a walk' in the opening pages of *Anti-Oedipus*, loses his normal sense of identity, where he might see himself as an individual subject – an autonomous agent who engages with things that are outside him and sees them as separate from himself. Instead of that, he internalizes everything he senses, so that he is overwhelmed by the rush of stimuli, and unable to know how to act. He becomes formless, because he loses all sense of where his self ends or begins. He inhales air, and the air in a sense *is* him, but then when he exhales, where does he end? And the mountains that he wanders among – they are part of him too – and the snowflakes that he sees and that make his skin tingle. It is all part of a big system, a big machine, and Lenz cannot feel himself as an autonomous part, but only as enmeshed in the whole of his *milieu*.

The great idea in Spinoza is immanence, which Deleuze in particular picked up as a preoccupation. 'Immanence' is almost the same as 'emergence', seen from an alternate point of view. Emergent properties are immanent in the initial conditions, but that is not initially apparent. The properties are noticed only later, when they emerge. Before they have become apparent they can be impossible to anticipate, but after they have become evident, we can understand that they were about to develop, given the necessary conditions. If we have not seen water boiling, then its heaving movements as it reaches boiling point will certainly take us by surprise. Where did that animation come from? Is it alive? We are habituated to the water's behaviour, so we do not ask the questions.

Andrew Ballantyne and Chris L. Smith

Intelligent Community

Dictyostelium discoideum is popularly known as slime mould, but popularity is not its most pronounced characteristic. It can take the form of a strangely malleable slug-like creature that wanders about in ways that are not always easy to understand, as its structureless body reconfigures itself in ways that make the slug look familiarly creature-like. Slime mould shows signs of intelligence. It can find its way through mazes – sorting out the quickest route among alternatives – despite not having an organ that looks anything like a brain. It can also on occasion disappear; and having disappeared, it can reappear. It can do this because it is composed of many thousands of microscopic amoeba-like organisms. In certain conditions they assemble into something that at first glance seems slug-like, which can do things that the individual cells cannot, like finding its way through a maze. The slime mould has been an important testing ground for thinking about emergence.[37] Understanding it turns out to involve people at an interface between biology and mathematics, with mathematicians leading the way.

The story does not have a clear beginning, but we could start with Alan Turing, who is best known for doing something like inventing the computer, and shortening the war against the Nazis; but he also published an essay entitled 'The Chemical Basis of Morphogenesis'.[38] What he argued was that, given a set of simple interactions between cells, and a large number of cells, some complex patterns of behaviour can arise. One might not have predicted it from the initial conditions, but once one has seen it happening then one can make an analysis that shows mathematically that enough is specified in the initial conditions to make the complex behaviour occur. One of the tendencies as this area of study has developed has been for the biologists to intuit a source of willpower in the collective organism – supposing for example that there must be 'leaders' among the slime mould cells, which influence how the collectivity behaves.

However, the mathematicians see no need for such a hypothesis, and see the description as being complete without it. The problem is that non-mathematicians cannot follow the logic of the highly technical mathematics that is involved, so it is difficult to realign one's intuitions. In the same way, if one had not seen a pan of water coming to the boil a few times, one might think that something had been added when it came to boiling point. The biologists' initial intuition was to see transcendence – here a transcendent will, that arrives from somewhere as yet unexplained. The mathematicians, by contrast, asserted that the collective organism's will is immanent in the thousands of microscopic, chemically determined wills of the cells.

It is difficult to think of slime mould cells as individuals, as we encounter them only in swarms. When they behave independently they disappear, but as they are microscopically indivisible, they better deserve to be called 'individuals' than do most other things. An important part of what has happened, which makes more of us intuitively accept the mathematicians' reasoning, is that computers now can perform complex calculations rapidly and repeatedly in order to generate sequences of behaviour. When a mathematically derived model is being used then we know completely what there is in the model. We might have a series of interdependent variables that produce unpredictable results, but we know for certain that the results are not being caused by anything outside the mathematics. There might be a tendency to resolve in one way or another, to implode or disintegrate, depending on the initial conditions and the *milieu*, but we cannot impute motive, or will, or transcendental guidance, unless we put those things into play ourselves, programmed into the initial conditions. We can project our own emotions into the circumstances that we observe, but if it is all mathematically defined at the outset then we know that we are doing just that – projecting. Whereas in the case of natural organisms we are more inclined to accept our projections as being observations.

Descartes was famously resistant to projecting his human feelings onto animals, and he reasoned that animals did not have the means to feel pain. He was probably wrong there. But if instead of conducting his experiments on birds he had conducted them on a mathematical model of *Dictyostelium discoideum* then we would have found it very surprising if anyone thought that the mathematical model could suffer. In the case of natural organisms there is always the possibility that by performing the right experiment, one might make a discovery of some subtle organ – a soul, perhaps – that determines volition. But if the mathematical model can produce equivalent behaviours without needing to introduce such a thing, then one would stop searching for it and could conclude that it is an effect of intuitive projection rather than a natural object. It is the difference between Spinoza and Descartes, the difference between immanence and transcendence.[39]

The Social Thought

Moving from slime mould to artificial intelligence is not such a big move, given that the slime mould as a collective seems to be intelligent, whereas slime mould individuals seem not to be. There is a wonderful book by Marvin Minsky, called *The Society of Mind*, in which Minsky – an important figure in the development of artificial intelligence – sets out in an accessible way his theory of how intelligence works.[40] It is a curious book to read, because there are times when it seems to be saying very little, or at least not enough. What it does is to set out, on page after page, with very clear, straightforward diagrams, small acts of decision-making that do not look intelligent at all. There might be something like recognition but often the decisions are simple binaries: yes or no; hit or miss; off or on. What happens is that one reaches the end, thinking 'is that all there is?' The book is full of ideas, but they all seem to be relatively small ideas with no sense of a grand vision opening up as we go along. And then in an epilogue Minsky mentions the key, which is not a missing part that he has withheld from us, but the fact that there are millions upon millions of connections to be made among all the parts that have already been presented. He is not a biologist, so perhaps the aim is not to model what is going on in a human brain, but to find a way of designing a process that makes thought at least theoretically possible. Nevertheless it is the case that our brains are composed of millions upon millions of connections between parts that are so simple they seem to be inadequate as an explanation of what our brains are. What we recognize as intelligence, though, would seem to be an emergent property of the swarming multiplicity of synapses, given a plethora of interconnections.

Perhaps the biggest of Minsky's ideas, which is so big that it might go unnoticed, is that the brain is made of many different parts that do many different things. There is no centralized zone that everything goes through for a final decision, but different zones that do different things and switch in and out of action as required. The 'society' in the book's title might be a metaphor, but it is so apt a metaphor that it seems to be a literal description. The millions of interconnected parts are a real society in the same way that Deleuze and Guattari's desiring machines are real machines, and of course we recognize the rhizome here – the non-centralized network that is the basis of the thousand plateaus.[41] Minsky's more recent book, *The Emotion Machine*, explores a territory that should overlap with Deleuze and Guattari's desiring machines, but in fact it comes from such a different background that it can arrive at its conclusions without having been inspired by them, or needing their support.[42] Much of what is going on in our bodies is not what anyone would ordinarily call 'thinking'. Is a kidney thinking when it filters the blood? Is the stomach thinking as it digests food? And what about the processes going on in the unconscious parts of the brain? Would they be 'thinking'? And how would they be different from the conscious thoughts? And those desires – where did they come from? If I am feeling hungry, and am in genuine need of food, then at what point in the process of development did thinking begin, and how did it find expression as a desire? Is there thinking in the stomach? And if we resist calling that 'thinking', then can we confidently say that it is entirely different from whatever it is that the creature I call 'me' says when it says 'I think I'm hungry'? And we all know how indigestion can interfere with our life in dreams. The boundaries tend to dissolve, and either thought becomes formless and empirically impossible to define, or else a definition is adopted as a given, in order to be able to exclude part of what is going on in order that we can have a clearly framed idea. But this exclusion is always arbitrary – a marking of a limit on a line that continues beyond it into unknown territory. The little fragments of thought of which we are aware – the 'conscious' part of these extravagant processes – are exceptional. Most of what is going on is nonconscious and habitual, murmuring in the background, shaping our lives and our sense of what we can do, suggesting things we might like, things we might avoid, but mostly seething away unnoticed in our *milieu*, flowing into us by way of food and drink, the air that we breathe and the images streaming through the screen, the genetic inheritance from long ago and far away controlling the capture of molecules of calcium for the bones and iron for the blood, without alerting us in any direct way to what it is doing or where it might be taking us. Let it have its way. We have other things to think about.

People in Crowds

Individual slime mould cells are microscopic, and by the time that a slime mould community is big enough to come to our attention without the aid of a microsope it is an aggregate of millions of the elements involved. At this point we switch scale, so that people become the elementary particles. If I think of myself as an autonomous individual I can plausibly portray myself as someone with a complicated life and finely nuanced emotions. There are various ways in which I would like to think

I am *better* than a cell of slime mould – more developed, more complex, better company. However, if one steps back to look at the millions of people going about the world, the differences do not seem so very great. When we see people in large crowds, we do not see individuals with personal inclinations making considered judgments. We see something more like particles that have a lot in common with one another. This aspect of people is brought out compellingly in the film *Koyaanisqatsi*, which distances itself from a person's-eye view of things by preferring high vantage points and by using time-lapse photography so that events do not happen at their normal human speed.[43] When people come into view, whether in passing through a railway station or driving along a city street, what we see is a sequence of interrupted flows.

If I happen to be one of the people in the scene then I do not have this point of view. I will be walking along, say, and looking in the shop windows, thinking 'I can do without a new coat right now', 'that one looks good', wondering if somewhere nearby I'll come across a shop that might sell me something good to eat later on this evening; potatoes, apples, lettuces and strawberries. I notice the way that the polished shop windows reflect so well the sunlit facades on the other side of the street, and subliminally think that the person lumbering towards me looks as if he is expecting me to move out of his way, which I can do with a slight variation of my path. The traffic lights at this junction are just changing, and I might get across if I hurry, but I am not in a mood to hurry. I will enjoy the reflections in the windows, saunter up to the lights and wait dreamily while the lights go through their programmed sequence and a little crowd of people gathers around me, also waiting to cross. And how this comes out on the film, seeing the scene from high above, is that a mass of people move along at a fairly steady speed, looking like dark particles, and then the flow is interrupted while the traffic flows across the other way, and then the first flow starts again and lasts a little while, and then it is interrupted again, and the cycle repeats and repeats. At this scale I do not look like an individual, but more like a corpuscle in the city's bloodstream – and at that scale of operation, that is what I am. What it is about me that matters in this context is that I behave in a particular way – I move down the street, and from time to time I go into a shop with my credit card and nourish the process of distribution that is happening there – and all the rest of me is irrelevant to this situation, no matter how much I might value it.

Wael Fahmi moves across different scales in Chapter 10, 'Navigating Flow: Architecture of the Blogosphere', where he explores the role of new media and information technology in the transformation of individuals at social scales. He suggests that the 'virtual public spheres' of the blog are at one scale a non-place, a new category of 'blogosphere landscape' of online interactions of individuals who more often than not have never met, and at another scale, at select moments, these interactions crystallize as mass socio-political events, occupations and dissolutions of streets and other public spaces.

In Roland Barthes' last moments, on a street in Paris, all the complexities and sophistications of his thought were set to one side, as he became a mis-placed particle, a pedestrian unavoidably in the way of a laundry van. For the smooth running of the city as an organism, it does not matter what is going on in my head. The only thing that matters is how I behave, and how others behave, and if nearly all of us do the things that we are expected to do, then everything runs smoothly and an aberration here and there will have little impact on the whole. Even a death in the street, which is devastating for the individual, is hardly noticed by the teeming city.

Dissolution

An important aspect of the understanding presented in Deleuze and Guattari's *Anti-Oedipus* is the way that boundaries dissolve as we focus on connections. When something like an architecture is assembled and it functions, then the irrelevant parts of the bodies, objects or concepts fade from view. Samuel Butler, in 'The Book of the Machines', explains how the steam engine – the advanced and rapidly developing technology of his day – evolved, not by organic reproduction but through the efforts of mechanics and engineers. Just as the mechanics are part of the steam engine's evolutionary mechanism in Butler's description of them, so the breast and the baby, the nipple and mouth, connect as a unified machine and it makes no sense to insist on the separateness of two distinct individuals, or two distinct organs.[44] The sense of where to draw the line to mark out an entity is pragmatic, and derives from the kind of description that we find it helpful to make in order to deal with the situation in which we have to act. The sense of the boundaries of the self dissolve into the things we engage with – people, places, furniture, stars, hills, wolves: machines. Inside and outside lose their meaning. 'Why have we kept our own names?' ask Deleuze and Guattari. 'Out of habit, purely out of habit. [. . .] Also because it's nice to talk like everybody else, to say the sun rises, when everybody knows it's only a manner of speaking.'[45]

Guattari opens his book *Chaosmosis* by explaining that his research as a psychoanalyst and activist has led him to 'put the emphasis on subjectivity as the product of individuals, groups and institutions' and depicts subjectivity as that which involves 'no dominant or determinant instance guiding all other forms according to a univocal causality'.[46] The human subject is not a 'given', but is produced through engagement with other people and things, including objects, ideas and language, so Guattari rejects the apolitical subjectivity that comes from phenomenology and psychology, but embraces a 'machinic', in which the subject is produced by engagement with the world (indifferently inside and outside itself). It is an account of pragmatic and continuing development. Rather than being inherent in or dependent upon bodies and contexts, subjectivity, Guattari declares, is produced by multiplicitous forces and social fields, the multitude of contexts and states of life to which a subject has access (or notably from which a subject is excluded). He defines this multitude and the exclusions as 'the ensemble of conditions which render possible the emergence of individual and/or collective instances as self-referential existential Territories, adjacent, or in a delimiting relation, to an alterity that is itself subjective'.[47]

Usually, even in big cities, we behave as fairly autonomous individuals, even though we might flow along fairly predictable trajectories, and have dealings with others as we go. But from time to time we coalesce into a more organized sort of crowd, which rallies to protest against a government's actions, or roars as a footballer scores a goal. The chanting that signals a rhythm across the group, or the military band that sets the pace for a march, are agents that discipline this collective organism. These are traditional organisms that make their interconnections in primitive ways, and can call to the surface surprisingly primitive behaviours that constituent individuals in the crowd would not have been moved to in isolation. The crowd can assemble and it can disperse. I can be part of it, behave in ways that take me by surprise, and then become my self again.

The Virtual Crowd

Moreover, in addition to the traditional ways of being part of a crowd, the level of interactivity that is now possible on the web makes it possible to form new temporary groupings. There was a case of a mobile phone that went missing in New York in circumstances that made it interesting to millions of people. There is a compelling and detailed account of it in Clay Shirky's book, *Here Comes Everybody*.[48] In itself it was a trivial event, but many people identified with it and embraced the problem as their own, so that what started out as a mislaid and then misappropriated phone, turned into something where the stakes escalated and the wrongdoer was arrested, which would not have happened without the resolution of a vast crowd of supporters who helped in various ways: in tracking down the person who had received the phone, in supplying specialized legal advice and arcane details of police procedures, in giving support and encouragement. The surprisingly large scale of the operation was crucial to its success – first, in giving the injured party the determination to go on, even though from a commonsense point of view she might have done better to have resigned herself to the fairly modest loss, and second, in capturing the necessary specialized information, such as the transgressor's address, which was found by someone recognizing the place from photos that were taken on the phone after it had changed hands. It was not that a million people worked hard on the case and therefore it succeeded, but rather that the million people who took an interest included someone with one vital bit of information, and someone else with another. Even with odds of a million-to-one against, if there are millions of people involved then the one-in-a-million chance is good enough for success. Most of the millions of people were not even very interested in the story. If they had nothing special to contribute then it would have had no very powerful claim on their attention. The incident happened over the course of ten days – just ten days between the phone being left on a taxi seat and being recovered – which is unremarkable for the phone and the individual, but astonishing for the setting-up of an organization of millions of people. The monstrous organism assembled quite spontaneously, achieved its ends and then dispersed. We can now behave as crowds without being within each other's physical presence. It can be formless – not even slug-like. And it can disappear, dissolve without trace into the flow.

Amplification

Just as subjectivity, subjects, shells and architectures can be extracted from the flow and dissipate back into it, so can these extractions articulate a flow: speak, express and amplify. Orhan Pamuk's essay 'When the Furniture Is Talking, How Can You Sleep?' opens:

> Some nights when I get out of bed, I cannot understand why the linoleum is like this. Every square has all these lines on it. Why? And every square is different from the others.[49]

It's not an essay that invites a rational response to its questions. It is a rehearsal of paranoia: 'The telephone is talking to another telephone, which is why it has fallen silent'; 'Have you ever looked at the fringe of the carpet? Or the hidden signs in its pattern?' In fact as one reads one begins to wonder whether it is actually an essay, or rather a fictional character who is being introduced to us independently of any plot. But going back to the beginning: every square of linoleum is different from every other.

The reason is straightforward enough – the linolueum is produced by a manufacturing process that involves pressing differently pigmented batches of paste between steel rollers, so the pigments squash hard up against one another without blending. The matter that is pigmented forms a continuous sheet, but the pigments remain substantially unmixed. The pigments can be contrasted or can be closely related in tone. Nowadays sheet floor coverings are often made from vinyl and other plastics, but real linoleum is made from linseed oil and sawdust called 'wood flour'. The simple version of the recipe is to mix sawdust with linseed oil to make a paste and then to squeeze it flat, pressing it into a backing of hessian or canvas so as to hold it together before it is put in place on a floor. Then of course one way to use it is for the manufacturer to cut it up into tiles, so that it can be laid bit by bit, and a pattern of regular 'rational' tile squares is superimposed on the randomness.

It is these tiles that Pamuk encounters, and finds so disturbing. It is the non-repeating patterns within the squares that feed his paranoia. Indeed it is interesting that they are seen as 'non-repeating patterns' – not just as chaos. There is pattern here, and we recognize it, but it also escapes being a pattern that we can grasp and reproduce. Here are two very different regimes acting on the pigmented paste. One is a strong force applied from above and outside the medium – the force of the steel rollers that forces the paste into a smooth sheet. It is this aspect of the process that makes the paste useful as a floor covering. It would be unusable if it remained as lumps to be pressed on to the floor by hand. The force of the rollers is much stronger than the forces that act within the paste, binding it together flexibly. The second force that is important in determining the appearance of the sheet is the force of one pigmented paste pressing on another. The pastes are mixed so that they have the same strength and consistency, so they act on one another equally. If we try to separate out cause and effect then we have a problem, because each of the pigments has its own 'point of view' from which it seems to be pushing outward and meeting with resistance from another pigment that surrounds it. One paste makes the *milieu* for the other, and they sort themselves out at a 'molecular' level, which in this instance is not really molecular but at the scale of grains of sawdust.

But the point is that the 'decisions' about the placing of the boundary between the different colours are taken within the substances of the pastes. It's not under the willed control of the person who operates the rollers. The decision is delegated to a level where human thought does not hold sway, and so even though every grain of sawdust might have the same properties as every other grain of sawdust, the minute differences in circumstances between their different environments means that they generate shapes that never identically repeat.

If I describe what is going on in the linoleum from the point of view of a grain of sawdust, then there are two very different dimensions to my experience. One is the unarguable force of the steel roller – a tyrannical oppression that ignores any dissent. The other is the jostling of my fellow grains of sawdust, which means that we sort things out so that we're evenly packed and all equally comfortable. This is more like the kinds of force that I feel acting on me as I walk along the street, approaching the traffic lights. I keep my feet on the ground – gravity sees to that, and I am in no position to argue with it. I could say that in one plane, a vertical plane, I have no freedom, while in the other I am relatively free. If I shrink myself so as to be able to join the sawdust particles, I find that I can say much the same thing. So the irregular patterns in the linoleum are expressions of this freedom – it is freedom within powerful constraints, but a freedom nonetheless.

It is worth pointing out that whatever freedom we feel is always a freedom-within-constraints. The things we desire to do are the things we can imagine ourselves doing. Spinoza said that if we were able to communicate with a rock hurtling at a steady velocity through space, that the rock would let it be known that that was exactly what it wanted to be doing just at that moment.[50] What else would it be wanting? Similarly we feel that we are free when we are allowed to do the things that we desire. On the whole we do not often stop to ask why we feel the desire, and whether it might have been avoided, though Spinoza suggests that we should be paying attention exactly to that. We feel that we are free to go out and spend our hard-earned money on things that buy us sustenance, or pleasure, or status, depending on what we are feeling the need for at that moment, but there is a whole profession of advertisers who understand how to create and channel our desires, so that the manufacturers who are paying them benefit from our freedom to act on them.

Moreover, there are some desires that I do not have just because I do not suppose that they would ever be met, and to nurture them would only lead to frustration. The law of gravity acts on me in a way that I think is inescapable, and so I don't find myself yearning to escape it. Perhaps this is a form of resignation, but I do not feel it as a version of Thoreau's desperation. It seems to be built into me, and the desires that I have would tend to take that for granted; but perhaps the reason it feels 'built-in' is because the circumstances of my life have 'produced' that effect as part of my subjectivity. If it had been innate in everyone then we would never have developed the aeroplane and the story of Icarus would never have had a hold on our imaginations. When I try to empathize with the sawdust particle in a sheet of linoleum, I find that I would be resigned to the action of the steel rollers as part of the nature of things, and I would be concentrating on aligning myself in solidarity with my fellow sawdust particles – at least the few around me with whom I was in contact – so that we all feel the same kind of pressure. That is the kind of freedom I would find, and that is the kind of freedom that finds expression in the pattern.

So there are two sorts of form-making going on here. The first, which is producing the useful sheet of hard-wearing, water-resistant floor covering, is 'hylomorphic' – producing a result that is precisely determined in advance by an agency that is outside and beyond the floor covering – a power acting from 'above'. The second, which is producing the pattern (if 'pattern' it is), is negotiated from within the flooring itself, by the particles that compose it. This aspect of the design is what Deleuze and Guattari call a 'plateau'; it has no definite beginning or end or edges – it can continue indefinitely in any direction – and all the decisions about it are made within the *milieu*, not from above.

Decisions, Decisions

It might sound fanciful to be talking about the grains of sawdust 'making decisions', but it is not as fanciful as all that. When the slime mould finds the shortest way through a maze, it does so despite the fact that it has nothing that even remotely resembles a brain. The individual cells of the mould are identical, and an individual cell cannot find its way through the maze; but when there is an agglomeration of thousands of them, they can do it. So are they thinking, or not? It is hard to say. Individually they certainly are not, but collectively they are doing something that might as easily be called 'thinking' as be called anything else.

Marc Godts and Nel Janssens' Chapter 2, 'Theoretical, Conceptual, Ethical and Methodological Stakes to Induce a New Age: M.U.D.', is one such engagement in a thinking that falls outside the usual logics and rationalisms of strict categories or imposed laws. Godts and Janssens look not to slime mould but to the multiple scales of the Belgium coastline and amplify its flows and floods in order to (re)think the architectural potency of land and liquid. This is literal but imaginary mud, which has its own internal logic and behavioural habits. Returning to Minsky's 'society of mind', one starts to wonder whether we ourselves would seem to be doing anything like 'thinking' if we were to separate out all the individual micro-decisions that go into the formulation of what is eventually expressed as a 'thought'. The individual little micro-machines do not think, but when they are connected together, so that one bit acts on the information supplied by another bit, and one runs through thousands of such links, then the assemblage can do something that looks from the outside very like thinking. If the two processes are the same, except in their scale and complexity, then we could see the two processes as instances of the same 'abstract machine', and then it becomes a question of custom and habit whether we feel comfortable talking about the sawdust designing the pattern in the lino, or seeing ourselves as particles in the city's arteries.

Things are going on – certain sorts of interaction – that operate across the boundaries of species and organisms, and different cultures can decide to draw in different places the lines that separate out the individuations involved. Moving in one direction we might be inclined to notice the mechanistic aspects of organisms;

Fluxions

moving in the other we would notice the life that animates machines.[51] The idea of simple processes interacting in complex ways is something that runs through a great many things, organic and inorganic, and we need not impose a rigid separation between these realms. We are, after all, composed of elements that in their most reductive state are inorganic: carbon, iron, calcium, oxygen and so on – a handful of dust. What matters are how these elements combine to build up into the entities that we know, and have the patterns of behaviour that we recognize.

Boh Tea

Another emergent pattern: a tea plantation in the Cameron Highlands in Malaysia. The tea trees are arranged so that people can walk in between them to pick the new shoots from the ends of the branches. The interdependent variables here are the conditions for growth of the trees, and the limits on growth that are imposed so as to keep the leaves accessible. These variables adjust to the irregular topography so the striations produced by the rows of planting have their regularities and their flexibilities, and they adjust to their circumstances in a way that is rational and visually appealing, but the point of it is pragmatic and effective. The decisions taken at local level – how far can I reach? How much space do we need between rows? – aggregate into a complex and sophisticated-looking pattern. The pattern is not defined from outside in a rigidly determined way, but is defined relationally, by the inclinations of the tree, the form of the land, and the reach of the workers (figure 1.2). These three things come together and produce something that looks like a pattern, but it is entirely defined from within, not by reference to an ideal form that it falls short of being.

Figure 1.2 Striated plantation, Boh tea, Cameron Highlands, Malaysia.

Andrew Ballantyne and Chris L. Smith

Manchester

At a larger scale again this kind of pattern-making can be found in the city. At that scale it is possible for humans to take decisions about what they are doing without those decisions necessarily being guided by a vision of the whole. So the order emerges from within, rather than being imposed from above. Such an order, an ordering, is described by Peter Mörtenböck and Helge Mooshammer in Chapter 6: 'Trade Flow: Architectures of Informal Markets'. Mörtenböck and Mooshammer describe an organization of space which has neither centre nor specific end; a space that is neither characterized in relation to a central authority nor through programmed identities and strict objectives. Such 'informal' ordering is not only the preserve of unregulated small markets. There is a wonderful description by Engels of the layout of Manchester, which when he knew it in the mid-nineteenth century was a booming town, not yet recognized as a city and with Waterhouse's town hall still a generation away from being built. He describes its generative logic in exactly these terms. It is built, he says:

> so that someone can live in it for years and travel into and out of it daily without ever coming into contact with a working-class quarter or even with workers – so long [. . .] as one confines himself to his business affairs or to strolling about for pleasure. This comes about mainly in the circumstances that through unconscious, tacit agreement as much as through conscious, explicit intention the working-class districts are most sharply separated from the parts of the city reserved for the middle class. [. . .]
>
> Manchester's monied aristocracy can now travel from their houses to their places of business in the centre of town by the shortest routes, which run right through the working-class districts, without even noticing how close they are to the most squalid misery which lies immediately about them on both sides of the road. This is because the main streets which run from the Exchange in all directions out of the city are occupied almost uninterruptedly on both sides by shops, which are kept by members of the middle and lower-middle classes. In their own interests these shopkeepers should keep up their shops in an outward appearance of cleanliness and respectability; and in fact they do so [. . .] Those shops which are situated in the commercial quarter or in the vicinity of the middle-class districts are more elegant than those which serve to cover the workers' grimy cottages. Nevertheless, even these latter adequately serve the purpose of hiding from the eyes of the wealthy gentlemen and ladies with strong stomachs and weak nerves the misery and squalor that form the completing counterpart, the indivisible complement, of their riches and luxury. I know perfectly well that this deceitful manner of building is more or less common to all big cities [. . .] I have never elsewhere seen a concealment of such fine sensibility of every thing that might offend the eyes and nerves of the middle

classes. And yet it is precisely Manchester that has been built less according to a plan and less within the limitations of official regulations – and indeed more through accident – than any other town.[52]

Engels explains how the pattern of the city is generated not by the imposition of form from a higher level, but by decisions taken within the *milieu*, especially but not exclusively by the small shopkeepers. He calls the manner of building 'deceitful', and in doing so places himself on a higher level. He does not himself subscribe to the values that are finding expression in the town. To someone who does subscribe to the town's values (which is to say, to someone who does not really think about them, but lives in the town) the manner of building does not look deceitful at all – it would not be conceived in those terms. There is nothing hypocritical here, only the exercise of a sense of decorum. Just as one would not do in public some things that seem perfectly natural in private, so it is that decisions are taken about what kind of activity is appropriate on different kinds on street. If I live in the Manchester that Engels describes, and am well adjusted to my life there, then whatever class of society I negotiate, I do not see the town's layout as deceitful and hypocritical, but as more or less natural. That is because my subjectivity has been produced in that *milieu* – I am part of that town and have its values in me as part of my identity. It would feel to me that as the town rapidly developed, although there might be inconveniences along the way, nevertheless everything would seem to be going swimmingly. As a particle in the town I would not need to take a view of the whole town – and Engels suggests that nobody in fact did so – I just need to decide whether I can find a place to live. Maybe I have to settle for somewhere squalid, but I can hope that I can afford to live somewhere, and with access to a means of subsistence I can thrive and look around. With a certain level of prosperity I can ask where it would be good to locate my shop, how to pass for a respectable citizen, how to make a decent living. It involves *not* thinking radically, but being absorbed in the *milieu*, participating in *its* common sense. From outside and above – from Engels' point of view – it might look as if I have been brainwashed; but *from within* everything looks just fine.

Order

If I think about the kind of order that I find around me, at a personal scale, I am rather aware that if I am going to keep it looking anything remotely *like* order, then a constant activity of maintenance and tidying up is required. If I just act unselfconsciously and do the things I'm inclined to do while I'm working, for example, then I end up with sheets of paper, open books and cups of coffee distributed more or less within reach of my computer. And for as long as I am at work, it feels like a fairly reasonable kind of order that is taking shape around me, beginning to make a provisional definition of a space that is adapted to my needs – a continuation of my activity – an emanation. When I break off from my work then everything stays in place, and that need not be a problem, as long as I have other space to use – ideally in another room. However, when I revisit the place, without the intention of continuing with the work, or even more acutely, if I have a visitor who is expecting to be able to sit down at this table to eat, then I have a crisis in my understanding of this emergent 'order'. Before, when it was in active use, it was convenient and supportive, and I could feel an order assembling itself around me as I was writing. Now, seeing it with a visitor's eyes, the room looks like a bomb has hit it. It looks terrible, neglected and problematic. I do not want my visitor to see the place looking like this, and somehow I have no confidence in the sense of order that I had only a short time before. That has altogether deserted me. I cannot work without making a mess, but while I am working it does not feel like a mess. The tidiness, that keeps being forcibly reimposed at intervals, is an order imposed from above, and it is instantly comprehended by a visitor coming in on the scene. The hylomorphic order imposed from above and outside is the kind of order that is immediately apparent to the visitor – like Le Corbusier's correct and magnificent play of forms in light. The order from within the plateau, the emergent order of immanence and emanation, the architecture of relations, is less tidy at first glance, but as a priority it accommodates (because it is generated by) the machinic relations that make things work.

Åsa Andersson's Chapter 4, 'Interpretive Flow: A 1930s Trans-Cultural Architectural Nexus', is a return to the personal and intensely particularized 'emergent orders' of her engagement with a summer cottage designed by the architect Georg Scherman and built on the east coast of Sweden in 1935. Andersson extracts the poetic resonances, material associations and architectural references from the flow of her continuing engagement – her ordering of this summer cottage.

Scales

This aspect of expression – of expressing an order from within – clearly relates to the idea that architecture might express the materials from which a thing is made, or find a way to let them find expression. Building materials are inescapably the substance of buildings, and it makes some sense to adopt materials that we can allow to find expression for various reasons, not the least of them being that by doing so one can enhance the sense of the building being real – which seems in constant danger of being lost in the contemporary world, where appearances can be manipulated in so many ways. The same issues are at work at various different scales, from the microscopic to the regional and beyond, but we relate most readily to things at the scales we can most readily perceive.

At the human scale we give these processes names like 'thought' and 'will', 'desire' and 'life'. We are uncomfortable about recognizing these same attributes at scales much larger or smaller than our own: it is significantly easier to for us to contemplate killing a gnat than a mammal of any size, because it is more of a stretch to feel empathy with it. Historically we have even had some problems recognizing them in non-human creatures that are about our own size, 'the ascidian and the crocodile', and with which we might expect to be able to feel some empathy, but Butler points to the sympathetic rapport that develops between an engineer and a steam engine, and nowadays portable computers and mobile telephones' enabling of social links make them part of our relational apparatus and therefore part of who we are. The idea of architecture can be generalized, from the starting point, where I think about myself in a room, to thinking about being in smaller and larger spaces, established through the relational content in the connections that are to be found in the space, whether they are the aggregates of molecules that make up materials, or the aggregates of people that make up a society. Somewhere in between these scales of operation there are buildings, which when we look at them at one scale are the cells of a greater organism that we call a city, and when we look at them at another they are environments for people. At a smaller scale again the building materials are sites of orderings for the grain of timber or for the wood flour of linoleums. Beyond this scale, buildings are environments for the molecules that bind together to make materials. And at a larger scale than the city, the surrounding countryside has a role to play in sustaining the city's need for resources, and it is in communication with other cities that in a way make up its environment. Even the individual human subject doesn't escape from the relations with others, and depending on the relations we are drawn into, we find ourselves developing different aspects of the character we might suppose ourselves to have. We call our interpersonal relations by the name 'politics', and similarly there is a politics in matter, in the relations between molecules, and politics in the relations between cities. Just so, we can think of the role of buildings as political mediators. The matter of which a building is made might find expression, or it might be actively suppressed. A building might promote the fellow feeling of the people who move in and out of it, or it might separate them out so that they never come into contact. People with different roles are often separated out, for example, in a large hotel, with service lifts and corridors, or in a theatre where the backstage areas are out of bounds for the general public, or even in a restaurant, where the dining space can have a very different ambience from the kitchen and service areas, which are reached by an altogether different route.

    Buildings help us to behave in certain ways, and obstruct us when we try to do otherwise. If I live in a city then I know that some doors are open to me, while others remain firmly closed. I am familiar with some places, and I go to them because I feel comfortable in those surroundings. There are some places that offer facilities that I want to use – like the university library, which is open to me, but is not open to everybody. There are shops that sell things that I want to buy today, others that sell things that I might want to buy someday, and some shops in which I cannot imagine I will ever set foot. The city that I occupy is subtly different from the one that my friends occupy, and hugely different from the city that is experienced by some of the other people who live in it. So far as the city-organism is concerned, we are as different from one another as the kidneys are from the heart – both necessary for the city to thrive in the way it does, but not interchangeable.

    This is a lesson learnt from Deleuze and Guattari, who move from one scale to another – the molecular to the molar – but see the same things going on at different scales. Ordinarily we have different names for these things, and we discuss them under separate headings. Things happening at a molecular scale are considered as physics. Things happening at the human scale are considered as psychological or medical or personal. Things happening at the scale of the environment are considered as ecological or political. But if we transfer the ideas across from one scale to another, we can find that the same sorts of things are going on.

Andrew Ballantyne and Chris L. Smith

There are ecologies of ideas, there are micropolitics within the individual, there is an ethics of geology. And – in all sorts of things around us – there are the beginnings of what we might want to call thought. It's not just that the furniture is speaking, not only the linoleum and the telephone, but the buildings they're in, and the buildings outside, and the sawdust and the clay, and the rolled sheets of steel and the drawn copper wires, the cast concrete blocks and the polished timber floors. They can all speak of their substance and their means of production; and they can speak of our relation with them, as we care for them or neglect them. That relation is probably most satisfactory when it is a dialogue. We make clear what it is that we want from the relation – a certain level of support, a non-slip surface, a clear passage of light – and then we allow a certain freedom so that the stuff can have its say; so that it can think for itself.

Machinic Phylum

The zone that is being described here is what Deleuze and Guattari call the 'machinic phylum' – a space where things are in flux and have not reached a determined form, but interact with one another to produce the next state of affairs. At some stage in the process things take on the shapes that we recognize and deal with, and that is the world in which we act – produced by states of affairs that we might not notice or understand, over which we have no direct control. The 'things' in the machinic phylum can be molecules or crowds, ideas or mountains. They can interact by bumping into one another or by being connected through electronically computed algorithms; however the interactions happen and it is the characteristics of the interactions that produce the 'grain' of the substance in question – the characteristics of the medium, or substance, or *milieu*.[53] In thinking of a substance with a grain, one thinks first, perhaps, of timber, which is a good model to hold in mind; but the idea is much more general than that. Georges Simondon engages with the idea in the discussion of electronic interations.[54] The fact that the mechanisms can as easily be physical, intellectual or instinctual makes it include, for example, a social fabric or any scale, from a colony of slime mould to a human city, a planet or a constellation. The world that we know from our own experience, a world of comfort and discomfort, of hunger and thirst, of consumer choices and personal desires, is a world of connections with other people, with lines of supply and access to (or separation from) resources – water and electricity, for example, which come into my personal world in a discontinuous flow – and then food, information and luxury goods, which find their way in by other means, sometimes with deliveries to the door, sometimes by my making journeys, always these days being tracked by the electronic media that make 'money' (whatever that is) flow in agreed quantities out of my accounts.

The machinic phylum includes, but is not limited to the 'space of flows', as it is defined by Manuel Castells in his sociological study of the 'network society'.[55] The space of flows is dominant in the culture of global capitalism, where anything can be liquidated, but in fact it is everywhere if we choose to see the world in those terms. Castells is inclined to see novelty where we are inclined to see continuity and intensification: flows that have been continuing for generations, gradually accelerating, seem novel when the gradual acceleration pushes us across thresholds so that we find a new way to deal with the information that is coming our way. The town crier and Twitter are both versions of the same abstract machine, that disseminates information, but a historical gulf separates them and we lose sight of the way that one gradually evolves into the other. There are differences, not least because they each bring into being a distinct social group of auditors of the information – people who live in the same neighbourhood in the first case, people who follow related tweets in the second. For as long as there has been society there has been information, and the circulation of certain sorts of information is what has constituted a society, so one could take issue with the idea of characterizing the present as the 'information age', the 'information society', or even the 'network society', since all societies have always been information-circulating networks even if they have not always been seen in that way.

The essays that follow in the rest of the book are more remarkable for their variety than for their similarities, but what they have in common is the continuing theme of giving priority to processes rather than rigidly defined geometric forms. The processes generate forms, but the forms are determined by the interactions of the parts, and the forms carry on developing, not reaching a static final result, but continuing endlessly to proliferate and flow. 'Forms' here are simply 'shapes', and carry none of the overtones of the ideal that the word 'form' would indicate in a Platonic context. The processes are machinic and productive, and involve variously the impact of literal flows – such as the flow of water, the rising of sea level with the melting of ice caps, the consequent production of vast acreages of mud in low-lying countries, and therefore the production of new ways of life and new building types to accommodate them.

The flow of sunlight is to be felt in varying degrees almost everywhere on Earth, but in some places it is given particular value and is embraced and allowed to shape the way of life to an uncommon degree, bringing in its train a particular method of economic development. Patricia Wise's Chapter 5, 'Solar Flow: The Uses of Light in Gold Coast Living', explores how sunlight itself can become mobile and translatable into the dollars, desires and the architectures of the Australian coastline. This economic development is itself another flow that has its own specific algorithms and a culture that goes with them, and is very much a part of Castells' space of flows.

Metamorphic Materials

All building materials come from the earth, but with some the journey from earth to building is short and obvious, while with others there is a transformative process that makes the origin far harder to detect. The buildings that are most characteristic of commercial developments in Castells' account of the space of flows have a character as powerful and non-place-specific as capital itself.

The steel frame is the structural basis of commercial buildings everywhere, not only the high-profile skyscrapers that make the places of commerce look so culturally assertive, from Manhattan to Kuala Lumpur and Dubai, but also the pervasive supermarkets, shopping malls, showrooms, offices and industrial units that make up the newer parts of our towns – the edges and out-of-town parts. Steel is adaptable and predictable. It is immensely strong and an engineer knows exactly how it will perform. Stone by contrast has veins of unpredictability running through it, which might cause the material to shear, so despite the fact that stone was the material used for the structure of all the world's surviving pre-modern monuments, it is seen as unreliable and therefore avoided as a structural material in normal commercial work. Steel comes from rock, but the rock is crushed and heated to make the steel run out of it as a liquid. It is purified, poured and rolled at controlled temperatures, and then cools into the product that arrives on the building site. The rolled steel joist (RSJ) that is installed in my local supermarket could have come from rock that was mined in Eastern Europe, China, Turkey or the USA, depending on the price that was negotiated when the supplier of RSJs placed the order for the steel. These markets are rational in their way, and the order would have gone to whoever was offering the best price. But the price would be influenced by international currency exchange rates, which themselves fluctuate to reflect the international business community's confidence in the future of a currency's economy; so the rational algorithm that determines where the order goes rests on a collective faith that is prone to influence by rumour and on the inductive expectation that on the whole things will continue much as before.

Craig Martin's Chapter 8, 'Controlling Flow: On the Logistics of Distributive Space', explores the dynamic logistics and management of mobility involved in the highly regulated and organized movement of materials through the port space of Thamesport in Kent. At the heart of this concern is the complexity of the relationship between materials, flow and control. Ultimately this chapter sets out to consider how forms of time and space are produced through a specific construction of logistical ordering which demonstrates the openness and unpredictability of space as well as time; and yet the finicky manipulations of logistics appear as a smooth motion at a global scale. When the steel arrives on-site in the UK it does exactly the job that it was specified to do, bearing no sign of its journey, and as a material it is indistinguishable from the steel that originated elsewhere. We do not know where a specific RSJ ultimately came from, and would not be able to find out by testing its chemical composition, any more than we would be able to determine where the fuel came from when we refilled the car at the supermarket. The food products inside are labelled so that we can tell where they are from, and the story of international connectivity that they tell is a powerful example of interdependence.[56] The seasonality of supermarket food products is more closely related to festivals and holidays than to what will grow locally at a particular time of year. There are more pumpkins available around Halloween, more sweet chestnuts around Christmas, but potatoes, apples, lettuces and strawberries are always available. They might have been grown in Peru or Thailand; they may be simultaneously being sold from a stall at the Rom-Hoob market explored by Soranart Sinuraibhan in Chapter 7, 'Local Flows'; but all I have to do is wonder whether the price looks reasonable and lift them off the shelf into my basket. In Australia I can find myself in an unremarkable supermarket wondering whether to drink water that was bottled in France or Italy. Once-liquid steel is equally mobile once it enters the marketplace.

Steel structures need sheet materials to make them usable. Plate glass is often used, which is satisfying because it leaves the steel frame more or less visible. It too has undergone a metamorphic transformation. In its raw state it is sand, but once heated, purified, infused with additives that modify its properties, then floated in a thin sheet on a bath of molten tin, cooled, tempered and solidified, it becomes the transparent veil that makes a secure showcase to display new cars, or the shiny armour of a sleek corporate tower. The transformation consumes a quantity of energy that would have amazed the pharaohs: a square metre of laminated plate glass takes about as much energy to make as would keep 135 labourers working for a day, or, to put it another way, if one person's energy were directed into the production of plate glass, he would be exhausted in the production of 3 square metres a year.[57] To see the glittering towers rising up from the desert sands around Dubai is to see the transformative power of vast quantities of energy, miraculating the grains of the earth into a shimmering iridescent mirage. One can imagine the process as a CGI effect in a film: the city conjured out of the desert by genii. In fact, though, the sand in the glass is unlikely to be local, as the industrial plant for transforming it could be in Europe or Asia.

The most routine covering for the steel frame is insulated steel sheet. The steel is rolled thin, and folded so as to make it stiff enough to span between joists, and is coated with a finish that protects it from weathering and makes it whatever colour is desired. It is the most pervasive material in the new edge-of-town developments, where there is a free choice of materials. In established town centres there is often an insistence on more traditional materials that match the older buildings, but out of town the steel-framed, glass-clad buildings are everywhere, often housing useful facilities. It is safe to say that they are hardly ever loved as buildings, but we keep building them because they answer the imperatives of the non-human system that humans sustain. They are flexible, adaptable and predictable (which is to say reliable). They cost significantly less money to build than would buildings of the same size made with traditional materials, and they can be put up far more quickly, their components coming from wherever in the world they are currently available at the best price. The appealing thing about these buildings is not on the plane of human experience, but on the plane of capital. They produce the best figures. They started in factories and as factories, as effective ways of protecting the expensive machines and their attendant workers, but now they house our hospitals and schools, shopping malls, museums and concert halls. There are steel-framed houses, which have architectural cachet when the steel frame is evident, but they often pass unnoticed because they are clad in reassuringly old-fashioned materials. The spaces in houses are smaller than those in factories, so timber frames have more often been able to do the job at a lower cost than steel, and so have been preferred. Again (at least in the UK) the structural frames are often concealed behind a veneer of brick that gives a desired illusion of permanence and solidity. The fabric of buildings has become something to order from a catalogue or a website, rather than something to be scouted for around the site.

The *milieu* in which buildings take shape is determined not only by the architect and the builder, but by the whole culture in which they operate, which determines what materials are available, how much time there is to make decisions about them, what seems possible and what seems to be out of the question because it would leave open too many professional liabilities. If we take the prudent cost-effective decisions that we (as a society) are bound to take most of the time, then without quite noticing it we generate the environment that is actually taking shape around us.

Background

It is this routine production that is the mainstream architecture of the space of flows, and we have a high propensity to take little notice of it. As a culture we tell ourselves that the really significant buildings are the rare exceptions that stand apart from the crowd as objects of admiration and as Michael Tawa suggests in our concluding *envoi* (Chapter 12, 'Limits of Fluxion'), stability and orthogonality too have the potential to unsettle. In a city we do tend to notice the few important 'cultural' buildings, while the rest of the fabric disappears into the background; but it is in this non-signifying background that most of us spend most of our lives. At a smaller scale the same pattern is apparent: in a shopping mall the quasi-industrial housing for the activity becomes invisible, and we learn to recognize and respond to the signs that are attached outside.[58] We respond to familiar signs – being drawn to some, avoiding others – as our way of navigating towards environments where we either feel comfortable or where we think we will be able to find what we want. This is taken furthest in mass-marketing, whether it is with populist or luxury brands. Some signs draw us towards glamour and awaken desires and instincts that mean we can find ourselves spending surprisingly large sums of money on products that somehow briefly persuaded us that we would be able to inspire lust and envy in others if only we owned these shoes, sunglasses, this fragrance, those clothes. Other signs beckon with the promise of an unpretentious atmosphere, safe familiar products and low prices. No one is going to be impressed by anything from these places, but at least they are affordable and do the job.

At a larger scale again the same process seems to operate, so that if we are far enough away from them some whole nations are adequately signified by a single monument: Egypt by a pyramid, France by the Eiffel Tower, India by the Taj Mahal. These iconic buildings attract the attention of tourists, but play no role at all in everyday life. They invite aesthetic contemplation, but our daily routines and our productive activities are housed in buildings that we hardly look at at all. They are the background buildings, which are produced by making prudent decisions about spending the limited amount of money that we have. If I need somewhere comfortable to sit, then I might think about the problem from first principles and consider making something myself or commissioning a craftsman to do a better job; however, statistically I would be much more likely to go and see what is available in the shops or on the internet. Similarly if I do decide that something is required that I cannot buy at a reasonable price ready-made, I am likely to go in search of materials at a place where they have already been processed – timber sawn into planks or joists, or bonded into sheets, no longer looking like the trunks of trees that they once were. I can in theory go in search of a twisting branch to cut for my own use, but in practice it takes too long and in any case would look too quaint and self-consciously rustic. It feels altogether more reasonable to buy it cut and planed, and to think of timber as something that comes in long, straight pieces. The decisions that come under my conscious scrutiny are quite limited in comparison with all the processes of transformation that the materials have undergone. If I want to fix two pieces of timber together then I wonder where I can buy a screw; I do not start by looking for ore to heat up to release the iron to make it, and so long as I know how to use a screwdriver I need know nothing of the process that put the screw into my hand – and indeed put the screwdriver there too. Those processes are part of the unconscious world that actually has a much more significant effect on what I can do to shape my world than do the decisions that I am aware of taking. If I have been to the DIY store and bought the components, I *feel* that I have freely invented and made the thing from first principles, but many presuppositions were made before the products came my way. In the same way I can *feel* that I am a unique individual in my carefully wrought and finely equipped home, but if I distance myself from it a little, I can see that really it is much the same in all the important ways as my neighbours' and friends' homes. The books and music here might be different from theirs, but they too have books and music, and in fact if I start browsing along their shelves they seem to have made some of the same choices. There are times when we overstate to ourselves our individuality, our intelligence and genius. If I am formed by this society and its culture at this time as the conditions of life, then these are the things I will have. The advertising people know a surprising amount about me. They may not know what I think, but they have a fair idea of what I will do and an accurate idea of how I will spend my money. They can see me coming.

Architecture that aspires to the condition of unconscious production that we find in the seashell is the result of conscious decisions about other things. It is produced when we are going about our lives, selecting a sofa here, a light fitting there, made available by the productive flow of the rest of the community that knows nothing of me personally but which knows quite a lot about people like me. The architect needs to know about or imagine the habits of the person (or the type of person) who will be inhabiting the place, but then equally, as we adjust to our dwellings we form habits in our dealings with them and they become part of the unconscious background of our lives, rather than the focus. They become part of the fabric of our lives and part of our identity. There are times when technically they are armatures that help to constitute living organisms that have nonconscious life, but which are as much organisms as is a sea squirt or slime mould. They do this as a matter of practical fact, regardless of their style or expression.

Buildings are above all instruments of living, and they participate in a dispersed vitalism that includes not only us, but – at the furthest reach – everything. Consciously we tell each other stories that have us as heroes in our own lives, exercising free will in taking desperate identity-defining decisions about upholstery or table lamps, but in the space of flows we are particles in a bigger organism, which acts without speaking. It does not have our interests at heart, but it is precisely our interests that power its nonconscious behaviour. We can infer its intentions only by projecting our own feelings on to its deeds in retrospect, when we try to interpret what it has done without us necessarily noticing. It melts iron in China to make girders scrape the sky in Abu Dhabi. It warms the air with its breathing and causes cities to sprout. It lays waste to forests and makes the ocean levels laugh. It moves populations and changes the weather.

Notes

1 Le Corbusier, *Vers une architecture* (Paris: Crès,1924), transl. John Goodman, *Toward an Architecture* (London: Frances Lincoln, 2008), 102.
2 Karl August Wittfogel, *The Hydraulic Civilizations* (Chicago: University of Chicago Press, 1956); ibid., *Oriental Despotism: A Comparative Study of Total Power* (New Haven, CT: Yale University Press, 1957).
3 Jonathan Barnes, *The Presocratic Philosophers* (London: Routledge, 1979), 66.
4 Gilles Deleuze and Félix Guattari, *Mille plateaux: Capitalisme et schizophrénie, tome 2* (Paris: Les Editions de Minuit, 1980) transl. Brian Massumi, *A Thousand Plateaus: Capitalism and Schizophrenia volume 2* (Minneapolis: University of Minnesota Press, 1987), 363.
5 Eileen Gray, cited by Peter Adam, *Eileen Gray: Architect/Designer* (New York: Abrams, 1987, revised edition 2000), 309. I have retranslated the French original.
6 Kensuke Naka, *Biomineralization 1: Crystallization and Self-Organization Process* (Berlin and Heidelberg: Springer, 2007).
7 Diogenes, see *What is Architecture?*, ed. Andrew Ballantyne (London: Routledge, 2002), 1; Henry Thoreau, *Walden*, cited in *Architecture Theory*, ed. Andrew Ballantyne (London: Continuum, 2005), 152.
8 Henry David Thoreau, *Walden* (1854) in *Walden and Civil Disobedience*, ed. Owen Thomas (New York: Norton, 1966), 5.
9 Samuel Butler, 'Quis Desiderio . . .?' in *Universal Review* (July 1888), republished in Samuel Butler, *Essays on Life, Art and Science*, ed. R.A. Streatfeild (London: A.C. Fifield, 1908), 2–3.
10 Ibid., 3; John Frost, *Lives of Eminent Christians* (Hartford, CT: Case, Tiffany and Co., 1850). The text was republished in New York in 1875 as the *Cyclopedia of Eminent Christians of Various Denominations*, but the new binding would no longer have suited Butler's purpose. Butler's most famous work, *The Way Of All Flesh* (London: Grant Richards, 1903) published posthumously, but written 1873–84, is a sustained critique of his father, a clergyman, and there is certainly mischief in his choice of book here.
11 Butler, 'Quis Desiderio . . .?', 3.
12 Samuel Butler, *Life and Habit* (London: 1877; 2nd edition, ed. R.A. Streatfeild, London: A.C. Fifield, 1910; reprinted London: Wildwood House, 1981).
13 Samuel Butler, *Evolution Old and New* (London: Hardwick and Bogue, 1879); Samuel Butler, *Unconscious Memory* (London: Hardwick and Bogue, 1880); Samuel Butler, *Luck or Cunning as the Main Means of Organic Modification* (London: A.C. Fifield, 1886); Samuel Butler, *The Notebooks of Samuel Butler* (London: A.C. Fifield, 1912; reprinted ed. P.N. Furbank, London: The Hogarth Press, 1985). See also Gregory Bateson, *Mind and Nature* (London: Wildwood House, 1979) and Donald R. Forsdyke, 'Samuel Butler and Human Long Term Memory: Is the Cupboard Bare?' in *Journal of Theoretical Biology*, No. 258 (2009), 156–64.
14 William Wordsworth, 'The Rainbow', 1802.
15 G.S. Kirk, J.E. Raven and M. Schofield, *The Presocratic Philosophers* (Cambridge: Cambridge University Press, 1957), 211.
16 Bernard Stiegler, *La Technique et le temps 2. La Désorientation* (Paris: Galilée, 1996), transl. Stephen Barker, *Technics and Time, 2: Disorientation* (Stanford, CA: Stanford University Press, 2009), 97–187.

17 Charles Darwin, *On the Origin of Species By Means of Natural Selection, or the Preservation of Favoured Races In the Struggle for Life* (London: John Murray, 1859); unless otherwise noted reference is to a facsimile of the first edition with an introduction by Ernst Mayr (Cambridge, MA: Harvard University Press, 1966).

18 'Darwin displays, categorises, and argues, but does not expect to contain the workings of the world in his mind, or ever fully to understand them. He believed that he had discovered the mechanism of evolution but he did not expect to encompass the whole process. Indeed his theory was necessarily hypothetical rather than traditionally inductive'; Gillian Beer, *Darwin's Plots: Evolutionary Narrative in Darwin, George Eliot and Nineteenth-Century Fiction* (Cambridge: Cambridge University Press, 1983, 2nd edition 2000), 51.

19 Gottfried Semper, 'Development of Architectural Style' in *The Inland Architect and News Record* (14, 1889), 58; cited in Philip Steadman, *The Evolution of Designs: Biological Analogy in Architecture and the Applied Arts* (Cambridge: Cambridge University Press, 1979), 73.

20 Oliver Stone (director), *Wall Street* (1987).

21 *Desperate Housewives* has been broadcast on ABC from 2004, attracting 24 million viewers in its first few seasons. It is still being recommissioned and sells worldwide.

22 Herman Melville, 'Bartleby the Scrivener, A Wall Street History' in *Putnam's Monthly Magazine* (1853); see 'Bartleby, The Scrivener: A Story of Wall-Street' in *The Library of America: Melville, volume 3* (New York: Literary Classics of the United States, 1984), 635–72.

23 It might be noted that Darwin's evolution-related phraseology centres on a notion of 'any organic being' and he often refers to an organism as 'form', 'organic being' or simply 'being'. The use of 'forms' to denote organic bodies should not be regarded as an instance of Platonism – indeed, Darwin was deeply anti-Platonic. See Walter F. Cannon, 'Darwin's Vision in On the Origin of Species' in *The Art of Victorian Prose*, ed. George Levine and William Madden (London: Oxford University Press, 1969), 154–76.

24 Stuart Brown, *Play* (New York: Avery, 2009), 70–3.

25 Gilles Deleuze, *Logique du sens* (Paris: Les Editions de Minuit, 1969) transl. Mark Lester and Charles Stivale, *The Logic of Sense*, ed. Constantin V. Boundas (New York: Columbia University Press, 1990).

26 Peter Adam, op. cit., 378.

27 Barnes, op. cit., 75.

28 Lucretius (Titus Lucretius Carus), 1st century BCE, *De rerum natura* (*On the Nature of Things*) many editions and translations including the Loeb edition by W.H.D. Rouse (London: Heinemann, 1966); Michel Serres, transl. Josué V. Harari and David F. Bell, 'Language and Space: From Oedipus to Zola' and 'Lucretius: Science and Religion' in *Hermes: Literature, Science, Philosophy* (Baltimore, MD: Johns Hopkins University Press: 1982), 39–53, 98–124; Michel Serres, *La Naissance de la physique dans la texte de Lucrèce* (Paris: Les Editions de Minuit, 1977) transl. Jack Hawkes, *The Birth of Physics* (Manchester: Clinamen Press, 2000).

29 John Ruskin, *Love's Meinie, Lectures on Greek and English Birds*, given before the University of Oxford (Keston, Kent: Allen, 1873), 59.

30 Beer, op. cit., 7.

31 Charles Lyell, *The Principles of Geology* (London: John Murray, 1830) cited Beer, op. cit., 21.

32 The argument of 'natural selection' is made in *On the Origin of Species* by introducing the notion of 'Variation under Domestication', or as 'artificial selection' where man is presented as the unconscious architect of domesticated species before subsequent chapters completely swallow the human into the discourse of 'organic being'; Darwin, *Origin of Species*, Chapter 1, 7–43.

33 This 'connection' was explored in Beer, op. cit., 62.

34 Jacques Derrida, 'La structure, le signe et le jeu dans le discours des sciences humaine' (lecture delivered at Johns Hopkins University, Baltimore, 21 October 1966) transl. Alan Bass, 'Structure,

Sign, and Play, in the Discourse of the Human Sciences' in *Writing and Difference* (Chicago: University of Chicago Press, 1978), 278–93. 'Freeplay' is Bass's translation of Derrida's *jeu*. See *The Structuralist Controversy: The Languages of Criticism and the Sciences of Man*, ed. Richard Macksey and Eugenio Donato (Baltimore, MD: Johns Hopkins University Press, 1972), 264.
35 Brian Massumi, *Parables for the Virtual: Movement, Affect, Sensation* (Durham, NC: Duke University Press, 2002), 16.
36 Julien Offray de La Mettrie, *L'Homme machine* (Paris: 1748), transl. G. Bussey, *Man a Machine* (New York: Open Court, 1977), 51.
37 Steve Johnson, *Emergence* (New York: Scribner, 2001), 11–17, 20–1, 63–4, 163–9. See also John H. Holland, *Emergence: From Chaos to Order* (Oxford: Oxford University Press, 1998); Scott Manazine, Jean-Louis Deneubourg, Nigel R. Franks, James Sneyd, Guy Theraulaz and Eric Bonabeau, *Self-Organization in Biological Systems* (Princeton, NJ: Princeton University Press, 2001); Richard Solé and Brian Goodwin, *Signs of Life: How Complexity Pervades Biology* (New York: Basic Books, 2000).
38 A.M. Turing, 'The Chemical Basis of Morphogenesis' in *Philosophical Transactions of the Royal Society of London*, Series B, Biological Sciences, Vol. 237, No. 641 (1952), 37–72.
39 See for example John C. Dallon and Hans G. Othmer, 'How cellular movement determines the collective force generated by the *Dictyostelium discoideum* slug' in *Journal of Theoretical Biology*, 23 (2004), 203–22.
40 Marvin Minsky, *The Society of Mind* (London: Heinemann, 1987). See also A.M. Turing, 'Computing Machinery and Intelligence' in *Minds and Machines*, ed. Alan Ross Anderson (Englewood Cliffs, NJ: Prentice-Hall, 1964), 4–30.
41 Deleuze and Guattari, *A Thousand Plateaus*, op. cit.
42 Marvin Minsky, *The Emotion Machine* (New York: Simon and Schuster, 2006).
43 Godfrey Reggio (director), *Koyaanisqatsi* (1982).
44 Samuel Butler, 'The Book of the Machines' in Ballantyne, *Architecture Theory*, op. cit., 126–43; cited by Deleuze and Guattari, *L'Anti-Oedipe: capitalisme et schizophrénie* (Paris: Editions de Minuit, 1972) transl. Robert Hurley, Mark Seem and Helen R. Lane, *Anti-Oedipus: Capitalism and Schizophrenia* (New York: Viking, 1977), 284–5; breast and baby, ibid., 1.
45 Deleuze and Guattari, *A Thousand Plateaus*, op. cit., 3.
46 Félix Guattari, *Chaosmose* (Paris: Galilée 1992), transl. Paul Bains and Julian Pefanis, *Chaosmosis: an Ethico-Aesthetic Paradigm* (Sydney: Power Publications, 1995), 1.
47 Ibid., 9.
48 Clay Shirky, *Here Comes Everybody: the Power of Organizing Without Organizations* (Harmondsworth: Allen Lane, 2008).
49 Orhan Pamuk, *Öteki Renkler: Seçme Yalizar ve Bir Hikâye* (Istanbul: İletisim, 1999), transl. Maureen Freely, *Other Colors* (New York: Knopf, 2007), 26.
50 Baruch Spinoza, Letter 62, to G. H. Schaller (The Hague, October, 1674).
51 Mark Rowlands, *The New Science of the Mind: From Extended Mind to Embodied Phenomenology* (Cambridge, MA: MIT Press, 2010); Jeremy Narby, *Intelligence in Nature: An Inquiry Into Knowledge* (New York: Tarcher/Penguin, 2006); *Shamans Through Time: Five Hundred Years on the Path to Knowledge*, ed. Jeremy Narby and Francis Huxley (London: Thames and Hudson, 2001); Michel Serres, *Hominescence* (Paris: Le Pommier, 2001).
52 Friedrich Engels, *Die Lagen der arbeitenden Klasse in England* (Leipzig: 1845), transl. Florence Wischnewetsky, *The Condition of the Working Classes in England in 1844* (Moscow: Progress, 1850, reprint 1973), 84–6; cited in Andrew Ballantyne, *Deleuze and Guattari for Architects* (London: Routledge, 2007), 89–90.
53 Deleuze and Guattari, *A Thousand Plateaus*, op. cit., 408–9.
54 Gilbert Simondon, *L'individuation à la lumière des notions de forme et d'information* (Grenoble:

Millon, 2005). This is the published text of Simondon's doctoral thesis from 1958. Deleuze and Guattari reference an earlier shorter version: Gilbert Simondon, *L'Individu et sa genèse physico-biologique* (Paris: Presses Universitaires de France, 1964). See also Jean-Hugues Barthélémy, *Penser l'individuation: Simondon et la philosophie de la nature* (Paris: L'Harmattan, 2005); Jean-Hugues Barthélémy, *Penser la connaissance et la technique après Simondon* (Paris: L'Harmattan, 2005); Jean-Hugues Barthélémy, *Simondon ou l'encyclopédisme génétique* (Paris: Presses Univesitaires de France, 2008).

55 Manual Castells, *The Information Age: Economy, Society and Culture*, 3 volumes (Oxford: Blackwell, 1996–8).

56 Andrew Ballantyne and Gill Ince, 'Rural and Urban *Milieux*' in *Rural and Urban: Architecture Between Two Cultures* (London: Routledge, 2010), 1–27.

57 Based on 4,000 kcals a day for a working person, and an embodied energy of 210,000 BTU per square foot for laminated glass (10 square feet per square metre).

58 Robert Venturi and Denise Scott Brown, *Architecture as Signs and Systems for a Mannerist Time* (Cambridge, MA: Belknap/Harvard University Press, 2004).

Part One

Places in Flux

Chapter 2

Theoretical, Conceptual, Ethical and Methodological Stakes to Induce a New Age: M.U.D.

Marc Godts and Nel Janssens

Lay out: Nel Janssens, Marc Godts and Ben Robberechts

Theoretical, Conceptual, Ethical and Methodological Stakes

ABSTRACT

The M.U.D project develops ways of thinking about shared territory (here: the Belgian coastline) and tries to be coherent with the ideas of flux/flood/floating/flows etc. Its design presents an 'artist's impression' pre-figuring the age of the hybrid called M.U.D. Its designers turn the coastal area into a zone of 'future conflict' where floods and flows are anticipated, accepted, even welcomed. In consequence the use of land as well of sea will be negotiated in permanence.

To compensate for 'loss' of land and 'solids', a new 'liquid' exploitation is proposed. Changing grids scan M.U.D for flow-through of source material, energy and waste, fluxes of data transport, population and migration and re-code all these as transactional knowledge, technology and culture. The 'urban network coast' formerly known as 'linear coastal city' and once, long ago, as 'coastal resorts', dissolves, atomizes, explodes further and further into a enormity of small interactions and changes, shifts of interstitial, making the coastal area, again, truly, a 'coast', that is: a Space of Flows.

A READER'S GUIDE

The different types of writing reflect different types of design and reflection.

One column reads like a story. It is the M.U.D narrative, a voice off, telling you bedtime-wise its story: M.U.D as a design and its working in the world. The second column like a glossary flips through a second level of design: the design of key concepts and instruments.

An extensive footnote, in its attempt to be the longest footnote in history ever, elaborates page bottom on the theoretical, conceptual, ethical and methodological stakes[1] that underpin the M.U.D project: reflection.

Images flash through the text and slide-show the first level of design: the evolving of the project from a reading of the existing situation (satellite image) to the designing of the M.U.D environment and its propaganda by means of the artist's impression.

With this specific layout we de- and (re-)construct the different levels of thinking, acting, designing that are active in the design process of M.U.D and the like, and how they intertwine: research by design, including the design of this paper in progress.

---

[1] **THE STAKES**

The M.U.D. project was designed by FLC. FLC is an ongoing sequel of designers working in free association and has everything to do with the
clashes between individuals, the clashing of individual aims, experiences, desires and intuitions into something more interesting than the unique expression of a unique identity and into something more flexible, workable and exciting: a collectivity, not a compromise. The coming together of designers with their individual backgrounds, motivations and practices naturally means FLC projects evolve around crucial points where everything meets: shared territories, no matter the size or medium.

Marc Godts and Nel Janssens

PROLOGUE

The FLC Glossary is a glossary of the technical terms, instruments, concepts and notions which have all been generated by the extended design activity of FLC. The terms are being constantly updated by that same activity, so this is a 'glossary in motion'. Its terms constitute a specific field of knowledge opened up by design and related to spaces of limits, shared territories, collective intelligence and collective behaviour.

Usage guide:

[unsyllabicated main entry/term out of the alphabetical list of terms related to the specific field of FLC and generated by their design activity] *(a reference to the origin of the term)* *defining cross-reference **0.1** the first of its meanings or accompanying definitions **0.2** a second meaning or accompanying definition **0.3** and so on. Definitions are presented with or without (*a cross-reference to related term). A ~ symbol stands for the term in question. Text between ( ) is a specification in relationship to a meaning or definition. Text between ' ' is a referential quote. *Italic illustrates the use of the term.*

Selection from the FLC GLOSSARY

A

[artificial flood] *(FLC2005 concept)* **0.1** desired even provoked flooding to produce an intentional rupture of a coastal or inner coastal membrane **0.2** similar to an arena of artificial life ~ unleashes some behavioural codes in order to provoke new, modified behaviour **0.3** ~ (re)defines and moves limits/borders/agreements (*HYPER-ECONOMY *CAPSULAR COAST).

Sixty-seven kilometres of Belgian coastline. Every metre of this heavily exploited strip along the North Sea is considered by its users to be a highly personal possession. A possession to whose many aspects they simultaneously lay claim. The Belgian coast is for individual consumers and is in no way attached to any sort of sense of collective responsibility whatsoever. Where hyper-individualism and the economy of experience intersect, that's where the sea is: ('our sea, my sea'). (from Andrew) Mare Nostrum Mare Meum.

Mare Meum, 'my own personal sea', is under threat, and with it the illusion of the enchanting world for which we, the consumers of experience, are constantly in search. With the possibility of a deluge and a number of social phenomena in the back of our minds, a manipulated satellite picture crystallizes, on a tapestry ¹⁄ₙ the premonition of a new era, one of mud.

What FLC started to do is emphasize in each job, commission or project, possibilities of turning conflicts into positive energy, introducing the imagination to future conflicts over which space can be negotiated continuously, mirrors for collective intelligence. (FLC extended, 2003)

FLC is part of this flipmode society where networking outsmarts bipolar routines, where reality and fiction merge, where references go tactile or extra-sensory and stop being simply visual.
And in this flipmode era of reorientation into daily life, planning and politics, some very big problems and contradictions emerge.

Theoretical, Conceptual, Ethical and Methodological Stakes

[ambient] *(picked up from the term (ambient music) a music that creates an environment and is intended to drift in and out of the listeners awareness while creating its effect on the listener's consciousness, FLC adaptation 2005 instrument)* **0.1** short for: ambient information and cognition system **0.2** (first level) a pleasant stay **0.3** (second level) an environment of communication and interaction **0.4** (third level) a display of information, instruments, rules and tools; *in M.U.D. the ~ was a vast carpet printed with an artist's impression and combined with television screens showing the communication on the project.*

[artist's impression] *(term used for designating artist's renders of applied projects like aircraft and spacecraft modelling, FLC adaptation 2005 instrument)* *PUBLIC IMPRESSION **0.1** one of many possible images that crystallizes a possible perspective on the issue; as such the ~ can stand on its own or function as a new starting point **0.2** a beautiful image playing an instrumental role as a strong visual synthesis, leaving an opening for multiple meaning and interpretation **0.3** a moment in time **0.4** an end product reflecting the designer's attitude of taking distance from the existing reality in order to create a new, plausible reality, leaving room for interpretation; the ~ has a relationship with reality but is not a (exact) representation of it; *in M.U.D the ~ was a manipulated satellite picture.*

In the MUD era there are ongoing negotiations over the dividing lines that were formerly fixed boundaries. Boundaries between water, land and air and also between use and development. In the MUD era concessions to the rising water are compensated by risk management and local super-defences. And each point within the MUD barrier zone is capable of transforming or upgrading itself economically, culturally and socially.

That is why there is a need for more imaginative design.

The particular philosophy and organization of FLC makes it an instrument designed to explore and gain understanding of emergent possibilities, a publicly intellectual, designed tool uncommonly apt to question alleged impossibilities imposed by daily practice and reality as it is commonly perceived.

The M.U.D. project in first instance resulted in a proactive projection (image) of a possible future. This kind of speculative projection points out that the current urban planning, in search for an impossible perfection, uses outdated procedures that have

Marc Godts and Nel Janssens

C

[capsular coast] *(FLC2005 concept)* **0.1** the entirety of coastal cities, villages, coastal fortresses, endogen clusters and singular infrastructures that appear as enclosed capsules in the (M.U.D.) landscape after the intentional rupture of the coastal membrane **0.2** specific development of the coastal urbanization after the intentional rupture of the coastal membrane **0.3** beyond the tidal coast, the coastal settlements, the coastal resorts, the linear coastal city and the urban coastal network: the next step **0.4** a ~ consists of *capsular entities (*CAPSULAR SOCIETY *CAPSULAR ENTITIES).

[capsular entity] *(FLC2005 concept)* **0.1** carefully selected city material, guaranteed waterproof and completely protected against the (M.U.D.) environment **0.2** defensible capsule: *coastal fortress, mall...*

[COASTOMIZE!] *(FLC2007 concept)* **0.1** literally the coast made to meet your customers' needs (customize your coast) **0.2** ~ is meant to be an interactive and ambient set-up that will open up to a larger public the notions and dynamics of individual and collective space, individual and collective behaviour, precariousness and the perennial **0.3** ~ shows how interactivity, chain reactions and the unpredictable shape shared territories; here the Belgian coast in particular and our everyday space in general. ~ questions the roles of design and planning in such a process and illustrates how daily life, science, art and technology can get us involved **0.4** multi-sensorial, multi-material (cfr. M.U.D. mud), multi-dimensional (cfr. M.U.D. MULTI USER), multi-user, multi-ideal, multi-capsular (cfr. M.U.D. MULTI DOMAINS) **0.5** ~ is an M.U.D. and like M.U.D. it is entirely process, the realm of ongoing serial creation its only reality.

This image is not a scenario for the distant future. It shows explicitly what is already under development – though scattered and fragmented – or is being kept under control. The division of land on the polders, the flooded fields after a downpour, the oversubsidization of agriculture, the holiday villages and tropical resorts, the reports on the coastal defence strategy, the urban beaches. These elements all had a significant influence on the creation of the final picture.

FLOOD/CAPSULAR
SOCIETY/HYPER-ECONOMY
THREE GLOBAL TRENDS AS THE
BASIS FOR A LOCAL SCENARIO

The design team picked up on three social trends as usable ingredients. Although floods, the capsular society and the hyper-economy are contemporary concepts, it has not yet been established to what extent they will influence the future. However, they do provide three original angles from which to look

their roots in archaic territorial concepts. This planning is retrieved by dynamics of a reality that is driven by processes and movements that are global, interchangeable, synchronic, relative, abstract and volatile. M.U.D. shows how the flood erases the landscape and demonstrates how relative planning is. (Goossens, 2007)

We could say that this kind of design reveals to urban planning a wider perspective by investigating the space of possibilities and showing alternative potentials. The critical, radicalizing perspective taken here, enables imagination to develop unconventional standpoints
and can be an antidote to what Harvey describes as 'the sclerosis that often reigns in planners' heads', and makes it hard for them to

Theoretical, Conceptual, Ethical and Methodological Stakes

[co-creative world] *(Daniel Wahl, FLC adaptation 2007)* **0.1** refers to 'The world as it is, and at any given moment, is the best that joint intelligence and collective behaviour produces throughout what should be considered as being the longest running open source project ever.' (M. Godts) (*KILL SPACE).

forward, from the existing reality to a possible reality.

D

[designers in free association] *(FLC1997 concept)* *flc **0.1** free associating designers **0.2** the coming together of designers with their individual backgrounds, motivations and practices.

F

FLC] *(FLC1997 concept)* **0.1** short for fucklecorbusier **0.2** ~ is a ongoing sequel of designers in free association and has everything

1) The changing climate and rising sea level force us to re-examine the relationship between land and water. The 'flood' phenomenon does not revolve solely around the danger of flooding, but around the interaction between water and land and the effect it has on the border area between the two. Belgian coastal defences are not based on the possibility of a deluge. Without additional measures, the sea will break through the dykes and reoccupy the old polders. What if we were not to stick to a strict dividing line but, instead of reinforcing the dyke, allow water and land to fight for their own territory? In this scenario the borderline would change into a transitional area in which the surf is free to play with time and space. The following perimeters might be used to fix the conflict zone behind the dyke: the line marking the expected rise in

'effectively check the possibilities of evolving a different urbanization process.' (Harvey, 2000: 30). The aim of designing such prospective alternatives is not to create a 'futuristic' reality but to prefigure a possible (future) reality by bringing to the foreground latent possibilities, ⅕ possibilities that are implicitly present but are not explicitly acknowledged. It is about considering and making explicit possibilities beyond what is known ⅕ possibilities that challenge the ruling principles of daily practice. This designer way of thinking is typical for a critical/conceptual design practice, such as FLC.

In this current flip-mode era, where reorientation in the face of various emerging problems is the key challenge, designers are urged to speculate on a different future reality and conceptualize prospective alternatives since many problems can't be solved to do with the clashes between individuals, the clashing of individual aims, experiences, desires and intuitions into something more interesting than the unique expression of a unique identity and into something more flexible, workable and exciting: a collectivity, not a compromise **0.3** ~projects evolve around crucial points where everything meets: shared territories no matter the size or medium **0.4** ~ emphasizes in each job, commission or project, possibilities to turn conflicts into positive energy, introducing the imagination of future conflicts over which space can be negotiated, mirrors for collective intelligence **0.5** ~ produces future conflict-orientated design **0.6** part of this flip-mode society where networking outsmarts bipolar routines, where reality and fiction merge, where references go tactile or extrasensory and stop being simply visual.

[future conflicts] *(FLC2003 concept)* **0.1** proactive revealing problems, free of us but not free of a rough and violent quality *(*revealing problems)* **0.2** designing ~ instead of short-lived solutions for relative problems for short-term profit **0.2** the imagination of ~ ; the opportunity of ~; the designing of ~.

[future conflict zone] *(FLC2005 concept)* **0.1** an area in which each point (economically, culturally, socially …) can be tuned or upgraded in a redefinition of what is called the Urban Network Coast: a capsular coast in a hyper-economy, a collection of coastal heterotopias and their networks, a series of continuously negotiable statuses, an economic-cultural-social entity next to the *Vlaamse Ruit, Randstad Holland* … **0.2** an area that oscillates between damage control, risk management and hyper-defence *vis-à-vis* every possible flooding (of water, migrations, manure surplus, etc.) **0.3** a new and hybrid situation where the line that once was the border between land, water and air together with the border between land use and development, from now on and each moment will be negotiated, with a probability of at least two times a day to once every 10.000 years.

sea level; the original polder landscape and the corresponding Pleistocene geological substratum; the historical territory of Flanders; the geographical zone where the beaches of fine sand are deposited. When the high-water line move inland, the resources not deployed for the additional reinforcement of the dykes would be invested in disaster management. Depending on the landscape behind, the sea would gush or seep through dyke breaches into the controlled flood areas.

2) Capsules are the nodes of a network society. A capsule is an artificial, strictly organized and controlled sphere. It provides physical and mental protection against an environment seen as chaotic and unsafe. In a world where non-places take the upper hand, capsules are an attempt to provide real places. They do this by simulating a parallel reality in which everything is focused on

---

anymore by 'curing symptoms'. This implicates that the emphasis should be put on the redefinition and subsequently the 'redesign' of problems. Here imagination and a designer way of thinking come into play rather than pure rationality or analysis (which is more oriented towards technical problem-solving).
Prefigurative designs like M.U.D. do not represent a search for variations, in the sense of perfections of existing or commonly accepted forms of urbanization. Instead, they question the conventional approaches by developing alternative perspectives from which to look at urbanization issues.
This questioning originates from the feeling that designing to solve the problem (in this case: coastal defence infrastructure to prevent flooding) doesn't satisfy anymore (we can't keep on heightening and thickening the dikes) and therefore the problem

Theoretical, Conceptual, Ethical and Methodological Stakes

[flipmode era] *(flipmode as in Busta Rhymes' Flipmode Squad, FLC adaptation 2007)* **0.1** era of reorientation in daily life, planning and politics, in response to very big problems and emerging contradictions.

[flipmode society] *(flipmode as in Busta Rhymes' Flipmode Squad, FLC adaptation 2007)* **0.1** society where networking outsmarts bipolar routines, where reality and fiction merge, where references go tactile or extrasensory and stop being simply visual.

G

[grid-bound hyper-economy] *(FLC2005 concept)* **0.1** soil-bound production gets replaced by ~ **0.2** grid that catches the hyper-relative fluxes of data (information, particles, transports, forces, populations …) and transforms those fluxes in transactional data, knowledge, technology, etc. **0.3** new kind of fluent exploitation **0.4** ~takes the form of a flexible structure that evolves with the dynamics of fluids and flows (*hyper-flux) **0.5** a technological grid of systems of references and coordinates that has the capacity to scan and probe and that only now and then crystallizes in a physical infrastructure (a eco-energetic floating field, a floating university …).

individual experience. The 'Atlantic Wall', the strip of high-rise holiday homes along the Belgian coast, is a form of capsular urbanism. Inwardly oriented and clearly distinct from their surroundings, the Belgian coastal towns satisfy specific needs. They develop as unambiguous spheres of experience which are explicitly intended to make an abstraction of everyday reality. This minimizes the chance of outside disturbance.

Breaking through the line of the coastal defences influences the capsular development of the coastal towns. Where major breaches of the dyke ensure the connection to the flood area, urban conurbations arise that throw up defences like a stronghold. No longer hindered by their connection with the land, they now arrange their walled beaches on the land side too. As capsules in a landscape of water and mud, these fortified coastal beach towns can continue to develop their own identity without interference: Ostend – cultural paradise;

---

should be reassessed and reconstructed (conceptualize a renewed relationship between land, water and urbanization where the territory is shared in a more flexible, interactive way).

The core of design projects like these is the redefining/redesigning of the (problematic) situation such that the answer goes far beyond the problem as it was presented or perceived. It is an exercise in reframing thinking, in 'naming and framing' instead of technical problem-solving. Therefore the emphasis is put on imagination and conceptualization.

M.U.D. however does more than create an image to communicate a certain idea. Donald Schön states that 'Through complementary acts of naming and framing, the practitioner selects things for attention and organizes them, guided by an appreciation of the situation that gives it coherence and sets a direction for action.' (Schön,1986: 4).

Marc Godts and Nel Janssens

H

[hyper-economy] *(FLC2005 concept)* **0.1** the next step in the evolution of economy. **0.2** economy based on less tangible, less material, less soil-bound and ever more volatile kinds of production (*LIQUID EXPLOITATION).

[hyper-flux] *(FLC2005 concept)* **0.1** the movements of flexible structures that themselves evolve with the dynamics of fluids and flows **0.2** in extenso the dynamics of fluids and flows to the second degree and more (*CREATIVE DESTRUCTION).

I

[interactive coast] *(FLC2005 concept)* **0.1** a coast with which you can interact

[interactive model] *(FLC adapted instrument)* **0.1** model with different levels of information and multiple choices, allowing the expression of preferences and offering possibilities to check/manipulate/interact/track …

[interstitial] *(FLC 2005 adapted)* **0.1** the ~ is the counter space of exaggerated fear that in the context of capsular society translates into lines upon lines of defence.

Blankenberge – family resort; Knokke-Heist-Duinbergen – luxury island. The installation of a flood area creates an inland coastal front with regular if not constant views of the sea. Towns in this zone can develop into water-based towns. They will acquire a 'bathing' side and will tend to make use of their enclosed areas of water, which are regularly connected to the sea. Motorways to this new coast are enclosed by dykes. Large-scale infrastructures will here and there attach themselves to their turn-offs. They will house accommodation, catering and shopping facilities, which will also be able to be transformed into sick-bays, relief centres and bases for emergency services.

3) The world economy is evolving rapidly. The place where things are produced and the nature of what is on offer is constantly changing. In the West the accent is shifting from an

---

Conceptual design practices like these have a strong capacity to prefigure possible futures and to develop provocative instruments to design more revealing problems.
Concrete situation-targeted solutions are then surpassed by the wider applicable elaborated concepts and instruments.
The core idea that M.U.D. embodies essentially is about an environment that is determined by dynamics and interactivity. This kind of environment can be expressed by spatial organizations that are expected to continuously redefine themselves to the finest grain (Goossens, 2007). An obvious point of focus therefore is the matter of dynamics and interactivity, which goes beyond the concrete project for the Belgian coast. Furthering the M.U.D. project from the concrete and very much situated level to a more general level is foremost a matter of refining the abstraction (Goossens, 2007).

M

[MARE MEUM] *(FLC2005 concept)* **0.1** ~refers to the particular way in which our coast is being consumed: as the highly personal possession the many aspects of which are simultaneously and individually claimable and are by no means attached to a collective feeling of responsibility.
[mirror] *(FLC2000 concept)* **0.1** ~ for collective intelligence and behavior.

[mixed reality continuum] *(Mixed Reality or MR, FLC2006 adaptation)* **0.1** a continuum established by the merging of the real and the virtual **0.2**. the ~ supersedes the modern continuum which superseded the classic continuum.

[M.U.D.] *(FLC2005 concept)* **0.1** a display of an interactive coast with its inner loops, catastrophes and singularities. The intentional rupture of the coastal membrane inspired by artificial flood, capsular society and hyper-economy **0.2** Mud, a hybrid, de- and re-composed state between land, water and air **0.3** Multi User Domain, a collection of desiring machines, aggregates of subjective desire, architectures of articulated longing **0.4** Multi User Dimension, the ability to respond to simultaneous and even controversial needs **0.5** a new Age – ~ standing combined for MUD/Multi User Domain/Multi User Dimension. In ~ there are no laws, only agreements. ~ is a test-bed for futurity. **0.6** ~ dissolves the coastal urban network into a state of positive emergency: changes surrounding the nodal points in the dynamics of current flows and future conflicts, vast flows of undifferentiated data, patterns of information. ~ is entirely process; infinitely more than the combined sum of its various selves.

oversupply of standardized products to a less material level: that of the idea, the design and the experience. The term 'hyper-economy' refers to this vaporization of the economy. The evolution from a commodity economy to a data and service economy means that the role of the polders as an agricultural area – the reason this area was reclaimed from the sea – is now outdated. We no longer need land for our economy. The context of a dynamic sea ⅟ₙ land conflict may lend support to the hyper-economy. In the flood zone, ground-based production is replaced by an invisible grid – an idea for possible economic development. To give one example, an eco-energetic floating field might attach itself to the grid, moving with the rhythm of the sea and using or converting this movement into an economic process. This grid might be the mooring for a floating university. It might be a drilling platform, a software company or a hotel. Everything is changeable within the grid: every point can at any time enter into relations with

---

A first step thereto can be seen in the development of the triple concept M.U.D. Mud – Multi User Dimension – Multi User Domain. M.U.D. is followed by another design project called COASTOMIZE! that precisely focuses on the matter of dynamics and interactivity. COASTOMIZE! elaborates on how interactivity, the unpredictable and the chain-reacting of more or less complex individual actions, shape shared territories. It confronts the public with notions of individual and collective space, collective intelligence and collective behaviour. It questions the roles of design and planning in such processes and illustrates how daily life, science, technology and design can get us involved on a co-creative basis. In its turn COASTOMIZE! resulted in several new concepts.

P

[PXL] *(FLC2007 concept)* *superpixel **0.1** pixel **0.2** ~behaviour: an enormous amount of little things, signal depending on resolution, redefining constantly (*silent white) **0.3** to act like ~, time/place/network related traces and a proactive memory: what are you going be next?

[provocative instrument] *(FLC2006 instrument)* **0.1** (design)project that inspires through a consequent magnification of reality **0.2** a challenging manifesto that stimulates imagination and triggers discussion **0.3** the strategy of the visionary pamphlet that is used because daring to think beyond what is thought possible is a prerequisite to achieving fundamental innovation **0.4** a ~ is used to get beyond the barriers of the rational 'no's.

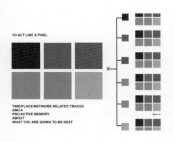

R

[reduction & magnification] *(FLC2007 concept)* **0.1** by enlarging the field of research/design, the specificity of the problem diminishes while the complexity of the problem enlarges **0.2** the specific kind of reduction – switching the resolution – makes it possible to think about a reality that in its complexity is ungraspable.

any other point(s). And any point can at any time change its nature and function, depending on circumstances. The hyper-economic grid is more of a concept than a material structure. This technological development zone would send out feelers to Lille, the metropolis, the Flemish Diamond and the Randstad.

CONCLUSION

M.U.D. spells 'mud', the substance that is a mixture of water and land. But M.U.D. also stands for Multi-User Dimension. When territory and ownership are subject to the dynamics of the sea, newly interested parties negotiate again and again on varying points inside the conflict zone. There are capsules, as atmospheric bastions of control and self-defence. And there is the regularly flooded outer area, where possibilities appear and

---

So, M.U.D. became more than a name for a project. It developed – through design – into a frame that encompasses different phenomena and from where other propositions can be developed. Through this design, theoretical and conceptual stakes as well as ethical and methodological stakes are developed.

M.U.D. looks upon problematic situations from a critical perspective and uses 'unconventional' research methods. In doing so the design enables the redefining and redesigning of the problem. The result is a conceptual frame (like M.U.D. or COASTOMIZE!) that in itself surpasses the particular, concrete design project. The production of 'conceptions', 'notions' and 'names & frames' is typical of the result of so-called 'research by design'.

Theoretical, Conceptual, Ethical and Methodological Stakes

[reset] *(FLC2005 concept)* **0.1**~rabbits called 'what I like' and 'what I don't like' (*PINK RABBIT).

disappear and where control is always relative. Mare Meum spreads out. That which is not wanted or claimed by anyone $\frac{1}{n}$ which is sometimes the case and sometimes not, $\frac{1}{n}$ cannot be set down in rules.

That creates freedom.

The M.U.D project develops ways of thinking about places (here: the Belgian coastline) and tries to be coherent with the ideas of flux/flood/floating/flows etc Therefore a strongly imaginative approach is used to think about phenomena in our contemporary world, from the concrete to the abstract level.
Projects like M.U.D. offer hypotheses for the futurity of our physical environment and a way to gain knowledge on latent reality. Therefore they should be considered as a beautifully imaged vehicle of knowledge building

Bibliography:
Vincent Brunetta and Véronique Patteeuw, eds., 02FLC *Future Conflicts:* 'Young Architects in Flanders' (Antwerpen-Brussels: Vai/A16, 2003)
Caroline Goossens 'M.U.D.' in Achtergrond 03: Architect/Ontwerper/Onderzoeker? Casus Mare Meum: een oefening op de zee (Antwerpen: Vai, 2007)
David Harvey, 'Possible Urban Worlds' in Megacities Lecture 4 (Amersfoort: Twynstra Gudde Management Consultants, 2000).
Donald Schön, *Educating the Reflective Practitioner* (San Francisco: Jossey-Bass Publishers, 1986).

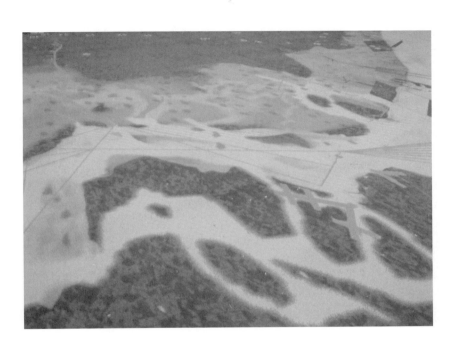

Chapter 3

Oceanic Spaces of Flow

Amanda Yates

Introduction

Proposing space as a phenomenon of time, this chapter frames architecture as an event condition, with interiority or exteriority produced through the performance of inhabitation. Temporal flow is understood here as that state to which all things – space, artefacts, individuals, molecules – are subject to the ceaseless flux of duration: eroding, accreting, deliquescing, everything is in movement, becoming other in the flow of time.[1] Architecture is always in a condition of flow, channelling people, rainwater, breezes, birdsong, energy, while architectural boundaries or material accumulate or abrade, swell or settle, transforming through time – yet architectural discourse remains inflected by its traditional concerns with spatial stability and temporal stasis, with the effect that the time–space relationship remains under-considered. Addressing time's place in architectural discourse and praxis this chapter explores the Oceanic region's customary and contemporary architectures of flow.

'Space is not a ground on which real motion is posited,' said Henri Bergson, 'rather it is real motion that deposits space beneath itself.'[2] In Western culture, architecture, landscape architecture, interior and performance design are understood as a group of distinct and separate spatial disciplines; within this group, though, architecture has a certain primacy through its concerns with structure, form and function, weather resistance, durability and spatial stasis. In redefining space via movement Bergson locates lived space in an explicitly temporal zone. His proposition that space awaits motion or event in order to come into being unsettles architecture's static discursive foundations.

Making architecture that intentionally enacts temporal flow requires an eroding of foundational thought and a liquefying of hermetic boundaries, both spatial and discursive. The architectural artefact that performance theorist Dorita Hannah describes as 'the discrete object of architecture',[3] is formed by its static and enclosing boundary: the space within the figured architectural boundary and the ground without establish interior and exterior as fixed identities rather than conditions dependent upon durational flow. Writing in *Parables for the Virtual*, Brian Massumi proposes that event space is characterized by porous rather than enclosing boundaries.[4] Durational flow is explored in this chapter as spatial flow, where interior and exterior, architectural figure and ground become temporal rather than spatial conditions, and architecture becomes event rather than object. As the architectural boundary is set into motion, the stable identities and established discursive and physical boundaries of the Western spatial disciplines dissolve, architecture becoming performative, interior becoming landscape, all subject to ongoing flux, becoming other through time.

Inconstant and shifting, the Oceanic region exists in a state of ceaseless flux: small island groups are subject to the vast Pacific Ocean; this liquid site marked by the repetitive rhythms of wave and tide, the fluid dynamics of circling gyres and emergent local turbulences, whether aerial or oceanic. The dual topology of constantly changing sea and sculpted land is reflected in Oceanic architectural typologies – light-weight, open and transient structures merge Pacific architecture with its changing environment while articulated architectural landscapes establish the ground as a fluid and protean space upon and within which to dwell. Western distinctions between figure and ground, architecture and landscape are undermined here as architectural enclosure is eroded and the landscape becomes an earthen architecture which problematizes distinctions between inside and outside. With its permeable and mobile boundaries and fluid distinctions between interior and exterior, customary Pacific architecture offers a model for contemporary spaces of flow.

My architectural work reflects Oceanic architectural typologies in order to open up my architectural practice to cultural and spatial difference. My ongoing project theorizes architecture as a complex and culturally inscribed condition with fluid and discontinuous identities rather than as hermetic discipline or static built form. The work then moves between different cultural practices, making architectural space informed by Oceanic and Western thought and practices, particularly the Oceanic spatio-temporal concept of *wa* (distance, or interval), Bergsonian becomings and Deleuzian formulations of difference and between-ness. The space of the in-between, the space of flow, becomes a primary site for the architectural praxis and an active mode by which the praxis operates.

Architecture is understood here as a way of thinking, a thinking as doing, rather than as a representation of thought or a semiotic text in the Derridean sense. Such a position builds from a Deleuzian model in which thinking itself is understood as active and generative. This cognitive and critical model establishes a fluid ground for an architectural praxis that is open to shifting alignments, to difference, and to becoming other than itself. Rather than engaging in the problematic application of theory to architecture the built work employs theories of between-ness and becoming as architectural praxis. This praxis has no codified aesthetic but is rather an active mode by which to generate space. The term praxis, rather than practice, is engaged for its etymological origins: praxis, or 'doing', sources from the Greek *prattein* or 'do' and is itself already an action, already in flow.

This text addresses concepts of flow through its subject matter and also through its composition: it describes fluid architectures but also seeks to enact flow in passages of text that describe spatial experience as a continuous, fluent sequence. An experiential text is interposed then between an analytical exegesis, these repeating sequentially, in waves.[5] The analytical text moves from a discussion of Western philosophies of flow, to a study of Oceanic spatial thought and practice, and finally to a close analysis of three built works by the author: Ground House, sited on an inlet in the lower North Island of New Zealand; the Sounds House, located in the Marlborough Sounds in the South Island; and Tokatea, situated on the Coromandel Peninsula, in the North Island. The experiential text explores spatio-temporal shifts in the course of a single day in the house Tokatea. This text is expressed in sense impression mode, a type of stream of consciousness writing, and seeks to evoke an experience of inhabitation and the temporal flow that is the living of the house.

Early morning, Tokatea, Coromandel Peninsula (figure 3.1)

Morning mist hangs heavy on the sea, different densities of fluid particles in suspension. The bulk of the headland to the east, with its sheltered bay, is shadowed, hazy. Liquid notes of tui sound, dampened by the weighty atmosphere. The sun, haloed, focuses as the mist burns off. Diurnal rhythms begin; runners' footsteps echo from the road beneath; the powerful speedboat sounds in the tight bay below, tracking its way out slowly from its mooring, then tracing a flow line into the smooth surface of the open sea.

In the house, blinds roll up, louvre walls open, fresh morning air flooding in; sliding doors move, under pressure, in fluid channels; the recessed concrete

Figure 3.1 Early morning, Tokatea, Coromandel Peninsula: open phase.

bath fills with stored rainwater, bathroom misting as hot liquid air encounters cooler zones. The enclosing strand-board wall of the bed-bath zone folds as a large panel pivots, opening the channel to the main vessel; lines of movement generate around and along the central island kitchen as drawers slide open, plates and cutlery are laid on the island table, vessels of liquid pool and circle on the stove, and the kettle steams, releasing fluid particles into the morning-cool atmosphere. Sliding panels to the outdoor room are opened, forming space in-between.

Flow

Bergson establishes temporal flow as that ceaseless force through which life is expressed and evolves: durational flow, or the continuous flux of becoming, enables the ongoing iterations, differentiations and divergences of life and is therefore inherently 'creative'.[6] In Bergson's ontology of becoming this flow is irreducible, real duration characterized by its resistance to stasis or division. The 'vital force' of becoming, as Bergson terms it, streams through all things, whether people, objects, rivers, molecules – all transient, all in vibratile motion, all becoming other through time. This theory establishes 'reality as a perpetual becoming'[7] and space as an ongoing product of temporal flux.

Deleuze's philosophy, influenced by Bergsonian becomings, describes a profoundly dynamic ontology concerned with trajectories of movement, multiple vectors, flows and transformations through time. In this temporal theory the built object is, like all things, subject to ongoing change in the stream of time as an object in transition. Deleuze names this object-as-event an *objectile* and describes it in terms of 'temporal modulations' rather than as static space.[8] Deleuze references Bernard Cache's digitally manufactured architectural elements as examples of the *objectile*. Extending the object-as-event concept to the architectural environment, performance theorist Dorita Hannah suggests that 'within the dilating layers of the architectural *objectile* the built environment can be interpreted as space-in-action'.[9] Architecture is in this sense intrinsically performative and 'no matter how seemingly still, is itself a slow performance: a spatial thing in perpetual motion – heating and cooling, contracting and expanding, eroding and accruing.'[10]

The framing of architectural artefacts as temporal events and performative objects rather than spatial forms challenges an architectural discourse which philosopher Elizabeth Grosz suggests 'has thought time, with notable exceptions, through history rather than through duration, as that to be preserved, as that which somehow or provisionally overcomes time by transcending or freezing it.'[11] Architecture's resistance to the notion of durational flow runs counter to much modernist discourse, which Hannah writes, 'revealed space as a temporal event, undermining the discrete object of architecture'.[12] Despite this Hannah notes that 'modern architecture has continued to rely on an ontology of stasis'[13] generating architecture figured by a 'timeless passivity of form'.[14]

Proposing a shift from architecture as form to architecture as time-based field, Sanford Kwinter in *Architectures of Time* asserts that architecture should be understood as a part of the system of forces that give shape and rhythm to the everyday life of the body. Thus the object – be it a building, a compound site, or an entire urban matrix . . . would be defined now *not by how it appears, but rather by practices*: those it partakes of and those that take place within it.[15]

Critiquing architectural convention, Bernard Tschumi asks '[c]an one attempt to make a contribution to architectural discourse by relentlessly stating there is no space without event, no architecture without programme?'[16] Proposing architecture as 'the discourse of events as much as the discourse of spaces',[17] Tschumi defines architecture as being a simultaneous combination of 'spaces, events, and movements'.[18] Tschumi's architectural practice is distinguished by its concern with programme, displaying a particular interest in how when architecture enacts the event it 'ceases to be a backdrop for actions, becoming action itself'.[19] In *Architecture from the Outside* Grosz too proposes the temporalization of space as a means of opening architecture up to its discursive outside.

While architecture's contained discourse resists the flow of time those spatial disciplines outside of architecture actively design in response to temporal flow. Landscape architecture and interior design, sited on either side of the architectural boundary, make space in relation to time's passage. Interior design, held within the architectural boundary, operates at the more temporary and temporal end of the architectural scale and is closely concerned with the embodied event. Landscape architecture, the exterior or ground to architecture's object, exceeds the architectural enclosure and is concerned with processes of vegetal emergence or decay. Landscape architecture plans space over time, designing for the careful phasing and sequencing of growth relative to season, and at times, operating on a monumental geologic timescale that transcends the arrested temporality of architecture. Performance design, an emerging field, makes space for and in relation to the performance event. Describing performance, theorist Barbara Kirshenblatt-Gimblett notes that first

> *to perform is to do* . . . [s]econd, to perform is to behave. This is what Erving Goffman calls the performance in everyday life . . . [t]hird, to perform is to show. When doing and behaving are displayed, when they are shown . . . events move towards the theatrical and more specifically towards the spectacular.[20]

These disciplines then, operating outside of the architectural boundary, exist also outside of architecture's traditional concerns with temporal stasis. I move now to a consideration of Oceania's temporalized spaces, whose mutable and porous constructions perform changing conditions of interiority and exteriority with little regard to an enclosing and static architectural boundary or to unitary discursive identities.

Morning, Tokatea, Coromandel Peninsula

The heat of the day builds as the sun climbs, solar waves propagating 150 million kilometres, energizing the mass of the concrete floor, casting dappling shadow. As the heat builds, the land-mass warms, energy gradients form, air shimmering up off concrete and rock, drawing in new air from the constant sea, drawing up the face of the hill, over the fluid contour of the house, displacing, refreshing. Louvre walls fan open as gills, making porous, patterned breathing boundaries which cast prismatic shadows; flow paths form along the glassy boundaries as sliding doors skim over each other until the interior–exterior boundary is eroded and multiplied. The exterior draws in, the interior extends out; fantails spiral through the air; blue-green sea below backgrounds lacy manuka trees; the tui's flight-path tracks the house diagonally from pohutukawa below to kowhai above; the speckled, particulate strand-board wall and ceiling lining mimics the local shell sand partially eroded by fluid force, this lining bleached, whitened, as if by the action of sun and salt; the sloping rock extends in to sloping concrete wall-floor; shelves on this sloping wall-floor offer nooks for books, flowers, reclusive sun-seeking readers; the bench of the wall-floor extends out into the shell beach on the eastern side of the vessel, and to the west into the pebbled courtyard.

Oceania

Concepts of motion and event shape the spatial practices of the Pacific. These concepts permeate the Oceanic region, with a generalized notion of space in time or space between, recognizable from the Maori and Hawaiian *wa*, to the Samoan, Tongan and Tahitian *va*, the Marquesan *ava* and the Japanese *ma*.[21] These reference, in subtly shifting ways, an idea of space in relation to time. The word *ma* means '"interval" between two (or more) spatial or temporal things and events. Thus it is not only used in compounds to suggest measurement but carries meanings such as gap, opening, space between, time between, and so forth.'[22] Japanese architect Arata Isozaki speaks of *ma* space as that which is 'perceived as identical with the events or phenomena occurring in it; that is, space recognized only in its relation to time flow.'[23] This is space as understood through embodied experience, an idea of spatiality as a profoundly active and shifting condition. This concept of space, like Bergson's, requires 'real motion' in order for a ground to be formed: this is a fluid ground then that is formed only in relation to the temporal event.

Such a conceptualization of space in relation to time mirrors a primary spatial characteristic of Oceania. Oceanic cultures are sited within a vast aqueous body – the Pacific Ocean – that is constantly in motion. Far-flung islands scatter across this extensive ocean. This sea becomes the fluid 'ground' of Oceania; a primary site of industry, source of sustenance, and mode for movement between islands. Writer and choreographer Lemi Ponifasio and academic Albert Refiti discuss this fluid element, and the effect the ocean has on the spatial practice of Pacific theatre. They comment that

> To be located in and around the Pacific is to confront the undifferentiated abyss that is the ocean. Of all grounds it is the most insubstantial because it has no particular identity, no fixed position(s), and if anything the sea severs the will to identify and tends to multiply and confuse the specificity of location – the oceanscape always pushes you hither

and thither and one literally floats on it. Thus Pacific theatre reflects the disparity of fixed identification and tends to deal with the moment, the temporal environment that is filled with (e)motion.[24]

Ponifasio and Refiti contend that the fluid spatial condition of the ocean strongly inflects spatial practice, engendering fluid identities and performative spatial ephemera.

Oceanic architecture is figured by ephemeral or interdeterminate boundaries that enable space to flow and thereby problematize fixed spatial identities of interior or exterior. Oceanic spatial practices encompass a use of the ground itself as a spatial matrix or material within which to form space; and a fibre-based lightweight construction typology that forms a partial or temporary containment. Such spatial constructs inhabit multiple zones at the same time, exhibiting an architectural monumentality, but one that is generated via the landscape and performs as spectacle (in the case of the terraced *pa* landscape) or as a site for performance (as in the *marae*); or forms an architectural enclosure, yet one which is porous and operable, space phasing from partial interior to exterior as mobile screens are deployed, their movements performing environmental or programmatic events. These articulated ground-scapes and porous enclosures are more easily aligned with the concerns and practices of the Western discourses of landscape architecture, interior and performance design than with architecture's contained stasis. Academic Mike Austin suggests that the openness of Oceanic architecture derives from the sea, this being most evident in the *marae*, or open meeting space, which Austin asserts echoes the 'ultimate open space [. . .] the marae roa the vast ocean itself, closed only by the horizon.'[25] Austin posits that this space of openness, which derives from the expansive sea, is a space of *ma*, *wa* or *va*: 'This openness can be compared to the well known *ma* of Japan [. . .] *Ma* is the gap, or the interval, the spacing, the in-between, and in the Pacific it becomes the *wa* or *va*' where space comes into being through the flow of time rather than through enclosure.[26]

Lacking a defined architectural boundary the landscape and the interior flow into each other in customary Oceanic architecture. In this tradition the land itself is utilized as a geo-spatial matrix, as matter within which to inscribe space. Throughout the Pacific, and particularly intensively in New Zealand, the land bears imprints from such interventions as the terracing of *pa* hill settlements to form defensible, habitable zones; the indenting of the interiors of sleeping houses; the recessing of *rua kai* to form storage vessels within the ground; and the insetting of *umu* to form earthen ovens. In this paradigm the relationship between inside and outside is contingent and indefinite as the exterior, or landscape, becomes itself a mode by which to make interiority. In spaces such as those within the partially sunken sleeping house, whose floors and partial walls are contiguous with the earth, inside and outside are in constant flux, interior-becoming-landscape, landscape-becoming-interior. This practice emerges from a notion of ground as a fluid, eroding and sedimenting in order to make pocketed space or elevated ground platforms for inhabitation and event. This ground, like Bergson's, requires 'motion' or event, in order to come into being.

The lightweight construction typology also surfaces from a fluid 'ground', the ocean, and associated spatial concepts and material practices. Austin writes that it is clear that

> water and boats affect Oceanic architecture in many ways from structure to construction to detail to ornament. In the Pacific, sails become floor mats (and vice versa), old boats are used as storage structures, and both buildings and boats are held together by a technology of weaving and tying.[27]

This building type is, as Austin notes

> thoroughly imbricated with the technologies, mythologies and aesthetics of movement. Furthermore, Pacific Island buildings are constructed in materials that decay rapidly giving the architecture a shifting and transient quality. [. . .] These dimensions of architecture in the Pacific contrast sharply with the fixity associated with Western architecture.[28]

This shifting, transient quality is evident in the temporary nature of these lightweight constructions, but also in the partial and porous character of the space formed. Austin describes this condition as one that allows the building to breathe: 'In Oceanic architecture solid walls are used only to define space that is open to the sky [. . .] Pacific walls breathe and are permeable as fences and screens. Often they are temporary and suspended.'[29] Referencing early colonial representations of the *whare*, or Maori indigenous house, academic Sarah Treadwell writes that 'the woven house is a container that leaks. It allows for the passage of wind [. . .] and denies the external skin as a closed surface.'[30] These spaces, formed from plant-based fibres and constructed with layered or woven technologies, are permeable. Like the articulated ground-scapes, these partial and temporary boundaries form space that blends or hybridizes interior and exterior environments, opening up space to the environment, to wind, to the smell of rain on the earth. This partial exposure to telluric flows is a primary quality of an Oceanic spatial practice characterized by permeability, mobility and responsiveness to weather and event. These spaces exist in a constant state of between-ness, interior-becoming-exterior as mobile screens are rolled up, exterior-becoming-interior as ground spaces are formed, these spatial conditions all in flux.

Noon, Tokatea, Coromandel Peninsula

The island-kitchen exerts strong tidal pulls upon the inhabitants; frequent but uncertain flow lines form here, tentative draws between fridge and bench, pantry and bench, flurries of movement as taps are opened, rainwater pooled, steam issues, fragrant leaves steep; a second high tide occurs as the sun centres in the sky, again generating an intricate criss-crossing of flow lines as plates, cups, cutlery, fridge, milk, hob, bread are sought until the island-table focuses movement. The island-table floats now in a space in between interior and exterior, focusing a point of intense flow between partial enclosure and artificial landscape, reconstituting itself in shifting registers in response to environmental flows of wind, rain, sun and the movement patterns of the inhabitants.

After this mid-day tidal pull, flow patterns disperse, then slow to stillness. Moving back through the slip-zone between bed-bath and main vessel small pauses occur; bookshelves lining one side of the slip-way slow flow as books are sought, keys are placed in storage vessels, photographs are viewed. Seeking cooling breezes, sliding doors track fully into their pockets, sliding windows stack over cladding, multiplying and emptying that boundary; the louvre wall offers a pause-space, a site from which to view the expansive sea and compact bay; the fragmented glass ripples as breezes are moderated; yachts rock and sway below, their masts tracing the magnitude of the pulsing waves; passing jetboats send sound tracking up.

Praxis

The contemporary praxis explored here is sited in a conceptual field between Oceanic thought and Western philosophies, drawing on the Oceanic spatio-temporal concept of *wa* and the western notions of becoming and its other formulations, between-ness and difference. *Wa* is understood here as space in relation to temporal flow or space or time between, while becoming is framed by Grosz as occurring in the space of the in-between, which is 'the only space of movement, of development or becoming . . . [and] the space of the bounding and undoing of the identities which constitute it'.[31] The space of the in-between becomes a primary site for the architectural praxis and an active mode by which the work is generated through a process of introducing difference, moving between these, enabling a becoming-other of architecture. In this moving between Western theories of duration and Oceanic spatio-temporal concepts the intent is not to conflate meaning, or confer relative status, but rather to move back and forth in a productive, and perhaps slippery, process between these differences. The built spaces are sited in a conceptual and discursive field between landscape, interior, performance and architectural disciplines and again the intent is to establish a spatial continuum within which to work, a space within which discursive identities can be rendered fluid and relational. The buildings exist in a spatial field between interior and exterior, these binarized pairings engaged in an oscillating trajectory, a moving between difference that generates new conditions. The buildings formed in relation to these conditions engage change, passage and movement in varying registers, scales and manners. Space flows under the effects of weather, time and the event.

Ground House, lower North Island, New Zealand[32]

Sited on a gently sloping terrain in Whitby, in the lower North Island, the Ground House is surrounded on three sides by housing with, to the north, a panoramic view to an inlet. Operating as a terraced, inhabited landscape, the Ground House blurs boundaries between landscape, architectural and interior space. A mutable architectural landscape begins below ground in the recessed winter lounge, which evokes recessed *whare* and *rua kai* in its siting within the earth, then folds up to the dining and then kitchen levels (figure 3.2). The concrete surface extends across the

Figure 3.2 Ground House: articulated concrete landscape.

summer lounge, level with the outdoor living spaces on either side. This continuous landscape folds to make and furnish space, remembering as it does the geo-spatial language of Oceania.

The ground plane is problematized in the winter lounge: when seated one is at eye level with the exterior ground plane (figure 3.3). This spatial strategy recalls Oceanic practice in which the ground is utilized as a spatial matrix, the 'natural' profile of the land moulded to form space as in the terraced *pa* landscapes, or

Figure 3.3 Ground House: recessed interior.

the small-scaled ground space of the recessed *whare puni* (sleeping house). Like Tongan *'esi* (earthen furniture) this mutable 'ground' furnishes the winter room, recessing 30 mm below the finished slab level to form an indented hearth; folding up to hold the fireplace, recessed within like the *taku-ahi* (recessed fire) and folding horizontal to become the mantelpiece and shelf over the fire, before becoming the ground datum of the adjacent dining space. This ground space is constantly in flux, performing as a recessed and furnished interior while also displaying itself as a spectacular 'landscape'.

In the other two terraces of the house, the undulating concrete 'ground' both defines spatial territories – marking the extent of the dining and kitchen zones through a level change – and furnishes space, as the concrete surface bends horizontally, becoming the kitchen bench. The surface of the bench, like the concrete floor slab, is ground back to expose the cut surfaces of aggregate and shell. Hobs are set into this cut 'ground' plane, the oven positioned below recalling the *hangi*. The grinding process is an erosive one, cutting back through the upper layer, the fines and slurry to expose sectioned spheres of aggregate and particles of shell just as ancient middens are exposed. The summer lounge, with its timber strip-flooring overlay, lies on the same terrace as the kitchen. Beyond the summer room a store area holds garden equipment and laundry. This space, like the service and storage zones of *rua kai*, is submerged within the ground as a kind of earthen vessel.

Extensive and moulded, the ground plane of the Ground House operates, in the manner of the geo-spatial architectures of Oceania, between the interior and the landscape. Space is formed and furnished in the Ground House by this articulated landscape, destabilizing Western distinctions between architecture, landscape architecture and the interior, and between surface and space, inside and outside. Architectural space becomes a complex event here, in flux between interior and exterior, landscape and furniture, geography and object.

Sounds House, Marlborough Sounds, South Island, New Zealand[33]

The Sounds House is sited on a steep bush-clad hill facing the channelled sea. An ambiguous interior–exterior field constitutes the public space of the house (figure 3.4). Inhabitation of this flux space is constituted as an experience of between-ness and of becoming as this space shifts register between exterior timber field and contained interior (figure 3.5). A fluid language is employed, expressed through spatial structures that facilitate movement such as channels, slip-ways and sliding glazing; through programming and the separation of living and sleeping functions, such that one must move outside to move between spaces; and though material selection and detail.

A chamfered folding roof partially encloses a timber platform. The surface, a liquid applied membrane, is continuous, extensive, flowing from wall, to roof, and back down as wall. The enfolding wrap is leaky, open at one end, only partially contained along the length of the timber field. The wrapped roof channels rainwater for domestic use; voided in one zone it folds down to the timber field, drawing water to a concrete vessel, an outdoor bath.

To enter the house one draws through a tight channel, entering into the exterior. The timber field, and sheltering roof, frame an expansive view of bush,

Figure 3.4 Sounds House: interior–exterior field.

Figure 3.5 Sounds House: open phase.

sea, sky. The space formed, between partially enclosing roof and timber landscape, shifts register, phase-changing between open and closed. In its open phase, glassy sliding doors retract into cavities in walls or slide over glass panels; in this mode kitchen, dining and living spaces are partially interior, partially exterior, contiguous with the timber platform, sheltered only by the folding roof (figure 3.6). In closed mode, the timber platform, sheltered by the partial wrapping roof-wall, remains an ambiguous space between inside and out, between interval and event.

Tokatea, Coromandel Peninsula, North Island, New Zealand[34]

Tokatea terraces into a steep hill facing a bush-clad headland on the Coromandel Peninsula. A concrete landscape folds over the sloping rock of the site, diverting to

Figure 3.6 Sounds House: open phase.

form a bench seat, inflecting up as a kitchen bench with inset fire (figure 3.7), deflecting down to form a sunken bath within which water swirls. Partially enclosed by an activated architectural boundary, the articulated landscape modulates over time, becoming landscape when the boundary opens or, when architectural closure is re-established, an interior ground-scape. Overhead a folded roof extends and inflects, functioning as both roof and inhabitable landscape, this open field establishing a circulation space that links the upper and lower terraces of the site.[35]

The flowing roof-scape enfolds a space for living; held between the roof and the main volume of the house is a self-contained studio (figure 3.8). Below the studio, the living space of the main house is lightly defined by a glassy evental boundary. This space is a permeable space of change, modulating between 'interior' and 'exterior' as full-height sliding glass panels shift in response to inhabitation and

Figure 3.7 Tokatea: open phase with concrete landscape.

75

Amanda Yates

Figure 3.8 Tokatea: articulated landscape.

elemental event. In open phase the space is 'exterior', enclosed only by a strand-board ceiling and storage wall, the timber floor of the dining zone contiguous with the outdoor timber, forming a space in-between inside and outside (figure 3.9), the rocky landscape extending inside as a concrete sloping wall-floor.

The extensive concrete ground is articulated to furnish the main living space, rendering it suitable for living and working. It forms a bench seat at the base of the angled wall-floor and folds up to form an over-sized concrete kitchen bench. The aggregate for kitchen bench and floor is sourced from the same site, flecked with white and grey stone and shells, reminiscent of middens. Recessed within the elevated surface is the hob; beneath it the oven. *Rua kai* of a sort are held within this extended ground plane, the pullout pantry stocked with cooking essentials – olive oil, tea, salt. Plates, cups, pots and pans are held within this folded 'earthen' vessel, as are pullout rubbish, recycling and compost bins and three different kinds of water vessel, two sinks and a dishdrawer. At the end of the concrete bench is the fire, held in a pocket within the artificial ground.

Overhead the continuous roof extends and, at the seaward end of the building, folds sideways and down to form a partially contained vessel which holds bedroom, bathroom and changing spaces. One moves through the thick storage

Figure 3.9 Tokatea: open phase, dining zone.

wall to access this space held in a gap in between the enveloping roof. Thin windows slide over the face of the exterior skin, creating full-height slotted openings in the bedroom, changing space and bathroom, rendering these porous and permeable through time. A wall of repeated glass louvres intensifies and dematerializes the bedroom's end wall, which focuses to the ocean below.

Tokatea's performative architectural boundary causes space to phase-change between interior and exterior as large glazed panels slide or louvre walls pivot open. When the evental boundary is open, the timber dining space blends with the outdoor timber platform, while the angling concrete wall-floor becomes contiguous with the sculpted rock slope, architecture becoming landscape (figure 3.10); when closed the articulated concrete landscape becomes an interior, recalling the recessed earthen interiors of Oceania. These spatio-temporal shifts perform the everyday inhabitation of the house, displaying Tokatea as architectural event and space of flows.

Evening, Tokatea, Coromandel Peninsula

A gather forms in the outdoor room, around the table floating at the level of the tree canopy; views extend out to the open sea or glance sideways to the enclosed

Amanda Yates

Figure 3.10 Tokatea: site and landscape.

bay below, glimpsed through manuka traceries. The fading sun angles, chamfering lozenges of light that extend, sliding sideways off the timber platform. In search of light-waves and a more expansive view, a flow-path draws up the stair, to the middle roof deck until, there too, the light evaporates, moving up into the sky as a generalized glow, until coral, indigo, ultramarine, the sun sets with only rippling clouds signalling its presence as we rotate away.

Slipping back down into the house, the morning routine plays backwards as louvre breathing walls rotate shut; bedroom-bathroom sliding window panels close from their register over the cladding; blinds extend down; and the sliding panels of the main vessel begin to seal in response to the sudden chill. The island generates multiple flow-zones now as the fire at the end of the island is lit, the oven is checked, hobs activated, and the table is set with steaming vessels around which movement coalesces. In time a draw builds, a current back along the length of the island to the fire, emitting a flickering orange light; the inhabitants recline onto the sloping wall-floor, movement slows, pools. The moon casts a line of light over the shifting surface of the sea, a reflected reminder of the next day, and the next, pulsing on in waves.

Spaces of Flow

Asserting that space is always being produced through time this chapter frames architecture as an interdisciplinary discourse of durational flows. Duration is established here as that most irreducible condition of life, the constant unfolding, differentiation and divergence of the new. To exist in time is to be subject to these ongoing transformations and emergences, subject to the vital forces of life. Like all things, architecture is inflected by temporal flows, yet Western architectural discourse has spent little time reflecting on temporality. Exploring time's effect on space, this essay considers theories and architectures of flow, both customary and current.

Influenced by its constantly changing fluid environment, Oceania both conceptualizes spatio-temporal flow and constructs architectures that perform change. Concepts of *wa, va* and *ma* merge space and time, forming these in architecture as intermeshed conditions. Oceanic space is in flow, conditions of interior and exterior intermixed as a result of temporalized or indeterminate boundaries which disrupt spatial containment.

Inflected by Oceanic constructions the contemporary architectures of flow explored here enact change, rendering interior and exterior or site and space as temporal, rather than spatial, conditions. Theory is engaged as generative practice, architecture becoming other, made in a space in between, between Oceania and the West, between landscape architecture, interior and performance design, between inside and outside. Space forms and reforms as and through the event and as architecture performs – activating space, enacting the everyday, or displaying itself as spectacle – it 'ceases to be a backdrop for actions, becoming action itself'.[36]

Rather than a discrete and enclosed object, architecture becomes an interactive and performative field that responds to its temporal environment. Experientially and doxically in between, these architectures of flow construct space as an always becoming other. As enclosing boundaries become thresholds, space opens up, sounds and scents drift, inhabitants move, and energies stream as architecture performs the ceaseless flux of life.

Notes

1 Henri Bergson, *Creative Evolution,* transl. Arthur Mitchell (London: Macmillan & Co Ltd, 1960).
2 Henri Bergson, *Matter and Memory* (New York: Cosimo, 2007), 289.
3 Dorita Hannah, 'Event-space: Theater Architecture and the Historical Avant-Garde' (unpublished PhD thesis, New York University, 2008), 22.
4 Brian Massumi, *Parables for the Virtual* (Durham, NC: Duke University Press, 2002), 85.
5 Virginia Woolf's text, *The Waves*, is remembered in this text construction.
6 Bergson, *Creative Evolution.*
7 Henri Bergson, *Introduction to Metaphysics*, transl. T.E. Hulme (Indianapolis, IN: Hackett Publishing, 1999), 41.
8 Gilles Deleuze, *The Fold: Leibniz and the Baroque,* transl. T. Conley (Minneapolis: University of Minnesota Press, 1993), 20.
9 Hannah, op. cit., 23–4.
10 Ibid., 40.
11 Elizabeth Grosz, *Architecture from the Outside* (Cambridge, MA: MIT Press, 2001), 111.
12 Hannah, op. cit., 22.
13 Ibid., 25.
14 Ibid., 23.
15 Sanford Kwinter, *Architectures of Time: Toward a Theory of the Event in Modernist Culture* (Cambridge, MA: MIT Press, 2001), 14.
16 Bernard Tschumi, *Architecture and Disjunction* (Cambridge, MA: MIT Press, 1998), 139.
17 Ibid., 149.
18 Ibid., 255.
19 Ibid., 22.
20 Barbara Kirshenblatt-Gimblett, 'Playing to the Senses: Food as a Performance Medium', ed. Richard Gough, *Performance Research: On Cooking*, Vol. 4, No. 1 (Spring 1999): 1–2.

21 *wa* 1) distance, definite space, interval; 2) an indefinite interval, unenclosed, open country; 3) The time, season or space in time; 4) Hawaiian: a space; *wayan*, time. *Va* 1) Samoan: a space in between; 2) Tahitian (obs): space in time. *Ava* Marquesan: space between, space in time; see *Maori-Polynesian Comparative Dictionary*, ed. Edward Robert Tregear (Christchurch: Cadsonbury Publications, 2001).
22 Richard B. Pilgrim, 'Intervals ("Ma") in Space and Time: Foundations for a Religio-Aesthetic Paradigm in Japan' in *History of Religions*, Vol. 25, No. 3 (February 1986), 255.
23 Arata Isozaki, cited in Richard Pilgrim, op. cit., 267.
24 Lemi Ponifasio and Albert Refiti, 'Sacred Space' in *The Labyrinth of the World and Paradise of the Theatre*. Catalogue for the 10th International Exhibition of Scenography and Theatre Architecture, Industrial Palace, Exhibition Grounds, Vystaviste, Prague (June 13–29, 2003).
25 Mike Austin, 'Pacific building: the construction of tradition' in *Additions to Architectural History: XIXth conference of the Society of Architectural Historians, Australia and New Zealand*, ed. John Macarthur and Anthony Moulis, 10 (Brisbane: SAHANZ 2002).
26 Ibid., 12.
27 Mike Austin, 'Pacific Island Migration' in *Drifting: Architecture and Migrancy*, ed. Stephen Cairns (London: Routledge, 2004), 226.
28 Ibid., 227.
29 Mike Austin, 'Pacific building: the construction of tradition', 13.
30 Sarah Treadwell, 'Categorical Weavings: European Representations of the Architecture of Hakari' in *Voyages and Beaches, Pacific Encounters, 1769–1840*, ed. Alex Calder, Jonathan Lamb and Bridget Orr (Honolulu: University of Hawai'i Press, 1999), 267.
31 Ibid., 92–3.
32 Ground House: Project leader.
33 Sounds House: Project leader with Stephen Bonnington.
34 Tokatea: Project leader.
35 Phase 2 of the Tokatea project involves the installation of a timber field over the roof, with stairs, enabling the roof to be inhabited as an artificial landscape and used as circulation route down and across the site.
36 Tschumi, op. cit., 149.

Chapter 4

Interpretive Flow: A 1930s Trans-Cultural Architectural Nexus

Åsa Andersson

Housed everywhere but nowhere shut in, this is the motto of the dreamer of dwellings.[1]

Introduction

This chapter will suggest a sense of the 'flow' that a Swedish 1930s summer cottage can provide. While I turn the now somewhat tinnitus-inducing, yet beloved, original kitchen tap to drink water from the well, the cottage highlights the conditions in which I live. One of the key motifs of the summer cottage has to do with ideas and applications of the 'open-air room' (*friluftsrum*) which I will return to as I set up an interpretive flow by drawing on examples of actual and fictive built constructions, literature and artworks.

Some of my interest in the summer cottage may stem from the enchanted watercolours of Elsa Beskow, found in her fairytale, *Ocke, Nutta och Pillerill* (*Woody, Hazel and Little Pip*) from 1939 (figure 4.1).[2] Fru Ollon (Mrs. Acorn) and her two children, Olle and Pillerill, live high up on the branch of a moss-clad oak tree. The tiny house is thus situated in the midst of the elements; it is breathing and oscillating upon the wind, and the rhyming verse says that the house rarely keeps still. Mrs. Acorn would probably rejoice with Gaston Bachelard when he notes: 'To ascend while breathing better, breathing directly not only air but also light, participating in the summit's wind, are all feelings and images that constantly exchange their values and that are mutually supportive.'[3]

My daydream of inhabiting Mrs. Acorn's levitating house, the privileged access to the summer cottage, and a few trips to Japan, have all contributed to a 1930s trans-cultural architectural nexus which I will attempt to reflect here. Although the chosen theme of a 1930s summer cottage is somewhat anachronistic, I will through this example address 'flow' as a concept reliant upon the flexibility of boundaries and methods of channelling. Although I have a mobile phone and an internet connection at the summer cottage, and thus can reach 'out' where capital and thoughts flow, the now aged and fragile structure forces me back to basics

Åsa Andersson

Figure 4.1 From Elsa Beskow, *Ocka, Nutte och Pillerill.*

– to processes of nesting, the production of well-being and the concrete tasks of maintaining one's living abode. I also become aware of how flow on a basic level is dependent upon trust – is this a place where I feel happy to leave my doors and windows open?

> The boulder-ridge stones roll under the rented car as I turn off the ignition key. The rustling of pine needles, birdsong and the smell of the nearby Baltic Sea hit me as I open the car door. I look up to the left and see the familiar sight of the summer cottage. I take a deep breath and walk up – I am home.

The summer cottage was built in 1934–6 on the east coast of Sweden and designed by the architect Georg Scherman (1899–1978). At the time, the summer cottage was nicknamed *Villa Hill* after the first owner, who also commissioned it. Due to its radical shape, it caused a lot of attention in the traditional fishing village. It was influenced by the 'functionalism' style of architecture and design that had been launched during the Stockholm Exhibition 1930. In an information sheet accompanying a current display of amateur photographs from the very same exhibition, it says: 'The [functionalist] home was to have a small kitchen and diminutive "sleep cabins", thus leaving space for a large, well-lit multi-purpose living room.'[4] As a frequent resident in the summer cottage, I would say it is still quite unusual and fits in very well with this description.

The summer cottage is embedded among old pine trees. Despite the damaging weight of snow, there are still branches that reach out and meet the roof, the veranda and the small 'shaving balcony'. In 1934 Junichiro Tanizaki writes: 'If the roof of a Japanese house is a parasol, the roof of a Western house is no more than a cap, with as small a visor as possible so as to allow the sunlight to penetrate directly beneath the eaves.'[5] Had he been able to 'listen in' while the functionalist summer cottage was more or less concurrently being constructed, he may have become curious to see its extended roof. And there is actually an intimation of a slight parasol shape too, as the summer cottage is conically built and opens up towards the front (figures 4.2 and 4.3).

I find an analogue to the experience of the summer cottage when Alain Robbe-Grillet writes about 'mental time' in relation to film. 'I saw Resnais' work,' he said, 'as an attempt to construct a purely mental space and time – those of

Figure 4.2 Summer cottage by Georg Scherman.

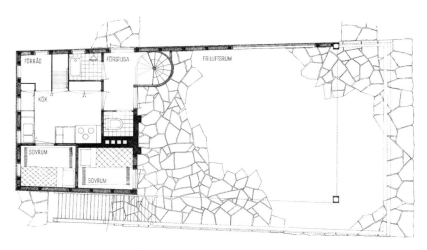

Figure 4.3 Ground floor plan.

dreams, perhaps, or of memory . . . And this *mental time*, with its peculiarities, its gaps, its obsessions, its obscure areas, is the one that interests us since it is the tempo of our emotions, of our *life*.'[6] Despite the assumed rationality of functionalism, the summer cottage sets up an affective scene for the ambivalent mental states that Robbe-Grillet mentions. This is also emphasized by the regularly required maintenance work, which highlights cyclical aspects of time and humbling notions of transience. In the photograph titled, 'In the House of my Father' (1996–7), the late Donald Rodney used his own skin to create a tiny house that is held together with a pin. In the image he tenderly balances the little house within his open hand.

> *As I yet again sand down the long wooden handrail running the length of the veranda and exterior set of stairs, My hands start to recognize every little knot and crack in the wood. If I could only learn the language of wood, I would become a better keeper.*

Bachelard speaks of intimate aspects of tactility by discussing hands that poetically dream: 'The hand also has its dreams and its hypotheses. It helps us to understand matter in its inmost being. Therefore it helps us to dream of it.'[7]

The exterior outline of the summer cottage has been described as being like a typical wooden bird box, built for humans. Yet through features of its design, which I will soon develop, and its asymmetrical placement on the 4,000-square-metre plot, it does also reach out into the landscape: 'Long reaches of faintly-tinted vapor cloud the far lake verge – long nebulous bands, such as you may have seen in old Japanese picture-books . . . (this singular appearance the Japanese call 'shelving')'[8] Lafcadio Hearn is here making a connection between depictions of lingering fog and the Japanese asymmetrical shelves called *chigaidana*. Masaharu Anesaki describes some of the fitting names for these shelf models: 'the "thin mist", the "one leaf", or the "plum branch" pattern.'[9] What these paintings and shelves suggest is a shifting world, where hidden depths and potential extensions, are possible.

> *When seeing a small tea caddy with a lid positioned on such a shelf, I think of Mrs. Acorn's tiny house far out on the oak tree branch.*

This sense of asymmetry is echoed in the ideals of the Stockholm Exhibition 1930: 'The furniture, according to the new ideal, could very well be of standard design and asymmetrically arranged.'[10]

Behind the sliding glass doors of a shop in Kyoto, I once noticed an accumulation of actual and imaginary landscapes (figure 4.4). There were maps, a printed fabric with a landscape motif, a photographic colour poster of a scenic location, and in the glass itself, a reflection of actual trees. Yet another landscape was presented through the backdrop pattern of the *noren*, or curtain. The layers of landscapes in the Kyoto shop mirrors the Japanese garden concept of *shakkei*, the spatial and aesthetic extension of a garden through the incorporation of distant features. *Shakkei* is often translated as 'borrowed scenery'. A traditional Japanese sliding door, a *fusuma*, can be decorated with paintings of landscapes,

Interpretive Flow: A 1930s Trans-Cultural Architectural Nexus

Figure 4.4 Sliding glass door in Kyoto.

plants, seashells and animals, and sets up a similar dialogue with spaces located on either side of the screen. A sensorial bleeding over of landscape, elemental time and daylight, also filter in through lattices or paper-covered *shoji* screens: 'the air passes freely through, snow-flakes or flower-petals come in driven by wind, or birds and butterflies fly through the rooms.'[11]

> At the summer cottage open doors and gaps in the weathered wooden facade invite spiders, grasshoppers and dragonflies, while the squirrels and deer still stay outside.

The circulation of air and inventions of flexibility create a sense of seamlessness between the summer cottage and the garden. On the original groundfloor plan, Scherman has written the word 'FRILUFTSRUM' at the edge of the space which is shaded by the floor above, while having two open sides to the garden (figures 4.3 and 4.5). A literal translation of the Swedish word is 'open-air room'. 'Frilufts-' is associated with outdoor leisure activities such as walking, cycling or camping. When the summer cottage was configured, this was an important political issue, as architects and urban planners had started to consider people's health to a larger extent, dividing areas for work and living. The vision was that everybody, regardless of income, should have access to light and greenery. At the summer cottage, the open-air room enables a connection between those who want to spend time in the garden and others who prefer protection from the sun while, for example, enjoying lunch. It also functions as a wintertime shelter for outdoor furniture, wooden screens and the occasional nesting bird. Five suspended and sliding, separately moveable glass doors were added to the *friluftsrum* in 1959 (figure 4.6). The room

85

Figure 4.5 View of the ground floor 'open-air room' and probably the family Hill, to whom Scherman was related.

can thus be fully or semi-glassed in, which allows the user to remain in a membrane-like contact with the garden. Additional heat can be provided through a fireplace and the (somewhat hazardous) ceiling-mounted electrical heaters.

Figure 4.6 View of the ground floor 'open-air room' (*friluftsrum*) with the added glass doors.

Interpretive Flow: A 1930s Trans-Cultural Architectural Nexus

I wonder what Mrs. Acorn would say about the idea of the *friluftsrum*, as she lives in something that could almost be deemed a rustic teahouse high up and tucked away by moss and twig fencing? In Sweden small houses, such as allotment cottages and romantic pavilions (*lusthus*), are quite common. Along the shoreline there are also some fanciful wooden bathing huts. There is even an authentic Japanese teahouse in central Stockholm. The first version of Zui-Ki-Tei, the House of the Promising Light, was built, dismantled and shipped from Japan and then later rebuilt at the Etnografiska Museet in the late summer of 1935. Mrs. Ida Trotzig, who had lived in Japan for many years and studied *ikebana* (flower arrangement) and *chado* (the tea ceremony), initiated the project. Visiting Japanese craftsmen and a gardener worked on site and I imagine that many people visited it. Curiously, this site is close to where the Stockholm Exhibition 1930 had been held a few years earlier. I like to think that Scherman also visited the Zui-Ki-Tei, which was built about the same time as the summer cottage. In 1969, the Zui-Ki-Tei was burnt down, but the *machiai* (a sheltered bench to sit on while awaiting the tea master's invitation) and *tsukubai* (stone wash-basin) are still there (figure 4.7). Luckily, a new Zui-Ki-Tei teahouse was inaugurated in 1990 near the original site. In May 2010 I helped out during the 20th anniversary of Zui-Ki-Tei, and could smell its cedar wood and *tatami* mats, while brushing off dried leaves and purifying the *tsukubai* with salt.

Juhani Pallasmaa talks about how 'elements of an architectural experience seem to have a verb form rather than being nouns. Authentic architectural

Figure 4.7 The *machiai*, *tsukubai* and garden of the old Zui-Ki-Tei teahouse, Stockholm.

experience consists then of . . . the act of entering and not simply the frame of the door.'[12] Similarly, while approaching the teahouse and the tea ceremony, the guests move through the charged zone of the small moss-covered garden where the stepping-stones become important. Kakuzo Okakura describes their role in the ritual:

> the *roji*, the garden path which leads from the *machiai* to the tea-room, signified the first stage of meditation – the passage into self-illumination. The *roji* was intended to break connection with the outside world, and to produce a fresh sensation conducive to the full enjoyment of aestheticism in the tea-room itself.[13]

The stepping-stones contribute to the experiential journey and enact a bridge-like function as the guests shed their mental attitudes. When I walk up the different paths that lead to the summer cottage, I similarly feel that I enter another zone, even if it is just the coffee percolator that greets me rather than a tea master. There is something valuable in having to stroll while nearing the cottage. Martin Heidegger discusses how nearness requires a sense of distance: 'What is nearness if it fails to come about despite the reduction of the longest distances to the shortest intervals? What is nearness if it is even repelled by the restless abolition of distances?'[14] Irregular-shaped paths, with paving made out of locally sourced limestone, blur the division between the cottage and the garden. The limestone is used for all the pathways and, within the *friluftsrum*, the floor and a fixed round table are made out of the same material. A feeling of anticipation is evoked by the meandering pathways, and the proximity of the forest is emphasized by the utilitarian wire fence, which only becomes a notional border surrounding the plot.

Inside the summer cottage, too, there are features that enable a sense of flow. With its brass railing, the interior spiral staircase makes the user feel as if on a boat, while being propelled up onto the second floor and into the day – or even full moonlight, coming through the large front window section (figure 4.8). The user can also reach the second floor, the veranda and the view of the sea, through the exterior staircase.

> *Once up on the veranda I feel like Mrs. Acorn, standing in the wind overlooking the trees and catching glimpses of the sea.*

Obsessions with specific natural substances, such as air, reverberate with what Bachelard says about reverie and matter: 'a reverie . . . must find its *matter*, a material element must give the reverie its own substance, its own law, its specific poetics.'[15] Over time these different material qualities become sensorially absorbed and form part of an embodied knowledge, expressed through culture. In the 1930s and 40s Tetsuro Watsuji used the term *fudo* (meaning wind and earth) as a term for a socio-historic cultural milieu of which the experiences of atmospheric phenomena were essential ingredients. He observed that 'Climatic characteristics . . . insinuate themselves into our experience to a depth far greater than we realize.'[16]

Interpretive Flow: A 1930s Trans-Cultural Architectural Nexus

Figure 4.8 Details from the summer cottage by Georg Scherman.

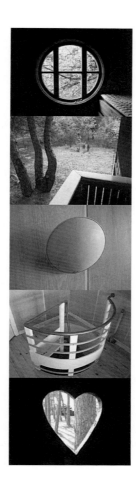

This 'environing' relationship has been suggested in a photographic series, *Camera Obscura, Interior Exterior* (1996–2002) by Marja Pirilä.[17] Through turning domestic living spaces into a camera obscura, she has portrayed the inhabitants who become draped by the projected imagery of the exterior world. Their bodies are interwoven with the external upside-down view of their dwellings that filters in through the pinhole, which links the room to the world outside. The images indirectly point to the external walls of the house itself, the fragile nature of our materially defined property boundaries, and the proximity of the elemental world.

At the summer cottage, the user becomes aware of the proximity of the surrounding garden by the various viewpoints that allow sightlines to the north, east, south and west. It is possible to follow the duration of the daylight while navigating or using the multiple seating areas. The garden and nearby forest and sea can be spotted through windows, doorways, the veranda and the small 'shaving balcony' (figure 4.8). Through the apertures' functions of framing we are, as Roland Barthes describes in relation to *ikebana*, seeing the production of 'the circulation of air, of which flowers, leaves, branches . . . are only the walls, the corridors, the baffles'.[18] These frames allow the mobilization of space. Even the heart-shaped view from the door of the outdoor toilet becomes expressive of proximity and distance, while making visible the long winding path, lined by moss and blueberry plants, leading back to the summer cottage (figure 4.8).

> *When in Japan, I have noticed how the nurtured looks of pine trees growing in gardens are different from the wind-twisted pine trees towering around the summer cottage. On a quiet suburban street in Kyoto, I observe a gardener who plucks away individual pine needles to promote airiness among the remaining cascades. Influenced, I later try this at the summer cottage and end up with an eye injury due to falling moss. I also cut off the tip of a juniper bush, thinking I will shape it, but stop quite soon. Every time I now look at it, I feel a sense of guilt.*

The semi-hidden black front facade of the Asakura Choso Museum in Yanaka, in the north of Tokyo, drew me in by chance. The museum houses work by the sculptor Asakura Fumio (1883–1964) and was designed by himself and completed in 1936. It reveals an intimate juxtaposition (and also an intertwining in terms of the interior) of the modernist vision (perhaps more *art deco* than functionalism) and traditional *sukiya*-architecture (dating from the late sixteenth century). The information guide describes the museum as a 'reinforced concrete building used as a studio and a *sukiya*-style house built mainly with logs and bamboo.'[19]

> *While stumbling along in the provided customary slippers, I follow narrow corridors and verandas. I move in a sensuous haze into the studio and view the sculptures, pour over the exquisite woodwork details of the domestic and representational areas. At close range I contemplate the enclosed pond garden, linger in the former greenhouse and embark upon the steep climb to the roof terrace.*

Mitsuo Inoue uses the term 'movement space' to describe spaces that are non-symmetrical and have non-fixed spatial arrangements, and this can be explored while visiting the museum.[20]

The overall museum offers a range of experiences such as the intimate viewing of the traditional pond garden, while the modernist section allows larger spaces and long distance views (figure 4.9). Although the two building styles are fairly different, they set up an intimate relation between inside and outside, while keeping a sense of restraint. The museum leaflet says: 'The major characteristic of the building lies in the *perfect harmony* created by *blending* the architectural styles of the West (bare concrete walls) and the East (the *sukiya*-style structure), which are basically *two completely opposing elements.*'[21] This embracing, rather than a rejection, of tradition and the modern, has also been discussed in a recent publication by Helena Mattson and Sven-Olov Wallenstein. They discuss *Acceptera*, a manifesto written by six Swedish architects who promoted the functionalist

Figure 4.9 The pond garden, Tokyo.

approach in 1931: 'the decisive rhetorical strategy put to use in *Acceptera* assumes two contradictory standpoints, so that a bridge between past and present can be created, instead of an opposition between the modern breakthrough and the persistence of tradition.'[22]

At the summer cottage, I experience that there is harmony between the natural materials used and the forest garden, together with a strong structural form. It allows an expansive annexation like the idea of *shakkei*, a correspondence between inner and outer landscape. It is an example of functionalism that has not gone to its programmatic extreme but is still making possible human values.

> While gently rocking in a hammock, in the shade of pine and cherry trees, I experience a symbiosis between my breathing body and the summer cottage itself.

Pallasmaa proposes a need for an *ecological functionalism*: 'architecture is likely to return to the aesthetics of necessity in which the metaphorical expression and practical craft fuse into each other again . . . an aesthetics of noble poverty, as well as the notion of responsibility.'[23] When he talks about noble poverty, I understand it as something like *wabi sabi* as made manifest in the refined seeming simplicity of the Japanese teahouse. The irony is that such a teahouse, including its typical utensils, can be very expensive to build. However, contemporary artists and architects frequently reinterpret the idea of the teahouse through using paper alone or found and/or cheap typical DIY materials which potentially widen the accessibility.

The unexpected disclosure, a wall that can be pushed to the side or temporarily removed, like a *shoji* or *fusuma*, has a suggestive air of freedom and fluidity. In 1940, the architect Erik Gunnar Asplund (1885–1940) completed Hoppets Kapell (the Holy Cross Chapel) at Skogskyrkogården (the Woodland Cemetery) in south Stockholm. Bengt O.H. Johansson describes some of Asplund's approach to the design:

> These courts are quiet and closed but not shut in; a >window< in the wall can open on to the great view. Nor do the walls always close up, but can miss each other so that a gap of a few centimetres opens up at the corners. Thus Asplund has achieved the effect that the walls only screen-off, but do not govern.[24]

This idea of openness and flexibility was taken further by Asplund as the large front section, made out of glass and metal, was planned to be lowered into the ground when the funeral ceremony had finished. The guests would thus proceed freely out into the open towards the water-lily pond and the Meditation grove.

Asplund may have been one of Scherman's teachers at the Royal Institute of Technology in Stockholm, and perhaps some ideas floated in the air, as the most radical feature of the summer cottage is the large window section on the upper floor. Not too dissimilar from the mechanics of a garage door, it could once be opened up through the help of handles, lead weights and hinges. The pivoting function is no longer working as one lead weight has fallen down after developing rust, but the handles and hinges can still be seen. As a side effect, the summer cottage is fairly unstable due to the fourth wall, i.e. the 'suspended' window section, only being attached at the top. My father describes the summer cottage as a three-sided wobbly shoe-box. Archival research has provided me with an opportunity to see what it was like when the window was folded up (figures 4.10 and 4.11).[25]

In the Swedish journal *Byggmästaren* from 1934, in which plans for the summer cottage were briefly presented, the large room on the second floor is also described as a *friluftsrum*. It seems like the ideal vision for the whole cottage is to be an open-air room, delimited only by a few walls. The panoramic view from the veranda, although now seriously challenged by growing trees, allows the user to see the long, narrow island of Öland. The island becomes an incorporated feature, like in the notion of *shakkei*, together with a lighthouse situated in the strait between the tip of the peninsula and the shore of Öland.

> Upon visiting the Katsura Imperial Villa in Kyoto, the famous 'lighthouse' stone lantern (a miniaturized representation of Ama-no-hashidate) surprises me by making me think of home.

The red-brown colour of the exterior wooden walls makes the summer cottage blend in among the tree trunks. Overall the dissolution between the inside and outside was emphasized through the original colour scheme. When my parents bought the summer cottage in the late 1970s, the shade of linden green was painted almost everywhere inside, apart from some blue details in one of the bedrooms.[26] Some redecorating was (regrettably) done as the persistent linden green made some of

Interpretive Flow: A 1930s Trans-Cultural Architectural Nexus

Figure 4.10 Summer cottage by Georg Scherman.

Figure 4.11 Summer cottage by Georg Scherman.

us nauseous. However, the interior frame of the large front window section is still green, providing a connection with the trees. The downstairs' outdoor ceiling still has the original blue hue and this adds to the aerial aspirations for the *friluftsrum*. The flat galvanized zinc roof is painted light green and all exterior window and door details are painted dark green to reflect the shade of the pine needles.

The journalist Hanna Hellquist compares the annual return to a summer cottage as a return to the site of a crime, where traces from last year can be found. 'It is eerie. Snowdrops and scilla are flowering on the lawn but inside it is still August.'[27] To some extent, I agree but the summer cottage is also a lived-in-house. Carpenter ants make the annual tour of the kitchen cupboards (and in the summer of 2010, most of the ground floor, necessitating extensive sanitation and the cutting down of a tree which had functioned as a nest). The cottage is continually exposed to coastal weather, snow and a number of other wood-loving insects. There are 'unruly elements' such as grass persistently popping up between the paving stones (perhaps the same grass that Scherman, in a 'prophetic' gesture, has added on some of the architectural plans). While residing in this floating summer cottage among the swaying pine trees, there are also moments of vulnerability as footsteps make the large window section rattle. Tensions between the aspects of idealism in the original design, and the architectural challenges to dualism, meet very practically located maintenance problems. During the cherry blossom season, and while taking close-up images of the then semi-dormant summer cottage, I became aware of the parallel transience of the blossoms, the decaying building materials, and by extension, of life. In Banana Yoshimoto's short novel *Moonlight Shadow*, the main character, after having seen the apparition of a lover by a river, says: 'Even as we exchange hellos, they [the people] seem to grow transparent. I must keep living with the flowing river before my eyes.'[28] I understand this in two ways, both as a memory of her encounter but also to live with an awareness of the ephemeral nature of existence. Pallasmaa says that: 'the mere experience of interiority implies peripheral perception . . . Peripheral perception transforms retinal images into a spatial and bodily involvement and encourages participation.'[29] This echoes Yoshimoto's suggestion of a semi-visible presence that moves us, and my embodied experience of the summer cottage. Thirsty, at night and in darkness, I reach out for the familiar chrome and bakelite door handles, and trace my way to the porcelain hand-basin which hides in a bedroom closet (figure 4.12).

I believe the summer cottage is a beacon of 'slow-flow' and harbours a 'tent poetics', as it can both be opened up and provide shelter. It is significant that Asplund's lowerable wall at Skogskyrkogården will now be reinstated after having been forgotten for many years. And Brunnberg & Forshed Arkitektkontor AB received Träpriset (the Timber Prize) 2008 for their housing development Östra Kvarnskogen (2006), where forty houses rest on stilts within a fir-tree clearing and having a 'Swedish Welfare State (*folkhems-*) standard'.[30] The jury's motivation reads: 'The area has a surprising feeling of informality and unfinished hut-architecture where the presence of the forest is notable. Here you live near the tops of the trees.'[31] I would say Elsa Beskow was a visionary architect of her own kind when creating Mrs. Acorn's hut. While visiting the interestingly sited show, *1:1 Architects Build*

Interpretive Flow: A 1930s Trans-Cultural Architectural Nexus

Figure 4.12 Details from the summer cottage.

Small Spaces at the Victoria and Albert Museum in London, July 2010, I climbed up into the Beetle House by Fujimori Terunobu, which is a fantastical 'teahouse' on stilts. Its surface is charred black to echo the look of a beetle. In my mind, this house becomes a fusion of all my projected desires, it appears as a mirage . . .

It is impossible to claim that Scherman was actually influenced by Japanese aesthetics.[32] Perhaps it is just a matter of coincidence? Birds know how to build their nests regardless of their geographic location, even if the availability of certain straws, snippets of electrical cables and the particular softness of moss will differ. The birds are builders of exquisite structures, mainly local 'resourcers', like the mentioned architects and the unnamed craftsmen, merging natural and conventional elements, while bravely incorporating the new.

> A couple of redbreasted robins decided to build a nest in my friend's boat shed this year; their uncanny choice was the metal pan he uses for melting lumps of lead.

An interesting contemporary example of architecture that also enables flow, and that Mrs. Acorn might approve of despite its urban setting, is Curtain Wall House (1995) by Shigeru Ban in Tokyo. Matilda McQuaid describes it as follows:

> The monumental, two-storey-high curtain that spans the second and third floors can be pulled back and the sliding glass doors along the east and south facades opened to reveal a wide deck that wraps around two sides of the house. The open facades and deck extend the interior so

95

that it can be completely exposed to the street. Standing on the deck, watching the activities of streetlife below, can seem like being on the prow of a ship.[33]

Documentation of the house shows the curtains blowing suggestively in the wind.

Bachelard quotes Georges Spyridaki who writes:

My house . . . is diaphanous, but it is not of glass. It is more the nature of vapor. Its walls contract and expand as I desire. At times, I draw them close about me like protective armour . . . But at others, I let the walls of my house blossom out in their own space, which is infinitely extensible.[34]

When Tadashi Ogawa concludes: 'Atmosphere is nothing but mood, air and wind', I agree, as the surplus effect of the summer cottage's spatial and material considerations affect the physical and psychological body.[35] The user becomes suspended among the 'visibles' as Maurice Merleau-Ponty suggests, in the 'tissue that lines them, sustains them, nourishes them, and which for its part is not a thing, but a possibility, a latency, and a *flesh* of things.'[36]

In *Architecture Pieces*, Yoko Ono dedicates the following instruction to a phantom architect: '[Build] A house that allows rain to be part of it and therefore the thought of a rainy day is not an unpleasant one anymore.'[37]

Figure 4.13 Details from the summer cottage.

As the raindrops tap on the flat metal roof, I would say Scherman achieved this, even if rumour has it that the front window section of the summer cottage required a whole group of people to hoist it down during a sudden thunderstorm and was thus not an easy task. This large window also had extra panes, which probably left it even heavier and shut, during the threats of World War II, when the Hill family temporarily relocated to the summer cottage, as it was regarded to be in a safe area. As I wash my cup using the kitchen sink, I can still see in the metal surface the welded trace of lightning that allegedly passed by Mrs. Hill by only a few centimetres (figure 4.13). This is a summer cottage that makes life felt.

Notes

1 Gaston Bachelard, *The Poetics of Space* (Boston: Beacon Press, 1994), 62.
2 Elsa Beskow, *Ocke, Nutta och Pillerill* (Stockholm: Albert Bonniers Förlag, 1960 reprint).
3 Gaston Bachelard, *Air and Dreams: An Essay On the Imagination of Movement* (Dallas, TX: The Dallas Institute Publications, 1988), 237.
4 Information sheet for the *Stockholm Exhibition 1930*. Autochrome photographs by Gustaf Wernersson Cronquist, Arkitekturmuseet in Stockholm, 8 June–29 August 2010.
5 Junichiro Tanizaki, *In Praise of Shadows* (London: Vintage, 2001), 29.
6 Alain Robbe-Grillet, *Last Year in Marienbad* (London: John Calder Ltd., 1962), 7.
7 Gaston Bachelard, *Water and Dreams, An Essay On the Imagination of Matter* (Dallas, TX: The Dallas Institute Publications, 1983), 107.
8 Lafcadio Hearn, *Glimpses of Unfamiliar Japan* (Tokyo: Charles E. Tuttle Company, Inc., 1984), 140 (italics added).
9 Masaharu Anesaki, *Art, Life and Nature in Japan* (Rutland, Vermont & Tokyo: Charles E. Tuttle Company, 1974), 36.
10 *Stockholm Exhibition 1930* information sheet.
11 Anesaki, op. cit., 34.
12 Juhani Pallasmaa, *An Architecture of the Seven Senses* in 'Questions of Perception, Phenomenology of Architecture' in *Architecture and Urbanism (AU)*, special issue (July 1994), 35.
13 Kakuzo Okakura, *The Book of Tea* (Tokyo: Kodansha, 2004), 177.
14 Martin Heidegger, *Poetry, Language, Thought* (New York: Harper & Row, Publishers Inc., 1971), 165–6.
15 Gaston Bachelard, *On Poetic Imagination and Reverie* (Dallas, TX: Spring Publications, Inc., 1994), 35.
16 Tetsuro Watsuji, *Culture and Climate: A Philosophical Study* (Tokyo: Hokuseido Press, 1971), 201.
17 Marja Pirilä, *Camera Obscura, Interior Exterior* (Helsinki: Kustannusosakeyhtiö Musta Taide, 2002).
18 Roland Barthes, *Empire of Signs* (New York: Hill and Wang, 2000), 44–5.
19 Museum guide: Asakura Choso Museum (Tokyo: Taito Ward Society of Art and History).
20 I benefited from the doctoral thesis by Kristina Fridh where she discusses the term 'movement space' taken from *Space in Japanese Architecture* by Mitsuo Inouse. Kristina Fridh, *Japanska Rum: En diskussion kring tomhet och föränderlighet i traditionell och nutida japansk arkitektur* (Göteborg: Chalmers Tekniska Högskola, 2001), 47.
21 Asakura Choso Museum guide.

Åsa Andersson

22 Helena Mattson, Sven-Olov Wallenstein, *1930/31 Den svenska modernismen vid vägskälet, Swedish Modernism at the Crossroads, Der schwedische Modernismus am Scheideweg* (Stockholm: Axl Books, 2009), 44.
23 Juhani Pallasmaa, *Encounters: Architectural Essays,* ed. Peter MacKeith (Helsinki: Rakennustieto Oy, 2005), 189.
24 Bengt O.H. Johansson, *Tallum, Gunnar Asplund's and Sigurd Lewerentz's Woodland Cemetery in Stockholm* (Stockholm: Byggförlaget, 1996), 102.
25 I would like to thank Marie Jansson, Jonas Malmdal, Annika Tengstrand and Torun Warne at the archive of Arkitekturmuseet in Stockholm for helping me to locate the material.
26 In the 1980s two windows were added to the summer cottage. Some fairly subtle changes have also since been made to the kitchen. During the 1950s the first floor interior horizontal wall cladding was covered over, probably due to the insulation creeping out. The indoor toilet has not been used since 1977.
27 Hanna Hellquist, 'Det är som att återvända till en brottsplats' in Stockholm: *Dagens Nyheter* (30 April 2010), 56 (author's translation).
28 Banana Yoshimoto, *Moonlight Shadow* in *Kitchen* (London: Faber and Faber, 2001), 150.
29 Pallasmaa, op. cit., 331.
30 A political concept and welfare programme promoted by the Swedish Social Democratic Party.
31 Fredrik Söderling, 'Pris till radhus bland trädtoppar' in Stockholm: *Dagens Nyheter* (23 April 2008) (author's translation).
32 Within the fields of architectural history and design history, research is currently undertaken to further uncover the influences from the Far East during the 1920s and 1950s. See for example, TrAIN – Research Centre for Transnational Art, Identity & Nation, based at the University of the Arts, London.
33 Matilda McQuaid, *Shigeru Ban* (London: Phaidon Press, 2003), 192.
34 Bachelard, *The Poetics of Space*, 51.
35 Tadashi Ogawa, 'Qi and the Phenomenology of Wind' in *Continental Philosophy Review*, Vol. 31, No. 3/July (Dordrecht: Kluwer Academic Publishers, 1998), 106.
36 Maurice Merleau-Ponty, *The Visible and the Invisible* (Evanston, IL: Northwestern University Press, 1992), 132–3.
37 Yoko Ono, *Grapefruit: A Book of Instructions + drawings: en instruktionsbok + teckningar* (Swedish-English edition) (Lund: Bakhåll Printers & Publishers, 2001), 238.

Chapter 5

Solar Flow: The Uses of Light in Gold Coast Living

Patricia Wise

Subtropical Australian light seems to get into everything, to flow more rapidly through spaces and buildings. It bounces, glances, shimmers on and between surfaces. Shapes are sharper. Shadows are deeper, penumbra somehow less diffuse. Movement is heightened – the phrase 'eye-catching' acquires an especially precise application. In such regions, which tend to be understood and represented primarily through how they make available libidinal engagements between bodies, nature and buildings, light becomes part of what Deleuze and Guattari describe as desiring-production,[1] 'operating beyond the nature/human distinction'.[2] Light, as a flow that connects, that produces regions of intensity, becomes implicated in the intimacy of flows of desire between people, and between people and place. But the lightness of space, the bigness of the sky, the clarity of the air also encourage habits of distance looking, of vistas, of gazing out towards horizons.

For Australians, the great majority of whom live in coastal cities incorporating wonderful beaches, or close to them, tourism has most often meant going to other beaches, and the iconic destination has long been Surfers Paradise, on the Gold Coast, in what was called 'sunny Queensland' until boosterism transformed it into 'the Sunshine State'. Queensland occupies the north-east portion of the continent. Its capital city, Brisbane, is in the state's south-east. Beginning about 20 kilometres south of Brisbane, the City of the Gold Coast stretches along some 70 kilometres to the New South Wales state border. In the national imagination, the Gold Coast equates with very bright sunlight, very long sandy beaches, very good waves, very high buildings, very big shopping malls, very active night life and very exciting theme parks. It equates with excess in the consumption of sun, surf, sex, shopping and the sensational.

To its core business of tourism, the city has added significant involvements in global entertainment production; education export; and an array of 'leisure industries', from building pleasure craft to golf course design, from Japanese wedding and honeymoon packages to cosmetic surgery holidays. But what the Gold Coast does first and best is sell, remake and develop itself. That is, the city has been and continues to be concerned with building and with image-building through buildings.

Over recent years, its high-rise hotels, apartment blocks and resorts have frequently been set among particularly extensive, landscaped, street-level precincts designed for mixed private, public and commercial uses. The consequent separation of tall buildings, even in the most densely developed parts of the coastal strip, means that the city's striking verticality is balanced by a considerable degree of horizontality. While the footprint of each Gold Coast high-rise development will commonly involve half a city block and sometimes much more, the high-rise building itself might occupy 50–70 per cent of the site while the rest is devoted to gardens, swimming pools, spas, tennis courts, retail and dining areas. A sense of urban spatial extravagance is intensified by the fact that in addition to the ocean and the mountains, a Gold Coast 'view' takes in expanses of plazas and low-rise apartments, shopping malls and carparks, waterways and marinas, parklands and golf courses, townhouses and suburbs. And while a breathtaking pace of development sees single dwellings, low-rise blocks, motels, caravan parks and corner shops make way for very high buildings in beachside areas, the city remains remarkably open. Its shape invites and harnesses flows of light at various speeds and intensities across, around, between, among and through its buildings (figure 5.1).

The Gold Coast has undergone particularly rapid growth over the past twenty years[3], and has benefited significantly from internal migration, especially from Sydney and Melbourne, the largest capital cities of southern states.[4] From the title of a highly successful television drama series involving a family undertaking a downshift from Melbourne to a small coastal town, the descriptor 'sea change'[5] has entered Australian popular, commercial and demographic discourse, along with its rural equivalent 'tree change'. Although it long ago ceased to share the qualities of small coastal towns, the Gold Coast has marketed itself effectively to 'sea changers' wanting to maintain the markers of sophistication and the advantages of urban life – high-rise apartment or low-rise enclave living, fine dining, elite retail outlets, coun-

Figure 5.1 Gold Coast City from Q1 – view to north.

try clubs, marinas and so on. Given the additional attractiveness of a burgeoning employment base and more affordable suburban real estate than Sydney and Melbourne, there has been a particularly rapid inflow of people in the 35–49 and 50–69 age brackets.[6] This is accompanied by a high degree of 'churn' within the region, as residents upshift due to increasing wealth, changes in family size, age or lifestyle preference. In the latest census (2006), almost a quarter of the total population (24.9 per cent; 117,737 people) had moved *within* the Gold Coast in the past five years.[7]

In smaller coastal areas elsewhere in Australia, while the economic benefits of regional growth are welcomed, it is commonplace for locals and sea changers alike to form residents' action groups to fight what is almost invariably called 'Gold Coast style development' – meaning high-rise buildings, large-scale tourism and showpiece shopping precincts. However, as a city-building strategy the Gold Coast's particular style has enabled it to represent itself, not inaccurately, as a global city – albeit a small global city, but still a player in the international space of flows, in Castell's sense.[8] Bell and Jayne ask:

> At what level in the global urban hierarchy does a small city 'trade'? To which other cities (and non urban places) does it link and what forms do those linkages take? It's not size, it's what you do with it. In a global urban order characterized at once by dense networks of interconnection and by intense inter-urban competition, absolute size is less important ... smallness is in the urban habitus; it's about ways of acting, self-image, the sedimented structures of feeling, sense of place and aspiration. You are only as small as you think you are – or as other cities make you feel.[9]

The Gold Coast is a small city that 'thinks big'. This can partly be attributed to how tourism is connected to global flows and partly to how the rapid growth of the region has been managed; how it has involved not only sprawl, but also the creation of an urban environment reminiscent of much larger cities. Early in the 'new economy' movement the Queensland Government put in place advanced optical fibre infrastructure and brokered the Gold Coast as the site for Warner Brothers' studios. By 2004 the Gold Coast had a greater proportion of its population engaged in 'creative industries' employment than any other Australian city except Sydney.[10] Internationally mobile creative people have been drawn by lifestyle factors; by technological and economic incentives; and by the city's location on the 'Pacific Rim', a growth area for the space of flows. But the Gold Coast does not offer the other markers of Landry's or Florida's 'creative cities', such as a richness of high culture or the kind of cool associated with regenerated and gentrified inner city cultural quarters that bring to city-branding the sense of historical continuity that Walter Benjamin recognized as central to urban identity: 'It may be that the continuity of tradition is mere semblance. But then precisely the persistence of this semblance of the persistence provides it with continuity.'[11]

Perpetually replacing itself, the Gold Coast seems to ignore history, to play out its (by now) clichéd role as a paradigmatically postmodern city, dipping into multiple 'semblances' taken from other cities to produce its next version of itself.

Patricia Wise

In his Arcades Project, Benjamin archived part of an essay 'On Present-Day Architecture' from Gogol's 1830's collection, *Arabesques*:

> Away with this academicism which commands that buildings be built all one size and in one style! A city should consist of many different styles of building, if we wish it to be pleasing to the eye. Let as many contrasting styles combine there as possible! Let the solemn Gothic and the richly embellished Byzantine arise in the same street, alongside colossal Egyptian halls and elegantly proportioned Greek structures! Let us see there the slightly concave milk-white cupola, the soaring church steeple, the oriental miter [sic], the Italianate flat roof, the steep and heavily ornamented Flemish roof, the quadrilateral pyramid, the cylindrical column, the faceted obelisk![12]

To someone from the twenty-first-century Gold Coast, this sounds uncannily like home. Gold Coast architecture plays with illusion and allusion, engaging in a complex form of intertextuality that invites international and local identifications. Yet there are some consistencies. From the first 12-storey apartment building, Kinkabool (1959),[13] several features have persisted in Gold Coast high-rise developments: basement car parking; (frequently) shops at ground level; penthouses on the top floor/s; a mix of permanent residents, long-term lessees and short-term rentals for tourists; and, most conspicuously, balconies for every apartment. As earlier buildings make way for very high high-rises, the balconies simply go higher, constituting a design opportunity, a comforting echo, and a motif that repeats across the city's landscape. Given the idiosyncratic architectural mélange, it had always seemed that developers could drop just about anything into this cityscape and it would somehow make itself at home. But when the 80-storey Q1 was advertised, exhibited and then began to take shape, many locals were disconcerted – it felt 'closed in', like an office tower in some other city. This was because, although Q1 has balconies, they are disguised behind sliding windows. In this city of spectacle, high-rise Gold Coasters are accustomed to living their private lives in view of each other, from balcony to balcony, in the sunshine and in the air. Similarly, while Benjamin understood Gogol's call for multiple architectural styles as 'a divinatory representation of the later world exhibitions', the Gold Coast is a *city-as-exhibition*, designed with the primary aim of attracting tourists, real estate investors and new residents.

Near the casino, The Oracle's 'two imposing towers' are marketed as

> set to create a destination within a destination . . . Its stylish boutique retail outlets, chic restaurants, dynamic commercial hub will be a magnet to holidaymakers and new residents looking for something new and different. It cleverly and seamlessly mixes urban chic and alfresco dining with beach culture.[14]

Benjamin saw 'arcades, winter gardens, panoramas, factories, wax museums, casinos and railroad stations' as 'the dream houses of the collective' for nineteenth-century Paris.[15] The Gold Coast's dream houses of the collective are clearly shopping malls, theme parks, viewing platforms, the wax museum, the casino and the airport but they are also the mixed-use spaces around the very big buildings that have come to represent the city in its own imagination. That is, despite its elite functions as part of a national and international desiring-machine in the speculative economy, Gold Coast high-rise real estate also participates in the local flows of residents and domestic tourists as consumers, in how they position themselves as bourgeois citizens.

The city's striking architectural discontinuities and its echoes of continuities combine to evoke apparently 'smooth' spaces[16] and apparently continuous flows. One effect of this is to produce a sense of time taking place differently from quotidian life – of time becoming 'holiday time', even for residents, drawing them into the pleasure and leisure aspects of the city as holiday destination. Another effect of the uses of space and light in architecture and city planning, of the ways in which the built environment works *with* the natural environment, is that distinctions between interiors and exteriors tend to break down, further intensifying the impression that the city accommodates itself to the relaxed and relatively uninhibited flow of bodies through it. Seamless and casual movement of people between the beach, the marinas and the city's streets and buildings brings the temporal, the spatial and the libidinal readily and comfortably into various alignments, connections, networks and nodes. The milieu of the Gold Coast is, in these ways, always already a milieu of flows.

Commentators tend to become so mesmerized by the excesses of the Gold Coast's built environment that they fail to notice that in fact the city only exists because of the natural setting it occupies. It is, of course, widely believed that cities inevitably work against nature and thus that the Gold Coast's high-rise and sprawl do what cities 'always' do – destroy nature. As Heynen, Kaika and Swyngedouw observe, 'Urbanization has long been discussed as a process whereby one kind of environment, namely the "natural" environment, is traded in for, or rather taken over by, a much more crude and unsavoury "built" environment.'[17]

There has been a confused double movement in how the West has viewed cities in relation to nature. One narrative positions the city, as *polis*, as the civilizing machine *par excellence* that enables Man (sic) to overcome brute nature and achieve culture, empire, science and so on. In the other narrative, the conventional city's chaos and complexity – its 'concrete jungle', overcrowding, disease and political corruption – replace the Arcadian simplicity of pre-urban life, for which people continue to express nostalgia in the suburbs and roof gardens, parks, allotments and hobby farms of contemporary metropolitan settings.

Lefebvre characteristically refused these dichotomized conventions by bringing into play a third term, 'second nature', in explaining how a town-becoming-city behaved like a 'vast machine', 'capturing natural energies and consuming them productively', and at the same time 'retained certain natural traits, notably the importance assigned to use'.[18] He stressed that the social, economic, political, infrastructural and natural flows involved in urban formations call for 'the immediate creation of something other than nature: a second, different or new nature, so to speak'. But Lefebvre's argument about city-building nevertheless bases itself in an acceptance of the old view that 'humankind is born in nature, emerges from nature and then turns against nature'.[19] As he had argued elsewhere:

> Nature, destroyed as such, has already had to be reconstructed at another level, the level of 'second nature' i.e. the town and the urban. The town, anti-nature or non-nature yet second nature, heralds the future world, the world of the generalized urban. Nature, as the sum of particularities which are external to each other and dispersed in space, dies. It gives way to produced space, to the urban.[20]

But there are quite other resonances when the term 'second nature' is used in the context of the Gold Coast. As a tourist destination, and as a desirable place to reside, it has always been about the ocean, beaches, estuaries, rivers, creeks, mountains and rainforest. Nature, still with its 'particularities . . . dispersed in space', has not 'died' and the urban is not constituted as 'anti-nature'. In its primary identity and representations, the socially produced space of the Gold Coast is a 'second nature' contrived out of the existing nature, a social-culture-nature assemblage. It is therefore not surprising that the discourses and practices of Gold Coast real estate development have increasingly produced a milieu, a stylistics for living, that depends on the commodification and consumption of rarefied aspects of a spectacular natural environment in which people are understood to be immersed, even as they inhabit the 60th floor of a tower.

Of course, other theorists of the urban (for example, Jacobs, Williams and Harvey) and, more recently, urban ecologists, have observed the many everyday and infrastructural ways in which 'cities are built out of natural resources, through socially mediated processes';[21] how the 'design, use, and meaning of urban space involve the transformation of nature into a new synthesis.'[22] But in the context of the Gold Coast, transformation *and* preservation of nature occur as commodification on a grand scale. It is commodification of space and place, of light and landscape, and it can be thought of as taking place almost as a precondition of the taking place of the rest of the city – its built environment, its more than half a million residents, its 10 million visitors per annum.

This is encountered most obviously in the management of nature. The beaches and the parks beside them are groomed daily. The rivers and creeks have been organized into a vast network of canals lined with expensive housing. There are residential developments on purpose-built islands. Among preserved or regenerated native coastal heath, along many kilometres of beachfront, eco-friendly boardwalks, pathways and esplanades cater for the leisurely strolls or power exercises of pedestrians and cyclists. There are several greenbelts of managed wetlands and bush. Winery trails, arts and crafts markets and so on draw tourists to the hinterland. Much of that hinterland is national park, of which a significant proportion on both sides of the New South Wales–Queensland border is World Heritage listed. Throughout these 'wilderness' areas, rangers manage free, well-maintained walking trails, disability provisions, picnic areas, vantage points, wildlife encounters, flora and fauna protection, information and education. There are also a range of commercial engagements with nature, such as the Currumbin Wildlife Sanctuary, where tourists in their many thousands weekly have photo opportunities cuddling koalas, feeding kangaroos, being bedecked with parrots, and gasping at crocodiles. The Currumbin Sanctuary is, though, a genuine sanctuary, and a leading site for the expert treatment and rehabilitation of injured native birds and animals. Similarly, Sea World is more than a theme park, being much admired in the community for its educational work, marine research, and whale and dolphin rescues. Rescued whales and dolphins have often become entangled in the shark-exclusion netting that runs many kilometres through the ocean to help prevent the untimely demise of tourists and locals alike. For regional residents, the many complex interactions of highly valued aspects of nature and environment with tourism and commerce are what make their city-region 'a great place to live'.

Equally important, however, is the milieu produced by how the city produces itself in its natural environment through the marketing of high-rise apartment buildings. In the northern end of the coastal strip, 50–60 per cent of residents live in high-rises, and the proportion of the population of Gold Coast City living in 'flats, units and apartments' is 22.6 per cent compared to a national proportion of 14.2 per cent.[23] But the Gold Coast spreads over an area of 1,402 square kilometres, including 70 kilometres of coastline. The great majority of residents occupy typically Australian suburban single-family dwellings, or low-rise gated communities.[24] In other words, Gold Coast residential high-rises have never been about how the city might fit more people in. They are to give more people access to the most important commodity the Gold Coast offers: proximity to the ocean and 'sweeping views'.

Benjamin explores the nineteenth century's fascination with 'panoramas' – painted exhibitions representing historical events or cities, which were popular attractions in the Paris arcades. He collected Labédolliare's description of one of Prévost's city panoramas: 'His spectators, situated on a platform surrounded by a balustrade, as though on the summit of a central building, commanded a view of the entire horizon.'[25] On the Gold Coast, spectators view the real city in its land- and seascape, encompassing 'the entire horizon', from real, very high buildings: from residential and tourist apartments and their balconies, from vantage points open to the public as 'viewing platforms' and 'observation decks', and in 360-degree procession from a revolving restaurant.

To lease or buy a Gold Coast high-rise apartment is to expect to consume the panoramic: the more extensive the panorama, the higher the value of the apartment from which the panorama is consumed. The proportion of the available panoramic amenity – the beach and ocean, the cityscape, the canals, the mountains and escarpments – contained in the view from an apartment, helps determine the exchange value of the real estate. Thus, at the most significant level of consumer capitalism, the natural environment is folded inextricably into the built environment by how it is seen. Because of the importance of both property markets and people-flow, this marriage of architecture and environment is a driving force for regional economic activity. It is also, I suggest, a significant part of urban identity formation, at the level of individual citizens and at the level of city branding. In Gold Coast high-rise living, nature has become *the* primary consumer item: that is, nature as it is framed by massive expanses of plate glass windows and sliding doors opening onto the liminal spaces of balconies where you can be in nature and not in nature all at once. The discourses of real estate sales, and increasingly the discourses of the community, transform these most artificial of human environments – massively high man-made structures containing large numbers of people in large numbers of dwellings stacked one above another – into the most 'natural' of spaces (figure 5.2).

It begins with the naming of buildings, which have begun to rarefy. Some have acquired a metaphysical connection – Zen, Avalon, Nirvana, Soul, Oracle; others have 'pure' atmospherics – Air, Windsong, Ambience, Reflection, Wave; and the current 'signature' buildings have names involving high-end global signifiers so floating that nothing much can attach to them at all – Circle, Q1 (figure 5.3).

When the buildings are marketed, visual and verbal discourses about light and space collapse the boundaries between their outsides and their insides. The following examples from real estate materials typify what has become an almost ubiquitous conjunction of light and landscape, nature and architecture in the discursive practices of Gold Coast development, and thus also of regional style magazines, interior decorating trends, landscape design preferences and personal expressions of local identity.

In the far south of the Gold Coast, Reflection at Coolangatta has two towers:

Figure 5.2 One of Q1's 'enclosed' balconies.

Solar Flow: The Uses of Light in Gold Coast Living

Figure 5.3 View to the south-east from Circle.

> Height alone does not confer views like this. The feeling of light and space that permeates every Ocean Skyhome is the luminous result of a stroke of design excellence: Stepping and feathering the higher floors so that bedrooms as well as living rooms are positioned to soak up the view. Glass balustrades are another view-enhancing design detail, curving around balconies of bountiful size. Above all else, the space of your Ocean Skyhome is a supremely luxurious expression of the beachfront lifestyle.[26]

This accompanies images that are flooded with golden light. It reflects off every surface, while the division between interior and exterior is almost indiscernible. The flow of light thus forms a conduit for the circulation of desire, so that the body is drawn smoothly into the visual and verbal representations. The sales material assumes desiring-production, carrying no traces that could be suggesting a lack to be filled. The person who will occupy this point of intensity where environment and built environment flow together, and where life and living space occupy a zone of indiscernibility, is positioned to feel as if s/he is already familiar with 'beachfront lifestyle'. Niecon's 'ocean skyhomes' are simply the living spaces that Australians used to call flats or home units, and that over the past thirty years have acquired the more globalized caché of 'apartments'. What transforms an apartment into an 'ocean skyhome' is the architectural enhancement of flows of light and air and vista, the actual and representational creation of a liminitrophe, whereby the resident will occupy a kind of borderless borderland between sea, sky and building. For Deleuze and Guattari, a zone of indiscernibility is not only the 'fuzzy zone of encounter, but also the margin wherein becomings occur that affect each dialect in the encounter.' They are 'found between singularities in any smooth space'.[27]

107

Although this particular encounter is taking place in the highly striated, powerfully organized context of a high-rise real estate development, the uses of light produce it as smooth space, in which each potential resident is invited to feel singularly 'at home' and multiply 'accommodated'. Among a wide array of amenities of the kind that have come to feature in almost all of the city's high-rise residential buildings, Reflection residents can enjoy the 'Executive Lounge', 'planted and designed to induce zen-like serenity', including restaurant and bar facilities and a private cinema. As if to emphasize its participation in a cosmopolitan space of flows, it's 'like an airline executive lounge without the uniforms', can be 'as casual or formal as your mood demands', and yet is 'akin to achieving membership in a supremely private club'.[28]

Nirvana is nearby at Kirra, 'the spiritual home of Australia's beach culture' where you can experience 'our coastline the way it should be: unspoiled, unhurried, unpretentious', a place that 'invites you to harness an indulgent and timeless way of life'. With 'sundrenched light sweeping through Nirvana's extensive glass exterior, glistening off polished timber, marble and stone in reflected hues', in this 'Nirvana for the fortunate few' you can enjoy a residents' lounge with private bar, temperature-controlled wine-lockers, teppanyaki barbeque and Zen garden, private cinema, gym, spa, sauna, lap pool, water garden.[29]

In pre-completion sales material for Ambience, a few kilometres north at Burleigh Heads, another developer asked consumers to:

> . . . imagine a place where golden mornings greet azure afternoons with the familiarity of old friends. Picture the natural beauty of sands, sparkling turquoise waters, golden sunshine and pristine parks lined with Norfolk Pines . . . The two towers feature organic curves . . . to form a sculptural expression which will fit comfortably with the urban landscape of the precinct. The smooth curve and 'soft' building outline will create a silhouette that will relate to the forms of the Norfolk Pines in the adjacent parkland.[30]

The apartments 'optimise their open plan design . . . to capture Burleigh's stunning views'. Given the curve of the coast at Burleigh, in these 'stunning views', natural features such as a headland nature reserve and a beachside park are folded into a particularly striking distance aspect on the high-rise skyline of the northern Gold Coast seen across a sweep of ocean.[31]

With The Wave, at Broadbeach, the balconies are offset against each other as 'waves', becoming sculptural features.[32] In marketing images, sunlight flows dramatically across and through the building, supplementing the architectural features with a sense of motion and transformation.[33] Nearby, Air becomes another kind of building-as-entertainment, with a nightly wash of changing colours across one side of the building.[34] It is not alone in using the whole building as a palette. Most of the Gold Coast's high-rises are predominantly white or cream to reflect the sunlight more spectacularly and to provide a suitable ground for lighting at night. Despite its core business of entertainment, its theme parks, nightclubs, hotels,

Solar Flow: The Uses of Light in Gold Coast Living

24-hour retail and leisure consumption, busy convention centre and major casino, the contemporary Gold Coast has not perpetuated a 1960s–70s preference for simulating Las Vegas in an extravagance of neon. Indeed, contemporary large building signage tends to be relatively inconspicuous, particularly above first-floor level. Taking advantage of its natural and built panoramas as much at night as it does by day, much of the city employs lighting techniques that throw relatively subtle floods of white, blue or green across water, buildings, parks, gardens, plazas, esplanades, beachside walkways and swathes of beach.

Unusually for Gold Coast real estate marketing, night shots predominate in the Sunland Group's brochure for Avalon, in Surfers Paradise. The deep blue tones in an image of the entrance area, strikingly lit against an evening sky, are reminiscent of the (Celtic) 'twilight' colours that were used in pre-completion representations. In a sweeping discursive gesture, we are drawn into the foyer and out again: 'Its unique and audacious design profile features a visually stunning three storey central lobby – granting unparalleled access to views in, out, through and beyond, to a landscape of greenery and serene water.'[35] When natural light is mentioned it is 'mellow morning sun'. Notions of serenity pervade the discourse, even though the building is 'in the dress circle of Australia's premier lifestyle city', 'enviably close to dynamic nightlife'. With the familiar 'exclusive access to exceptional facilities',[36] Avalon is 'positioned to enjoy every advantage of proximity, peace and privacy'. Its gardens abut an 'inviting parkland precinct', so that it 'presents a way of life that's best of both worlds: stimulating and tranquil, set apart and yet right at the heart of urban beach living'.[37] Against another deep blue evening sky, Avalon-by-night occupies the foreground of an arcing northerly aspect on the cityscape, the gold, blue and green lights of other high-rises reflected off a mirror-still river. However, while Avalon looks impressive, it is what the building looks *at* that visually and verbally steals the 360 degree show:

> Silhouetted in the curve of the river, Avalon is a haven of privacy enjoying the most expansive outlooks: with magnificent view corridors over the Nerang River towards Chevron Island, the ocean, out to the west, and the breathtaking panorama of the Surfers Paradise skyline.[38]

Sunland's Circle on Cavill in central Surfers Paradise is a substantial residential, resort, retail and entertainment development with an extensive multi-use precinct. It's marketing evokes fluid, sophisticated engagement in an urban milieu:

> Circle on Cavill. Two stunning residential towers, integrated with a fabulous retail precinct, fulfil every ultra-modern lifestyle need. Creating a rare convergence of inner-city energy, beach proximity and luxury resort facilities. At the forefront of the exciting revival of the historic heart of Surfers Paradise, Circle on Cavill sets new parameters for contemporary liveability – striking architecture in turn with spacious design, in an urban beach village showcasing the exceptional pleasures of living the high life.[39]

But it is sunlight and panorama that permeate the sales material when it comes to inviting the consumer to imagine living in a Circle apartment. For example, in one image part of an interior wall holds a circular mirror beside glass ornaments and an all-glass table lamp that glows brightly (and redundantly) in front of the blues of the ocean and sky that occupy only slightly less than half of the image (figure 5.4). Low in the frame, a sliver of white sand evokes the beach, and the top of an older high-rise suggests the uninterrupted views as does the adjoining text:

> A calm habitat of open outlooks and natural light, where floor to ceiling glass frames hypnotic views of the ocean, the river and the hinterland. And huge balconies extend expansive living spaces even further.[40]

In the next spread, the left side centres, within wide, white borders, a view to the east over buildings, beach and breakers, which together stretch across the lower quarter of the image, the other three-quarters being filled with ocean and sky. The right side is a borderless sky in which the sun is a translucent white ball beside lighter blue text: 'Just three minutes from Surfers Paradise Beach and one minute from the Nerang River, Circle on Cavill sits poised at the meeting-place of urban style and tranquil beachside.' Almost as if an after thought, much smaller, gold text, follows: 'From its unprecedented vantage point, Circle on Cavill captures ocean and city views to all aspects.'[41] The visuals are such that it is almost unnecessary to spell out that sunlight and spectacle attend the purchase of a Circle apartment. And

Figure 5.4 Circle interior.

Solar Flow: The Uses of Light in Gold Coast Living

when one lives in one, as the next spread illustrates, 'interiors . . . put the emphasis on natural light . . .'; '[s]pecially commissioned finishes in glass, polished stone and stainless steel add an understated gleam . . .'[42] Circle's two-storey foyer 'sculpts a one-of-a-kind ambience, composed of light and space'.[43] Consumers are thus taken to appreciate the relations between light and space and style and lived experience; to recognize how these all work together in the performance of desire in the context of the Gold Coast. Explaining Deleuze and Guattari's desiring-production, Bonta and Protevi stress that

> desire is not subjective hankering after what you don't have (that is, desire is not oriented to lack . . .), but is the material process of connection, registration and enjoyment of flows of matter and energy coursing through bodies in networks of production in all registers, be they geologic, organic, or social.[44]

Sunland's 80-storey Q1, which was briefly 'the world's tallest residential building',[45] has a number of its amenities for the care of the body – swimming pools, spas, gymnasium, leisure areas – set on ground level in a terraced array of gardens, waterfalls, sculptural features and decorative pools that flow into a retail, gallery and dining precinct under a soaring open roof of glass and metal, which in turn spirals a visitor towards and into a dramatic glass-walled foyer where half of the floor is water, visually connecting with the pool outside.

For the public visiting Q1's observation deck, there is a separate entrance with ticket sales and souvenirs. The observation deck has its own pamphlet and website[46] which enables 'Your QDeck experience' to be promoted as a generalized tourist attraction without diminishing the 'exclusivity' of the building as private residences and luxury resort. QDeck materials feature the slogan 'As far as the eye can see'. The 'EXHILARATING high speed lift ride of less than 43 seconds' might almost constitute an extension of the 'Xtreme' experiences available in the Gold Coast's theme parks and adventure holiday packages. But to arrive at level 77 with its 'breathtaking, panoramic views from Brisbane to Byron Bay' is to be delivered into nature, immersed in 'spectacular 360 degree views from the surf to the hinterland and beyond'. From '230m above ground' you can 'gaze in awe at the humpback whales' in what is certainly the most unexpected iteration on the regional speciality of whale-watching.[47] Even 'By Night' the visitor is discursively folded into the natural world: 'view the shimmering city lights of the Gold Coast, experience the brilliance of a full moon . . .' QDeck is an architecturally exciting space, with metal-framed glass all around and above, so that the visitor can see through to the engineering marvel of the building's huge mast, to the design feature of its open metal 'crown', and to the sky (figure 5.5).

Q1 sells a 56-page souvenir book featuring striking images of construction and of workers, frequently in dizzying positions against spectacular backdrops of city, mountains and ocean. 'It must be kept in mind,' Benjamin commented, 'that the magnificent urban views opened up by new constructions in iron . . . for a long time were evident only to workers and engineers.'[48] Steel, reinforced and pre-stressed concrete, and elevators, have made such views available to everyone.

Figure 5.5 Q1's 'crown' observation deck and upper floors.

Benjamin cites Meyer's recognition of 1907: '[w]e stand here at the beginning of a development that is sure to proceed at a furious pace . . . The . . . conditions of the material . . . are volatilised in limitless possibilities'.[49] Among Gold Coast developers, the Sunland Group is notable for how it overtly aligns itself with the continuing imaginative implications of large-scale architecture. Various facts about the building and several quotations from famous architects are set into a wide band of beautiful Australian hardwood flooring that abuts QDeck's vast windows all the way around. On my first visit sunlight streamed onto the timber at my feet to highlight:

> *Space and light and order. These are the things men need just as much as they need bread and a place to sleep.* Le Corbusier

Meyer argued that 'the origin of all present-day architecture in iron and glass is the greenhouse', causing Benjamin to reflect how 'curious' it was that arcade architecture 'is bound in its origin to the existence of plants' and to remind us that the central hall of the Crystal Palace incorporated pre-existing elms in that part of Hyde Park – because no-one wanted to fell the trees.[50]

On the Gold Coast, there is an opposite relationship with nature that involves bringing in mature trees, especially various palms, native figs and other subtropical trees, to produce 'established' gardens around new buildings. Instant landscapes are so common in retail, commercial, resort, high-rise and low-rise residential development that there are numbers of nurseries specializing in growing trees to movable maturity, companies specializing in transporting them and lifting them by truck-mounted crane into their positions, and landscapers who ensure that the rest of the garden (with reticulated, computer-controlled, 'water wise' irrigation system) is rapidly placed around them. When showpiece buildings open, there is no indication that less than a month before, their precincts were being cleared of builder's rubble. The trees, cycads, tree ferns and lush in-fills of broad-leaved foliage plants or flowering shrubs, suggest that the surrounds have been in place for years. It can be quite surreal until you get used to it – as if they had managed to throw up fifty or more storeys without disturbing 'nature' at all.

But Q1 also undertakes an even more dramatic reterritorialization of the built by the 'natural' environment. Just as Australian suburban homes conventionally have large gardens, Q1's apartments share its 'Skygarden'. Since the hinterland is famous for its subtropical rainforest, Q1 has a 'rainforest' planted in a 10-storey atrium that begins at Level 60. There, 180 metres above the ground, well-grown palms, trees and other rainforest plants thrive, with some expected to reach at least 30 metres in height, in what is doubtless one of the world's highest *and* tallest greenhouses.

Despite its aforementioned enclosed balconies, Q1 turned out to be a very photogenic building. It seems almost impossible to photograph it without capturing how light bounces off it and through the building, the neighbouring buildings, the ocean, the beach, the sweep of the city. That most modernist technology of light, the camera, draws our attention to how deeply and variously this engineered environment is connected to the environment in which it is set.

Deleuze and Guattari observe that 'beneath linear conceptions and segmentary decisions, an evaluation of flows and their quanta' must take place. In their usage:

> . . . 'connection' indicates the way in which decoded and deterritorialized flows boost one another, accelerate their shared escape, and augment or stoke their quanta; the 'conjugation' of these same flows, on the other hand, indicates their relative stoppage, like a point of accumulation that plugs or seals the lines of flight, performs a general reterritorialization, and brings flows under the dominance of a single flow capable of overcoding them. But it is precisely the most deterritorialized flow . . . that always brings about the accumulation or conjunction of the process, determines the overcoding, and serves as the basis for reterritorialization.[51]

In the context of the Gold Coast, light functions as 'connection', as the most deterritorialized flow, between nature, people and the built environment. But in considering the uses of light through an idea of flows, we must notice how this city depends on and trades in nature as a spectacle for consumption *and* as a flow in which people and buildings are interimplicated. In the discursive strategies of developers, light becomes the 'particle accelerator', the hyperdrive, that determines the overcoding, and serves as the basis for reterritorialization that manifests as commodification of the nature-panorama-architecture assemblage. These multiple flows make multiplicities and produce the Gold Coast's stylistics.

After a description of a Wintergarden, Benjamin says:

> When the sphere of planning creates such entanglements of closed room and airy nature, then it serves in this way to meet the deep human

need for daydreaming – a propensity that perhaps proves the true efficacy of idleness in human affairs.[52]

And so to return to those other paradoxes about the Gold Coast, about how it goes about being a city, attracting more creative people than might be expected, a small city acting like a much bigger one: perhaps Benjamin gives us part of an answer. The uses of light, the invitation to gaze at and immerse oneself in nature, to bring the light inside living spaces and to look out across the Pacific or towards the mountains involves the kind of idleness that opens out to imagination.

Notes

1 Gilles Deleuze and Félix Guattari, transl. Robert Hurley, Mark Seem and Helen R. Lane, *Anti-Oedipus: Capitalism and Schizophrenia* (London: Athlone Press, 1984), 4.
2 Mark Bonta and John Protevi, *Deleuze and Geophilosophy: A Guide and Glossary* (Edinburgh: Edinburgh University Press, 2004), 77.
3 In the period 1997–2007, annual population growth was 3.4–4.3% per annum, averaging 3.7%. (Gold Coast City Council homepage [GCCC] <http//www.goldcoast.qld.au>, *Gold Coast City: Community Profile*. Source: Australian Bureau of Statistics) <http//www.id.com.au/profile/Default.aspx?id=292>.
4 For example, of the total 2006 population 10.8% (51,162) moved to the Gold Coast from another part of Australia between 2001 and 2006, while 6.9% (32,601) moved from elsewhere in Queensland and 5.8% (27,582) from another country. Total growth 2001–2006 was therefore 23.5% (GCCC, *Gold Coast City: Community Profile* Source: ABS, Census of Population, Housing, 2006. Note that 2006 was the most recent Australian census.). There is continuing growth in Sydney and Melbourne, due especially to migration from other countries, while the rapid growth of Perth and Brisbane is due to migration from other states as well as other countries.
5 *Sea Change*, Australian Broadcasting Corporation, ran to three series, with the final episode broadcast in December 2000.
6 While, as with areas such as Miami in the United States, there is a national impression of the Gold Coast as overburdened with suntanned geriatrics, '*there were no major differences between Gold Coast City and Australia's age structure data in 2006*' (italics in original). The increasing attractiveness of the region to various age groups is indicated by the fact that 'the largest changes in age structure data . . . between 2001 and 2006 were in the age groups: 35 to 49 (+14,136 persons); 50 to 59 (+9,710 persons); 60 to 69 (+9,561 persons); and 18 to 24 (+7,378 persons)' (GCCC, *Gold Coast City: Community Profile*. Source: ABS Census of Population and Housing, 2006 and 2001).
7 The striking nature of the regional demographic data is underscored by the fact that only 36.3% of the population had *not* moved either into or within the Gold Coast in the past five years (GCCC, *Gold Coast City: Community Profile*. Source: ABS, Census of Population and Housing, 2006).
8 Manuel Castells, *The Rise of the Network Society* (Cambridge, MA: Blackwell, 1996) Vol. 1, 412.
9 David Bell, and Mark Jayne, eds, *Small Cities: Urban Experience Beyond the Metropolis* (Oxford and New York: Routledge, 2006), 5.
10 Queensland Department of State Development, *Creativity is Big Business: A Framework for the Future* (Brisbane: Queensland Government, 2004), 15. In terms of a national comparison of employment in the creative industries as a proportion of employment in all industries the Gold Coast was 3.32%, behind Sydney 3.91%. Melbourne ranked third (2.88%) and Brisbane fourth (2.38%).
11 Walter Benjamin, transl. Howard Eiland and Kevin McLaughlin, *The Arcades Project* (Harvard: Harvard University Press, 2002), 198.

12. Gogol, cited in Benjamin, ibid., 198.
13. Caroline Butler-Bowden and Charles Pickett, *Homes in the Sky: Apartment Living in Australia* (Carlton: The Miegunyah Press, 2007), 177. Kinkabool is now heritage listed.
14. Neicon Developments, *The Oracle*, pdf brochure, 4. <http//www.oraclebroadbeach.com/>.
15. Benjamin, op. cit., 405.
16. Gilles Deleuze and Félix Guattari, transl. Brian Massumi, *A Thousand Plateaus: Capitalism and Schizophrenia* (Minneapolis: University of Minnesota Press, 1987), 474.
17. Nik Heynen, Maria Kaika and Eric Swyngedouw, eds, *In the Nature of Cities: Urban Political Ecology and the Politics of Urban Metabolism* (London and New York: Routledge, 2006), 4.
18. Henri Lefebvre, transl. Donald Nicholson-Smith, *The Production of Space* (Oxford: Blackwell, 1991), 345.
19. Ibid., 109.
20. Lefebvre in Heynen, Kaika and Swyngedouw, op. cit., 5.
21. Heynen, Kaika and Swyngedouw, op. cit., 5.
22. Matthew Gandy cited in ibid., 5.
23. GCCC/ABS
24. In Surfers Paradise in 2006, 50.6% of residents occupied high-density housing, 11% medium density, and 7.5% separate houses compared to a city-wide 14.9% high density, 21.3% medium density and 50.4% separate houses (GCCC, *Gold Coast City: Community Profile*. Source: ABS, Census of Population and Housing, 2006). The current population density of Surfers Paradise is estimated to be 3,701 people per square kilometre compared to a city-wide density of 362 people per square kilometre and average suburban density of 800–1,000 people per square kilometre (GCCC/ABS).
25. Benjamin, op. cit., 532.
26. Niecon Developments, *Ocean Skyhomes: Reflection on the Sea*, pdf brochure, 6. <http//www.reflectiononthesea.com/>.
27. Bonta and Protevi, op. cit., 168.
28. Niecon, *Reflection Tower Two* brochure, n.p.
29. Niecon, *Nirvana by the Sea*, interactive brochure, 1. <http//www.nirvanabythesea.com/>.
30. Pacific Lifestyle Property <http://www.plproperty.com.au/burleigh-heads-ambience/burleigh-ambience-index.html>.
31. While its concentration of high-rise buildings means that from any distance Surfers Paradise appears to be the 'downtown' of Gold Coast City, this is an illusion. The Gold Coast's 'downtown' functions – banking and finance, local government headquarters, law courts, cultural institutions etc. are dispersed across other parts of the city.
32. The Wave won a Silver Award in the Emporis 2006 Skyscraper Awards.
33. The Wave Resort, <http//www.thewavesresort.com.au/index.htm>.
34. Air on Broadbeach, <http//www.airbroadbeach.com.au>.
35. Sunland Group, *Avalon Riverfront Apartments*, pdf brochure, <http//www.avalongoldcoast.com>.
36. Including 'a heated lap pool, gymnasium, spa, sauna and steam room, barbeque areas, the comfort and privacy of a fully equipped cinema and a club lounge that's the perfect setting for parties.'
37. Sunland Group, *Avalon Riverfront Apartments*, pdf brochure.
38. Ibid.
39. Sunland Group, *Circle on Cavill*, pdf brochure, 3. <http//www.circleoncavill.com>. The notion of 'historic' needs to be understood in its Gold Coast usage. In the demolition that cut through two city blocks for this development, it is very unlikely that any building was over fifty years old and the great majority would have been built after 1975.
40. Ibid., 5.
41. Ibid., 6–7.

Patricia Wise

42 Ibid., 9.
43 Sunland Group, Circle on Cavill, print brochure. Circle residents enjoy an excess of the usual amenities, including for example, 'privileged access to a Residents' Club Lounge with its own private balcony and barbeque terrace'; a heated lap pool and 'a large lagoon pool'; gymnasium; and 'exclusive in-house cinema and internet lounge, seminar and function rooms'. Each tower has further 'barbeque facilities, big screen viewing area, recreation and exercise decks, spa and steam room' and the whole complex is, of course, comprehensively landscaped with mature trees and so on (pdf brochure, 11). The private cinema and big screens are in addition to a huge public video screen that occupies a dramatic space between the two towers. From Circle's 'piazza' or any of the bars, cafés and restaurants around it, the public can view the screen, or look through to the western panorama of city and hinterland framed beneath it.
44 Bonta and Protevi, op. cit., 76.
45 Sunland has built an 80-storey sister building to Q1, called D1, in Dubai. Further, having built the famously opulent Versace Hotel on the Gold Coast, it will soon complete another Versace Hotel in Dubai.
46 http//www.QDeck.com.au
47 You can also have coffee and cakes at QBar café, which occupies a raised dais in the centre of QDeck, and becomes a cocktail bar at night. A short flight of stairs above there is a silver-service function centre, the 'Skylight Room' – what else?
48 Benjamin, op. cit., 156.
49 Meyer cited by Benjamin, op. cit., 156–7.
50 Benjamin, op. cit., 158.
51 Deleuze and Guattari, op. cit., 220–1.
52 Benjamin, op. cit., 422.

Chapter 6

Trade Flow: Architectures of Informal Markets

*Peter Mörtenböck and
Helge Mooshammer*

Over the past decades, the flows of the global economy have arguably gained a tight grip on the territorial distribution of human capital as well as on the boundary regimes that regulate its spatial and cultural accumulations. The current reorganization of human habitats in relation to market-driven choices seems to portray a system of unilateral appropriation that knows no alternative. Yet, if one looks beyond the boundaries imposed on the world by the global economic regime, one can recognize the manifestation of the boundary as a political space that cannot be controlled through the workings of the economy alone. In this sphere, one can make out the lines of flight of a potential for redrawing social, economic and political order. As the agonistic organisms that evolve from contemporary economic flows are ever more aligned to a globally distributed and flexibly interconnected trans-urban realm – markets unleashing markets, riots triggering riots, socialities engendering socialities – an intensifying network of nodalized informality has emerged on a global scale in which different cultures coincide locally and yield volatile, contradictory and contested space-time ecosystems.

So far, investigations into the expansion of such informal operations have for the most part been employing economic, developmental or sociological parameters, for instance with regard to the informalization of work and its social consequences. Yet there is an explicitly spatial and cultural component to informality as well, one that needs to be addressed through investigations into the spaces of informal cultural exchange and through the flows that create and sustain them. Here, we want to focus on informal markets as paradigmatic sites from where to explore how the complex flows of informal network economies constitute an important technology of extra-state power – a trans-territorial spatial articulation that fuses multiple politico-economic interests with processes of subject formation.

Informal markets are a decisive yet often overlooked theatre of the flows that make the livelihood of millions work. Responding to political upheaval and economic destabilization, shifting populations and new labour situations, they shape complex systems of alternate relations wherever and whenever institutional protocols have come to a deadlock – a volatile shadow system, whose relationship to the homogenizing forces of global capital markets is characterized by its paradoxical production of culturally heterogeneous micro-locations. In the current discourse, the term 'informal market' refers to widely scattered trading phenomena that are generally tied to processes of political and economic transformation but whose dynamics and forms of spatial materialization differ greatly in character. At the economic level, the term is applied to incomes whose generation escapes the regulations of the institutions of society, in a legal and social environment in which similar activities are regulated.[1] At the spatial level, the term refers to the rampant agglomerations of black markets on metropolitan fringes, the make-shift architectures of irregular trade along urban infrastructures or the mobile and border-crossing networks of the so-called 'suitcase trade'. Built around simple forms of economic exchange with an anonymous outside and often linked to the presence of immigrant populations, informal markets offer many traces of emerging modes of sociality, as does the associated network of transient commercial establishments that fill abandoned urban spaces. But although the makeshift structures of such markets – metal containers, tent-like constructions, cardboard stalls and other improvised sales areas – are obvious signs to manifest this presence, many 'market deals' appear to escape the usual regulatory mechanisms.

The informal market has its own regulatory forces, which thrive on a climate of murky deals, vague figures, dubious contacts, liabilities and unregulated control. It is because of family ties, the prospects of a quick sale and the opportunity to sell items at other markets, and because of friendships, dependencies, debts to suppliers, as well as unexpected twists in people's lives and the development of new relationships that people come together in an environment where they can benefit from worlds different from their own. This is the place to buy smuggled cigarettes and bootleg versions of brand-name goods: imitation Adidas tracksuits, fake fragrances, fashionable sunglasses, car accessories and counterfeit CDs can all be purchased quickly here.

Today, these widespread nodes of the informal economy emerge in a period of transition towards globally oriented market economies, in which the state's role is more and more confined to optimizing the flows of provisional arrangements. Driven by new imperatives of social mobility and the expansion of trans-national spaces brought about by the unequal movements of tourism, migration and flight, informal market types have come into being that have created novel and extreme physical configurations. These spatial structures are intermediate zones that are seized by diverse interest groups, no matter whether they are local or global, formal or informal, and own much or little capital. This unstable positioning is allied to the ambivalent logics of mobility and containment which keep informal markets deeply intertwined with the flows of the world economy.

In this sense, informal markets are shifting and vulnerable spaces that do not appear in the matrix of territorial and ideological affiliation of individuals and cultures. They are channels through which goods and commodities are transported and through which cultures outside the designated places of encounter interact directly with the forces of globalization. As labour conditions become increasingly precarious, the transport of goods and commodities becomes increasingly individualized, spreading across a large number of smaller towns and localities, where finely meshed networks participate in informal trading structures. Accelerating the surge of one-to-one exchanges, informal markets are part of global processes of geocultural fragmentation and diffusing economic flows that propel transition in many different ways. They serve, on the one hand, as places for brief stays and are themselves often seen as mere 'transitional effects': as adapters between unregulated relationships and order. This perspective, however, views the flows between one state and another as a foreseeable process. It assumes the existence of a central intention that controls change, the existence of both an order-generating plan and the latter's ability to capture a development in its totality. But what if this transition generates an accelerated space which, in the case of informal markets, is saturated with a surfeit of conflicting symbols and practices of signification? Then arguably, the cultural paradoxes of globalization and the inpredictability of the flows it aims to contain become evident.

    Diasporic cultures and the opportunities they find in global cities don't just combine to constitute the local presence of migrant subjectivities within a uniform worldwide labour regime. Interacting with the flexible technologies of governing and citizenship, they produce conditions that change the rationalities of urban space and provide the grounds for an unexpected and unsolicited place-making in its most elementary form. Against this backdrop of market-driven spatial fragmentations and a range of situated practices that tend to challenge unilateral control, we are interested in the ways in which the globally distributed nodes of the informal economy create new zones, characterized by social and cultural relations rich in endogenous development. In our studies we aim to approach geophysical conflicts not in a top-down view but from the perspective of creating social environments, foregrounding the spontaneity of social interaction and the ways in which it fashions a complex network of detours, back doors, 'underground relays', hiding places, tunnels and tricks that make up everyday life on the fringes.

    What emerges through such examinations is a horizontal and relational character of global economic, political and cultural processes, which complicates the clear distinction between formality and informality, legality and illegality, inside and outside in dealing with material and symbolic goods. Each of these sites engages singular transgressions and violations against existing spatial arrangements and produces a set of openings in the matrix of economic inclusions and exclusions, hubs and peripheries. What is common to all these endeavours is the question of how to organize a space which has neither centre nor specific end, a space that is neither characterized in relation to a central authority nor through programmed identities and strict objectives.

    Looking at three selected informal markets in and around Europe, the following sections aim to trace the multi-level network of 'operators', 'intermediaries' and 'marketeers' who provide the spatial and political context of informalized urbanization and link different levels of societal mobility: local migrant networks to global economic flows and the spatiality of national borders to the processes of trans-urbanization. We will explore how these practices act as performative frames for new modes of trans-local sociality and mark a radical shift in urban organization from geographically fixed territories to a networked ecology of flows, filters and channels.

Arizona Market: Inter-Ethnic Collaboration in Brčko

Not far from the north Bosnian town of Brčko lies one of the most notorious marketplaces in south-eastern Europe: Arizona Market. It has 2,500 stalls on an area covering 40 hectares, receives 3 million visitors a year and employs directly or indirectly an estimated 100,000 people. Apart from these statistics, what distinguishes the market depends on participants' perspectives and interests, and these can differ considerably. For some, it is a model of a multi-ethnic community, for others it is the largest open-air shopping mall in the Balkans, while still others experience it as hell on earth. The difference in perspective rests upon the numerous stages and transformations of what is commonly called Arizona Market (figure 6.1).

The strip of land occupied by the present Arizona Market is a part of the war zone that was fiercely fought over by Serbian, Croatian and Bosnian Muslim units because of its strategic position after Bosnia–Herzegovina had left the federal state of Yugoslavia in 1991. Besides the entities set out in the Dayton Peace Accords of November 1995, i.e. the Serbian Republic and the Federation of Bosnia–Herzegovina, the disputed territory around the town of Brčko, whose future was to be decided in an international arbitration process, was granted special status. It was placed under the direct supervision of a special supervisor from the Office of the High Representative (OHR) of the international community of states for Bosnia and

Figure 6.1 Arizona Market, Bosnia and Herzegovina.

Herzegovina. Along the so-called Arizona Corridor (the north–south link between Bosnia and Croatia, which divides the Serbian Republic into a western and an eastern part), thus named by the Ifor/Sfor troops, an economic hub has established itself whose importance extends far beyond the area occupied by the Special District of Brčko.

In 1996, after the checkpoint set up at the interface between the three ethnic groupings had evolved into an informal meeting place where cigarettes and cattle were traded and coffee was served at the roadside, the local commander decided to encourage initial encounters between members of the different ethnic communities by establishing a 'free-trade zone', with the aim of consolidating peace. Sfor soldiers levelled several hectares of farmland, cleared the mines and supplied building materials. In next to no time, the largest informal market for goods in Southern Europe arose on the opposite side of the road to the checkpoint: with wooden huts, improvised stalls, smuggled goods and bootleg versions of brand-name goods. Textiles, food, electronic products, building materials, cosmetics, car accessories and CDs could all be purchased at favourable prices there. The cheapest goods could be acquired directly from the lorries.

Decisive for the continued development of Arizona Market was the fact that, unlike most other informal markets, it arose on the open fields with the support of the armed forces. In the years that followed, the convergence of economic activities at the site and the self-organization of this grey trade area were extolled as a model for promoting the sustained development of communications and community structures between former wartime enemies. Supplementing the simple market facilities and mobile sales, the first houses soon arose, presaging the emergence of a self-organized urbanization process on the site. As time went by, ever more bars and motels operating in these huts and houses started to accommodate a form of trade that made it increasingly difficult to sell – at an international level – the success story of peace based on the market economy. For at Arizona Market, the real money was made through prostitution and trafficking in human beings: with women and girls who were being brought in from Eastern Europe. According to reports, they were rounded up on the streets and resold like cattle from one bar owner to the next. On 26 October 2000, the International Community (OHR, OSCE, UNMIBH and SFOR) announced a package of measures designed to purge Arizona Market of such illegal activities. These measures focused on regulating the issue of licences and tax revenues, and relocating the market by June 2001 to a new site that would offer all the necessary facilities and safety features (figure 6.2).[2]

The resulting transformation of the informal market into a shopping centre signalled a critical turning point, revealing the limits of translating between formal and informal systems. The 'spontaneous' evolution of a public–urban space in the shape of an informal market surrounded by transporters and huts was replaced by enclosed fee-charging parking spaces. The coming together of diverse cultures was now regulated by fixed opening hours and private security guards. In summer 2006, there was little sign of the original Arizona Market with its thousands of wooden huts standing around a tarpaulin and metal-roofed bazaar. The present Arizona Market contains the market halls operated by ItalProject – an Italian–Bosnian–Serbian

Figure 6.2 Arizona Market, Bosnia and Herzegovina.

consortium, which won the tender to establish and operate a new market – and a hybrid urban entity whose gravel roads and wooden verandas not only make it look like a wild-west town (a rudimentary social and economic frontier) but also conjure up images of an embryonic self-organized town where people can live and trade.

A new type of local structure is emerging here which is composed of the remains of the former 'rampant' developments and the newly partitioned plots of the master plan whose module structures are being appropriated through individual aesthetics. A residential settlement has evolved polymorphously above two clearly arranged sales floors, inspired by urban models. At the same time, the wide variety of roof extensions, window apertures, balustrades and other forms of decoration signal the advent of individual inhabitation of the large-scale structures of strategic investments. The site's remarkable form reflects the struggle of official planners to control the dynamics of the black market. In this segment of the market, the convergence of the two systems has led to the proliferating parallel existence of cultural claims and practices. Here, the tension between informally and formally regulated organizational forms has enhanced the aesthetics of spatial use which Srdjan Jovanović Weiss describes as 'turbo architecture' – a kind of aesthetics that takes its orientation from self-made truths about national tradition, rules and architectural style, and invents new typologies from a combination of diffuse repertoires of forms, colours, materials and standards. Turbo architecture is one of the unconcealable and unrestrainable results of the black market. It is 'proof that architectural production depends neither on a stable market nor on a stable political system'.[3]

Turbo architecture is a self-created niche marking out its own field of operation by skilfully manoeuvring through a combination of half-truths, misunderstandings and local reactions; it is the antithesis of the firmly laid-down rules of the master plan. In this sense it counterbalances the design envisaged for the new Arizona Market. Indeed, at Arizona Market, at the interface between the grown settlement and the new developments on allotted plots, 'Balkanized' house models respond to a landscape of unstable policies with powerful gestures of invulnerability and success, hyper-materialism and hyper-identifiables. In their study on the Arizona Market, Harvard Business School economists have concluded that democracy is not necessarily a precondition for launching capitalist economies.[4] The armed forces, they argue, are more efficient than a democratically elected government at triggering urban processes, because they, like their market counterparts, go into operation when states of emergency present themselves . . .

The convoluted flows of international money and goods at Arizona Market may have now entered a new phase, yet the form of capitalism that prevails there is no less 'rampant' than it used to be. Its aggressiveness resides with an all-pervading motivation to gain some form of control – ranging from the need to survive, at one end of the scale, to international relations at the other – by seizing anything that is not yet subject to controls. All these many different levels of exchange have created the countless trade situations that one finds at Arizona Market, which promise everyone an opportunity to exploit the market to their own ends. What appears to be a random remaking of territorial, economic and cultural claims, eventually marks a continuous displacement of boundaries that results from local interpretations, arrangements and deals. In this sense, then, there is no specific logic shared by all participants, but only a contingent operating mechanism – an economic fabric geared to situational opportunities, instead of being subject to the dictates of rational calculation. If we thus localize decision-making in the different temporal rhythms of individuals, groups, communities, networks and markets, in the flowing movements of societal praxis itself, then we gain an insight into the ways in which the flows of trade manoeuvres are spread across the individual zones of a region and stream across the different modes of cultural organization.

Istanbul Topkapı: Transient Traffic

In July 2005, one of the leading forums for international architecture – the 22nd World Congress of Architecture – was held in Istanbul under the motto 'Grand bazaar of architecture'. The central theme of the congress was the utopian idea of a pluralistic world in which cultural differences are not a source of animosity and atrocities, but a resource to help people find a way to live together in harmony.[5] The leading lights in contemporary architectural design presented their models and discussed them in the context of Istanbul's struggle for recognition as a cosmopolitan city. Outstanding engineering achievements, sustainable planning and cultural heritage formed part of a well-orchestrated protocol of declarations of intent to participate in the exclusive set of global cities. The allegorical motto of the congress as well as its point of reference – the legendary oriental bazaar that leaves no desires unfulfilled – transfigure the socio-spatial challenge posed by a rapidly expanding megacity and its hope that it will be saved by quick responses from architects and urban planners (figure 6.3).

Figure 6.3 Istanbul Topkapı, informal market, Turkey.

Outside the tourist centres, and escaping international attention, lies a very different type of bazaar. It is composed of a vast network of provisional, informal street markets that establish themselves right alongside building sites where urban renewal plans are being realized, beneath terraces of city motorways, and next to newly constructed tramway lines. These markets disappear as quickly as they materialize, only to reappear elsewhere. This bazaar is not so much a location for trading goods as a space under negotiation. It is a threatening and threatened space which winds its way through the city from site to site and temporarily uses (as the intermediary user of the newly planned infrastructure) the wastelands along the development axes of the planned city.

One of these arose in 2005 before the gates of the Byzantine city wall in the district of Topkapı, where the building sites of two of the main enterprises that took on the job of tidying up the city in the 1980s converge. On the one hand, a traffic network of urban motorways has been created there in the style of modernist US urbanism. On the other hand, the 1,500-year-old Byzantine city fortifications have been reinstated there in their original condition. In nationalist literature, their continual decline and the living conditions in the wretched areas bordering the fortifications had come to symbolize both the impoverishment of Istanbul and the stronghold of true Turkish values.[6] Between newly delivered and unused building materials, impassable heaps of crushed stone, and eight-lane motorways, a swarm-like mass fills a black market covering several kilometres. Piles of second-hand goods and fabrics are mixed up on bare ground with new TV sets, refrigerators, pieces of furniture and computers. On days when visitors turn out in strength, several thousand people can been seen negotiating this construction site of the new Istanbul.

The informal market evokes an archaic model of a city that arises organically as trading centre at the junction of transport and trading routes. In the case of

Trade Flow: Architectures of Informal Markets

Topkapı, however, it is also moving in the shadows of official town planning, which it temporarily turns into a vehicle serving informality. This market makes use of the semi-finished building structures in a way that has less to do with their intended uses or with any conceptions or images of modern urban planning than with unplanned utilization and the economic situation of the rural population that has migrated to the city. Land has been occupied here on an improvised basis, bypassing the planners. This approach is not based on how things will look after the plans have been realized, but seeks instead to realize alternatives to this process.

The innovatory power of this informal economy is evident not only in its sheer size, but also in its far-reaching ramifications, with all the emerging services systems such as shuttle buses, street kitchens, middlemen, suppliers, livestock sales, the attendant forms of cultural entertainment and ad hoc shooting ranges. With its bizarre combination of modern transport systems, its symbolic sites of a national renaissance, spontaneously arising market activities, rich visual display of the intricacies of legally authorized work, and its third market and informal trading, Topkapı represents more than just a coincidental clash of diverse forces. The growing perviousness of official and informal structures, the rampant appropriation of urban space, and the accelerated disintegration of cultural territories are typical moments in the evolution of a city structure dictated by the new world economy, in which full control over a territory is no longer a relevant issue. In contrast to the territorially based economic forms, large and small spatial structures are evolving which circumvent the functional separation of space and embed themselves in the prevailing geography as a mesh of networks (figure 6.4).

Participation in socio-spatial processes, for which the informal market situated amidst the hustle and bustle of Istanbul stands, echoes the performance – used as a metaphor by Ernesto Laclau – at which we always arrive too late. We live as *bricoleurs* in a world of imperfect systems, whose rules we co-determine and transform by retracing them. It is in this very moment, according to Laclau,

Figure 6.4 Istanbul Topkapı, informal market, Turkey.

that we find the key to (acts of) emancipation: in the middle of a performance that has started unexpectedly, we search for mythical and impossible origins but are unable to rise above the impossible task facing us. What counts, however, is that we struggle and strive to arrive at decisions that have to be made because there is no superordinate monitoring or control system. Running counter to the radical foundation of a democratic society and operational structures sketched out in the great narrations of modernity, a model of political praxis is taking shape that is continuing to develop through a plurality of acts of democratization.[7] At Topkapı Market, we only know that the minibus we try to stop by waving it down really is going to stop once we are inside it.

Moscow Izmailovo: Visiting Stalin

In the north-east of Moscow, on an area three times the size of that occupied by the Kremlin, 15 specialized trading areas form a rampantly growing bazaar structure that completely surrounds Izmailovo Stadium and includes all sorts of attractions: from Eurasian wholesale markets to a reconstruction of Tsar Alexander's wooden palace in the Vernisazh complex, which was specially erected for tourists and the sale of arts and crafts (figure 6.5). The market's 'owners' are among Russia's new millionaires, while at the lower end of the new market-economy scale, there are thousands of migrants from Tajikistan, Uzbekistan, China and an extended Southeast Asia, who have come to seek work at the market as stall-minders, carriers and tea-sellers seven days a week. They sleep in the metal storage containers (above the stalls or on the periphery of the market) or in the cellars of the stadium. In this state of modern slavery, they are not only at the mercy of exploitative employers, but also of arbitrary police behaviour and gangs of young thugs. As a result, many of them never dare to go more than a few hundred meters from the market.

Figure 6.5 'The Russian Court', Moscow Izmailovo, Russia.

In September 2006, one month after a bombing which killed 13 people and left 53 badly wounded, the vice-speaker of Moscow City Council announced that the market would be closing at the end of 2006. A few weeks later, the head of the Department of the Consumer Market of Moscow announced that most of the trading places on the site of the Russian State University of Physical Education (RGUFK) would be taken down by 1 July 2007, and the remainder by the end of 2007. This, it was said, would allow the site to be returned to its proper use, as a space where people could devote themselves to physical culture. But how is it possible to determine the 'proper' use of a space, especially in an age of global restructuring? Does its use as a venue for sports events really do justice to the original plans? Or isn't it simply a by-product, a parasitical use of its potential?

During the XXII Olympic Summer Games in 1980, the RGUFK site served as one of the locations of the Moscow Games. For the weight-lifting events, a new indoor arena, the Izmailovo Sports Palace, was erected. At the southern end of the site, next to Izmailovo Park underground station, the Olympic village was constructed in the form of a four-tower hotel complex with 8,000 beds. The stadium itself, which stands in the middle of the grounds, was built during the 1930s. It is a fragment of the envisaged 'Central Stadium of the Soviet Union' planned by Stalin to accommodate 120,000 spectators. Never completed, it also served to camouflage the 'Reserve Command Centre of the Supreme Commander-in-Chief of the Red Army, I.V. Stalin'.

Ultimately, the construction of the stadium was inspired by more than purely sporting considerations. Not only was the stadium intended to be bigger than Berlin's Olympic Stadium, and its peculiar asymmetrical form designed to hold grandiose military parades at which the columns of tanks could roll into the stadium unhindered from the parade ground to the east; it was also conceived as part of a vast military infrastructure covering the entire Soviet Union. Situated 17 kilometres to the east of the Kremlin, a bunker beneath the stadium was designed as an intermediary stop-over point in case Hitler should launch a surprise attack on Moscow and the Soviet Command have to be evacuated to Samara, 1,000 kilometres away in the Urals. Consequently, sports events in Izmailovo have always been part of a far greater system of deceptions and compensatory gestures. Cultural events are just as important as strategically embedded building structures for preserving this system. Events such as these helped to sustain policies that were imitated with ever greater rapidity when the RGUFK site was converted into one of the largest informal trading centres in the Russian Federation.

Cherkizovsky Market was a product of the politics of individual initiatives promoted by Perestroika. Under its banner, members of the state sports institute began to use the grounds and buildings commercially. In June 1989, Sergei Korniyenko and a 'collective of enthusiasts' leased the stadium buildings. Under the terms of the contract, the spectators stands and the sports fields are to be available for events such as Spartakiade 2000 ('For a United and Healthy Russia in the 21st Century'). The remaining spaces, like those beneath the stands, can be used commercially. FOP, the Sports Health Enterprise founded in 1989, proved to be extremely innovative. Nowadays, in conjunction with the New Historical

Cultural Centre Izmailovo (NIC Izmailovo, founded in 1995), it operates enterprises as diverse as an arbalest shooting range, the Aero Fitness Club, various bars, the Lux Sauna, the Alain Beauty Salon (up to 'European standard') and the Preobrazheniye (Transformation) School for the Spiritual Development of Man, which is run by a cosmic artist-healer.

Furthermore, FOP played a vital role in the 'rediscovery' of Stalin's old bunker. In 1994, the Iron Division club helped to organize a museum exhibition which was taken over from the Central Museum of the Armed Forces and opened as a branch on 1 September 1999. Adjacent to the bunker rooms, FOP operates a Georgian-style restaurant called Visiting Stalin, as well as a concert hall (holding 200 people) used for performances by the Prince Sergei Korniyenko Orchestra. Even though the bunker was apparently never used by Stalin himself – just as the stadium never performed the function originally anticipated – one can now book a bunker tour for a little over 100 US dollars. The price includes a visit to the reconstructed conference hall of the Supreme Command of the Red Army, as well as to Stalin's study and recreational and leisure areas, plus a dinner at 'Stalin'.

Whereas the stadium was originally supposed to provide an arena for mass performances demonstrating the superiority of the political order of the Soviet Union, it has now become the archaeological site testifying to the inner emptiness of a Babylonian city-within-a-city, into the cracks of which the ants of globalization have now moved. No longer do revolutionary tanks roll or patriotic armies march on the parade ground, which has disappeared beneath the Eurasia Market. Instead, thousands of carriers and tea-sellers swarm out around the endless labyrinth of its kilometres-long halls to keep this rough trading organism alive.

As a central trading place for the sheer necessities of life, the Cherkizovsky Market has become the contested scene of cultural identities, where attempts to reconstruct a Russian national identity encounter the complex realities of a globalized migration-economy (figure 6.6). The progressive commercialization of even the tiniest of niches has generated a large number of unforeseen spaces for micro-cultural negotiations, like the one for the 3,000 Mountain Jews from the Caucasus, for whom a 20-square-metre room – laid out with carpets and located between the shoe storerooms and the sportsmen and women's toilets in the caverns of the stadium stands – serves as a synagogue. Like the majority of the hundreds of thousands of people whose existences are inextricably tied up with the market, they, too, are both marginalized and transformed into targets of a global tug-o-war over cultural identity. To some, they are 'blacks', to some they are not orthodox enough, while some doubt whether they are Jews at all.

While the owners' good contacts with the government and the mayor have led to repeated delays in implementing the plans to close the markets, a ruling to restrict the share of foreign workers at markets to 40 per cent, which came into effect on 1 April 2007, really did have a widespread impact. From Moscow to Vladivostock, there are reports of markets collapsing completely. This has not only affected immigrants working at the market, but also all those impoverished sections of the Russian population who are dependent on the cheap products available at these markets. These policies (Russia for the Russians), which are propagated by

Trade Flow: Architectures of Informal Markets

Figure 6.6
Cherkizovsky Market, Moscow Izmailovo, Russia.

Russia's prime minister and former president Vladimir Putin, are frequently seen as a tactically motivated response to the increase in racially inspired attacks. Consequently, the bombers of 12 August 2006, who felt that there were 'too many Asians at the market', ultimately did not only kill 13 people and wound 53 others, but also affected, with their actions, the existence(s) of an estimated 5 million illegal immigrants in Russia.

On 29 June 2009 the market was finally shut down by Russia's consumer watchdog Rospotrebnadzor due to 464 alleged violations of fire safety regulations and after earlier raids had unearthed 6,000 containers of counterfeit goods. Though having been anticipated for some time,[8] this lockdown took many of the 100,000 migrant workers, who suddenly found themselves locked out with no access to their trading stock, by surprise. Stallholders and suitcase traders protested for days outside the locked market gates. A group of Vietnamese market workers trying to block a nearby highway were arrested and given deportation orders.[9] Immediate crisis talks between Chinese officials and the Russian government about the implications of the closure for the 60,000-strong Chinese community involved in the market lead to arrangements for traders to withdraw their stock from the market at regulated times. In a step forward, Russia and China expressed their mutual interest in establishing a standardized, transparent and convenient trade environment. In order to achieve sustained and sound development of bilateral trade, both parties agreed that it would be essential to tackle the problem of 'grey customs clearance' as it had been practised at Cherkizovsky market.[10] Work to bring the market stuctures down began in September 2009 and the RGUFK is keen to get its territory back. On 20 October 2009 Moscow mayor Yuri Luzhkov signed a decree on a revised listing

129

of Moscow's markets that no longer includes Cherkizovsky Market. On that day, Cherkizovsky Market officially ceased to exist.

Amphibian Configurations

The complex transformations of the three sites dealt with here reveal how markets function as a dynamic force that generates new flows of collective exchange, and how this process relates to the aesthetics of establishing new social orders. Despite the very different ways in which historical developments and local microprocesses converge, there are similarities between the informal trading areas along the Byzantine city wall in Istanbul, the establishment of an economy in the district of Brčko and the never-ending transformation of a cultural site of national importance in Moscow. All three markets arose and expanded in a hybrid situation, meandering between informality and planning, and in a close dialogue with strategically important typologies of modern urban planning – among sports and training centres, traffic buildings and facilities, and military complexes in the stadium area of Moscow's Cherkizovsky Market; between the newly constructed rapid transport systems and the historical fortifications in Istanbul; and at a checkpoint controlled by international troops in a Bosnian war zone. These three markets are now being demolished (Moscow), transformed into legal structures (Brčko) or forced to move to new locations (Istanbul).

The fate of these three junctions of self-organized trade is similar to that of other informal markets, following, for example, the pattern of the slow dismantlement of the Jarmark Europa at the Dziesięciolecia Stadium in Warsaw and the removal of the Polish market near Potsdamer Platz in Berlin around the time the Wall opened in 1989. These markets are able to survive for a short while as platforms for an experimental urbanity at the micro-level of everyday life; they then give way to the political pressure to create a new architectural order, which is supposed to restore some form of normative urbanity; later, they reappear somewhere else. Although these experimental structures repeatedly disappear from the face of the earth, they leave their mark on the fabric of the city. Their flows transport images, ideas and values between different worlds. And with their improvised technologies, infrastructures and spatial policies, they create openings for new urban situations and new links between the local and the global levels.

Yet these realities also raise questions about the convenient co-optation of survival strategies of the global South by neoliberal myths that equate informality with a nebulous expression of free individuality. Mobile and transient accumulation seem to be as much a constituent mechanism of black market worlds as of efficient capital markets. Elmar Altvater and Brigitte Mahnkopf have argued a certain structural alliance behind this kind of ephemeral accumulation, describing informality as 'shock absorber of globalisation' beyond the means of the welfare state. It ought to be located through structural changes in the interaction between global, national and local economy following the requirements of global competition.[11] Indeed, this complex entanglement of neoliberal technologies of government and forms of self organization along with the incorporation of market mentality (Karl Polanyi)[12] into the organization of creative processes and critical practices has led to a tricky point of departure in approaching the question of how we can organize cultural experience that creates a space for expressions whose outlines are yet to come.

According to Saskia Sassen, informal markets are the low-cost equivalent of global deregulation and serve, first and foremost, as the suppliers of advanced urban economies, with the sole difference that, at the lower end of the scale, the risks and costs have to be borne by the actors themselves.[13] With her argumentation, she finds herself in the same boat as Mike Davis, who, in *Planet of Slums* (2006), presents an ensemble of epistemological fallacies on informality in order to expose the strategic nature of the ideology of informal organization. From the myriad of concealed forms of exploitation and seduction to the fanatic obsession with quasi-magic ways of acquiring money (gambling, pyramid schemes, etc.) to the diminution of social capital as a result of increasing competition within the informal sector, Davis lists all the erroneous beliefs held by the advocates of an 'invisible revolution' of informal capital, such as the Peruvian economist Hernando de Soto.[14] Instead of fulfilling the promise of greater upward mobility, the boom that began in the informal sector in the 1980s led to greater ethno-religious differentiation, as well as to increased exploitation of the poor and urban violence. Davis's notion of a counter-offensive to the neoliberal version of informality involves strengthening trade union structures and radical political parties and, last but not least, reviving a community based on worldwide solidarity within the framework of a militant refusal to accept the assigned marginal role within global capitalism.[15]

The wealth of arguments and evidence, as well as all the statistics, maps and diagrams that have been presented, seem to demand a condemnation of the state of informality – a condemnation that can draw on well-documented material on the dynamics of poverty, exploitation and oppression. The roles of power seem to be too clearly allocated and consolidated to imagine how – through the way they function – they can allow alternative social formations to develop. But what if we refuse to accept this logic for a moment and take a look at an entire series of shortcomings in the apparatus of global economic control that we have just criticized – shortcomings that can create space for social experiences outside the boundaries within which this apparatus exercises control?

Attempts to explain informal activities from the standpoint of the totality usually ignore the way in which local spaces are changed by a large number of actors and spontaneously coordinated modes of behaviour that cannot be determined by knowing the overall situation. Thus, the type of habitable formation and the potential for change offered by networks of informal organizations are often overlooked. Although power circulates in such networks, people are not merely the consenting targets of those who exercise power, but, as Michel Foucault argues, the relays of power. Power flows through them, which means that it can be seized and redirected.[16] Hence, one of the ways of thinking the flows of power architecturally is to search – beyond the world of hackneyed concepts such as slum culture, chaos economy, social mobility and transitional societies – for ideas, constructions, images and experiences that help to show ways of making local coordination work in these flows of self-organized exchange, and to demonstrate how the forces of change are not appropriated or passed on in the same way as property and commodities, but are, instead, directed through networks with differentiated structures. This is not a question of establishing what the markets represent in themselves or are supposed to achieve, but of ascertaining what they can help to realize at a different level. Informal markets create a conflict-ridden terrain of accesses without explaining the principles behind accessibility. They are not a concept of space, but an expression of social praxis.

Consequently, informal markets often come into conflict with the official social order because the economic system operates with different framings from those the victims of globalization need in order to survive. Owing to the pressure to exclude their sociality in different ways, the migratory economies that are linked informally with one another also come into conflict with one another. The question arising in this conflictuous situation then is whether the networked operations of informal market worlds can provide the means to utilize the experience of difference as a political arena. A key moment in this discussion centres on operating outside existing political taxonomies. Many of the traditional taxonomies employed to gauge the dynamics of market activities are based on a conception of network structures as spatially linked phenomena with clear goals. The exact opposite applies, however, when we consider, say, the spatial reality of global network migration, where abrupt mobility, extreme uncertainty and radical openness are the defining parameters of this kind of social and economic structure.

This kind of knowledge production does not limit its own scope by opting to apply the most elaborate and consensual methodological canon. It favours the principle of good enough, which is in fact a common protocol of software and systems design to enable a system to evolve and gain complexity as it goes along. The benefit of this approach lies in focussing on what is gained in a network process rather than contemplating its formal weaknesses and failures. To enhance the flows of trade, informality veils the epistemological dimensions of the market. Informality filters knowledge, so that only some of the activities on the market remain intelligible, while murky segments, dubious contacts and risky transactions are supposed to go undiscovered. Precisely this aspect of knowledge production – the displacement, blacking out and the active suppression of knowledge – is responsible for a great deal of those activities that define not only informal trade, but also the spatial appearance, dissolution and reconstitution of informal markets. The informal market is an instrument of concealed trade. If they are to attract further transactions, as AbdouMaliq Simone argues, the forms of urban sociality arising in the shadows of the informal economy need to be able to shield themselves from the public eye, scrutiny and comparison. He writes:

> This process of assembling proceeds not by a specific logic shared by the participants but rather can be seen as a recombination of contingency. In other words, a coincidence of perspectives, interpretations, engagements, and practices that enable different residents in different positions to either incrementally or radically, converge and/or diverge from one another and, in the process of doing so, remake what is considered possible to do.[17]

One reason why deals are never complete when it comes to informal markets is rooted in the very nature of informal organization itself. Out of concern that such types of organization will become known, their set of operational frames are always provisional and mobile, so that they cannot be identified as having a tangible form or be assigned a familiar taxonomy. The movement of endless transfers is the dominant image of these global microstructures. Objects are transported ever further afield instead of being unloaded once at the 'right' place. The process of becoming of this particular place is rooted in the paths of movement themselves. Consequently, the process of transport is endless.

These parameters of mobile and transient production, the deferral, obfuscation and active fragmentation of archival composition account for many of the activities that define informal trade as well as for the spatial emergence, dispersal and re-aggregation of informal markets: the lack of price tags, the false trade descriptions, the improvised trading places, the mutability of constellations, the devalued spaces filled with cultural hybridities, the abundance of strange objects that can be used for almost anything. They allow us to consider the potential of cultural encounters outside the formal market prerequisites of clarity, transparent calculation and disentanglement. The market, with all its hustling and bustling, creates a cacophony of sounds, voices and accents which finds its own social audience despite the fact that it does not resound in an 'ideal speech situation'. Scattered informal arrangements of stalls, trailers, trucks and tent cities arise that do not constitute what modernist planning would consider a rich form of cultural cohabitation, but rather places that always exist outside the conceptual framework of urban planning. Irregularities appear that characterize the 'mosaic universe' of diasporic movements where things and beings don't converge on a totality, but assert their mutual relatedness by 'inventing junctions and disjunctions that construct combinations that are always singular, contingent and not totalising'.[18]

Arguably, the organizing principles of informal markets are not ideal blueprints for sustainable alternative economies, open community projects and new bonds of worldwide solidarity. They may, however, destabilize processes occurring within larger ecologies that have been taken for granted for quite some time. This destabilization does not represent the transition from one system to another, but the slow and conflict-ridden process of multiplying systems in an amalgam of synchronicities that are mutually dependent and use one another. It is not despite, but because of this entanglement such structures transform themselves into something novel: they become amphibian configurations. They multiply instead of disentangling themselves, producing a volatile body of knowledge which passes between informal global trade and the architectures emerging from it.

Notes

1 Alejandro Portes and William Haller, 'The Informal Economy' in *Handbook of Economic Sociology*, 2nd edition, ed. Neil J. Smelser and Richard Swedberg (New York: Russell Sage Foundation, 2005).

2 Office of the High Representative (OHR) and EU Special Representative (EUSR) in Bosnia and Herzegovina, 'International Community to clean up trade at the Arizona Market, Brcko' press release (26 October 2000), http://www.ohr.int/ohr-dept/presso/pressr/default.asp?content_id=4092

3 Srdjan Jovanović Weiss, 'What Was Turbo Architecture?' in *Almost Architecture* (Stuttgart: edition kuda.nao, merz&solitude, 2006), 28.
4 Bruce Scott and William Nash, 'Global Poverty: Business Solutions and Approaches', paper given at the Harvard Business School conference: 'Brčko and the Arizona Market' (1–3 December 2005), http://www.hbs.edu/socialenterprise/globalpoverty.html
5 Suha Özkan, 'The welcoming speech of the President of the 22nd UIA World Congress of Architecture' *Programme* (Istanbul: UIA 2005), 10f.
6 Orhan Pamuk, *Istanbul. Memories and the City* (New York: Alfred A. Knopf, 2005), 245f.
7 Ernesto Laclau, *Emancipation(s)* (London and New York: Verso, 1996), 79–82.
8 A number of international media have reported that growing alienation between former close allies Moscow Mayor Yuri Luzhkov and the oligarch Telman Ismailov which built up during June 2009 may have contributed to the market's sudden closure. See 'Oligarch pays for party that enraged Putin' in *The Independent*, 16 July 2009, http://www.independent.co.uk/news/world/europe/oligarch-pays-for-party-that-enraged-putin-1748289.html or 'Vladimir Putin "furious" over flaunting oligarch Telman Ismailov' in the *Sunday Times*, 28 June 2009, http://www.timesonline.co.uk/tol/news/world/europe/article6591398.ece
9 'Notorious Moscow market unlikely to reopen – watchdog', *RIA novosti*, 14 July 2009, http://en.rian.ru/russia/20090714/155523059.html
10 'Cherkizovsky Market closure heralds transformation of trade' in *China Daily*, 6 August 2009, http://www.chinadaily.com.cn/world/2009-08/06/content_8533540.htm
11 Elmar Altvater and Brigitte Mahnkopf, 'Die Informalisierung des urbanen Raums' in *Learning from* * – Städte von Welt, Phantasmen der Zivilgesellscnaft, informelle Organisation*, ed. Jochen Becker et al. (Berlin: NGBK, 2003), 24f.
12 Karl Polanyi, 'Our Obsolete Market Mentality: Civilization must find a New Thought Pattern' in *Commentary, Vol. 3* (February 1947), 109–17 [reprinted in *Primitive, Archaic and Modern Economies: Essays of Karl Polanyi*, ed. G. Dalton (Garden City, NY: Doubleday Anchor, 1968)].
13 Saskia Sassen, 'Why Cities Matter' in *Cities. Architecture and Society,* Vol.1, ed. La Biennale di Venezia (Venice: Marsilio Editori, 2006), 47–8.
14 Mike Davis, *Planet of Slums* (London and New York: Verso, 2006), 178–85.
15 Ibid., 202.
16 Michel Foucault, *Society Must Be Defended – Lectures at the Collège de France 1975–76* (London: Penguin Books, 2004, 1975), 29.
17 AbdouMaliq Simone, *For the City Yet to Come. Changing Life in Four African Cities* (Durham, NC and London: Duke University Press, 2004), 14.
18 Maurizio Lazzarato, 'To See and Be Seen: A Micropolitics of the Image' in *B-Zone: Becoming Europe and Beyond*, ed. Anselm Franke (Barcelona: Actar, 2006), 296.

Chapter 7

Local Flows: Rom-Hoob's Phenomena of Transition

Soranart Sinuraibhan

Introduction

This chapter delineates the everyday design that emerges within the space of flows and examines how local populations have integrated this concept into their everyday life in a way that embodies the energy of flows and in turn informs architectural practice.[1]

It begins with the space of flows defined by Manuel Castells, who analyses societies as being constructed around flows and organized in the space of flow (the flow of capital, the flow of information, the flow of technology, the flow of organizational interactions and the flow of images, sounds and symbols).[2] Such space is constructed by the interaction of distributed social actors and their actions, and shaped by the constant movement of information, technology, organizational interaction, goods, traffic, people and so on. This space is not so much organized to move things from one place to another, but to keep them moving around.[3]

Functions in society are organized according to these flows. However, the ascendance of flows and the structural domination of their logic dictate design principles, and alter the meaning and dynamics of place. Even though place remains important in people's everyday lives, its role is apparently decreasing and becoming more opaque. As Castells notes, the spaces of flows are supplanting and displacing the spaces of places.[4] Space understood as place-based consequently turns out to be more abstract, which excludes the everyday users. This is in part because the language of space is attenuated by some of today's architects, who search for emergent possibilities or new sensibilities in reshaping architecture in today's fluid world. This chapter positions itself critically in respect to contemporary attempts to design and build architecture that can merge with and respond to the space of flows with the use of viscous forms.

All too often the architect is concerned only with the manipulation of certain spaces, ignoring various factors that are of predominant interest to the users, wanting only to capture and represent such space as can be merged with the discourse of flow. Architecture is developed and subjected towards a certain set of criteria and consequently becomes part of the architectural mass media. Forms and spaces are therefore objectified and stand for a particular condition of space and time, which finally becomes one of the products by which architectural culture expresses itself.

Mae-Klong Market, the so-called 'Rom-Hoob Market', in Thailand is therefore presented here as an informative example of a different conception of what architecture in the flows and fluid world can be.

The Everyday and the Space of Flows

Rom-Hoob ('Shrinking Umbrella') Market is located within the centre of Samut Songkhram province, 72 kilometres from Bangkok. It runs about 500 metres along both sides of the railway track and is always crowded with buyers from nearby provinces. The placement of this market along a railway track raises interesting questions, especially given that it has become such a popular local junction, where people come to buy food and household products. The locals claim that this market has actually expanded from the rear of the central market where the railway track is located. The track ends at nearby Mae-Klong railway station, which is a transit hub for travellers from other areas. There is a constant influx of passengers, and the resulting mass of people effected a gradual transformation of the area into a small market running along the track. People came to trade their products, converting the area into a *de facto* commercial node. Subsequently temporary stalls and structures were erected and started to sprawl further, until the space finally became the Rom-Hoob Market as we see it today (figures 7.1 and 7.2).[5]

It has no definite entrance. People can, and do, reach it from where it begins adjacent to Mae-Klong station; or through small passageways that are situated at oblique angles through the market and connect the main road with the central market. All stalls are set up next to the railway track with overhanging sunshades that informally establish a defined corridor through the whole market. This arrangement turns the railway track into a footpath, and the entire structure is simply designed and constructed by locals. The sunshade is improvised simply from a tent sheet, ropes, a bamboo pole, a steel post and whatever else can be found at the site. It is easy to operate and can be erected and collapsed by just one or two people. After assembly, the tent sheet can be stretched out up to 2 metres in length and lifted up to 2–3 metres high. Interestingly, the sunshade attached to each stall and its stands is designed to be able to close and move each time the train passes through, six times daily (figures 7.3, 7.4 and 7.5).

Through critical examination of each stall, the relationship between the everyday architecture (occupied by its inhabitants) and the flows of space are revealed. The stalls can be categorized into several forms according to different foods and products. Vegetables and fruits are put in baskets and placed next to or immediately on top of the track. There is no need to move these baskets when the train comes as the space between the wheels allows the train to pass completely over the baskets. Seafood, chilli paste or lightweight products are laid on small tables, which are readily assembled from a piece of wood and metal stands. These can be easily dismantled, lifted up and moved. Heavier products, such as meats

Figure 7.1 Aerial photograph of Samut Songkhram.

Figure 7.2 Rom-Hoob Market and surrounding area.

Local Flows: Rom-Hoob's Phenomena of Transition

Figure 7.3
market
ce in trans-
nation.

or household items, are placed on bigger and stronger stainless steel tables with wheels attached. These tables are custom-made and come in different sizes. They can slide in and out when the train passes through and are simply operated by hand. Most sellers, however, prefer to sit on the floor or existing railings, as in one view, it is more convenient and easier to move when the train comes (figures 7.6 and 7.7).

This place is considered a space of common sense, of social practice: a space that enshrines everyday discourse, where design simply and completely follows function and combines with the flows (of communication, goods, vendors, buyers and, in particular, of the trains). The stalls and temporary structures designed by locals are essentially affected and formed by the movement of trains that are flowing in and out of the Mae-Klong station, as well as being bounded by the human body in movement though this fluid space. These movements can be seen as a means of experiencing everyday space, and the paths emerge in relation to the space (as place-based) of flows.

This place can also be considered an architecture of events as much as an architecture of spaces. It is unmediated, being brought about by real forces,

Soranart Sinuraibhan

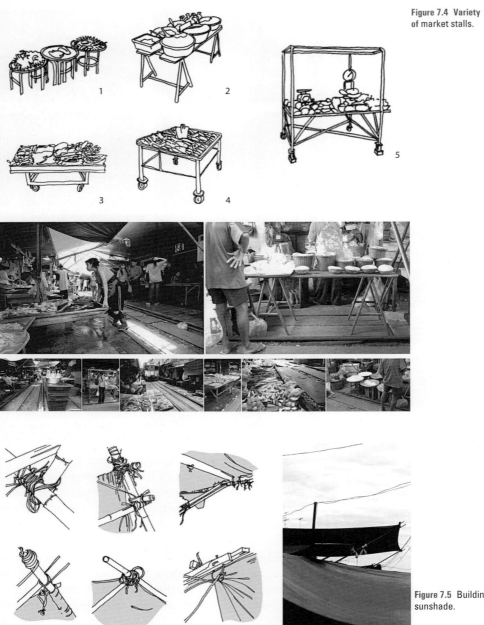

Figure 7.4 Variety of market stalls.

Figure 7.5 Building a sunshade.

real movements and real bodies in real space. This forms an organization of events within the space of flows, where functions, activities and programmes are merged. The meaning of the space is dynamically revealed and reconfigured through the everyday activities that are important barometers of socio-spatial practice of the

Local Flows: Rom-Hoob's Phenomena of Transition

Figure 7.6 Supporting structure.

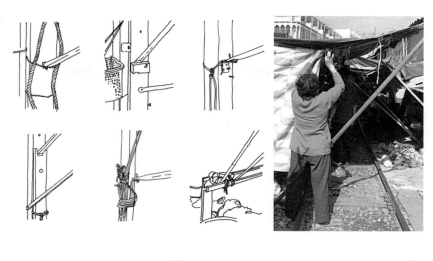

Figure 7.7 Rom-Hoob Market, where the everyday space is enfolded.

site. Finally this in turn informs the language of the architecture within this context and how inhabitants construct their everyday lives.

Though architecture has normally locked itself into patterns of thinking, which are inscribed into its ideology and its codes, Rom-Hoob Market, as completely intuitive and easy to construct, stands in stark contrast. Its construction can be performed by people without substantial prior knowledge and makes use of existing and easily found materials.[6] One might conceive of architecture as something artificial, distinct from the natural. One might view architects as separated from ordinary people by their profession as the agents and (re)presenters of architecture. Rom-Hoob Market, though, suggests these assumptions need re-examining.[7] It illustrates that people here are, to a large degree, architects. They exist in a dynamic relationship with the local environment and construct their shelters in creative ways that retain a sense of local ownership by subverting local materials for novel purposes. They are all continually involved in co-constructing places for themselves, and enact a complex range of relationships between them and their space in

141

order to do so. They generate subtle and complex patterns of conceptual structure, instinctually taking into account relationships and geometries. In this organic, self-directed enterprise, we see that the language of architecture, at least at its fundamental level, is shared by all.[8] This represents a shift from the perfect Euclidean geometries to a colloquial architecture, which contains a certain kind of appreciation for space, thereby yielding a different kind of spatial experience to users as well as a distinct interaction with flows.

Conclusions

By looking at the urban context of Rom-Hoob Market, we see that it is not only shaped by the movement of trains and users, but by the flows of capital and economics themselves (as in Castells' sense of flows). The form of the market is squeezed and stretched along the railway track because of the limited space within the city, which is in turn affected by the flows and growth of capital. Moreover, the utilized spaces within the market are similarly defined by the particular flows of transportation and goods. The language of the colloquial architecture that emerges within this context is then constructed by the everyday lives and needs of the community; and in particular the energy of flows. This suggests that the Rom-Hoob Market's very existence disproves Castells' historical claim, namely that flows displace spaces of places. Today's architecture seems to survive only when it reflects what the society or culture expects of it and particularly when our society and (architectural) culture rely on flows. But Rom-Hoob Market offers a way in which places are perceived and appropriated across the internal space of time and culture. This suggests that it may not be necessary to search for emergent possibilities in constructing architecture in our fluid world. Perhaps by looking to the local and the everyday discourses, an idea or alternative conception of what architecture in the space of flows can be will emerge.

Furthermore, it is necessary that the architect becomes concerned with the discourse of the everyday and collaborates both with this and the user of space in order to co-create architectural spaces. Architecture in the space of flows should not be based on a static universal concept, but rather constructed in a specific location where people can live comfortably in the flows of their environment. In striving towards this end, architects must be concerned more with their perceptual capacities, spatial awareness and sensory recognition in relation to the site and users. It is also valuable for architects to acquire an intense awareness of the actual direct experience of sites and structures and to learn to convert this into sensitivity towards the creative possibilities of architectural production.[9] This realization has consequences for how the architectural 'production' of space can be seen as part of a much wider condition of the social production of space, with architects placing themselves *within* and acknowledging the full range of material forces that shape a society and space of flows. Taken together, it is hoped that these realizations may form a new awareness about how architecture in the space of flows may be perceived, received and, finally, instituted.

Notes

1 This chapter was supported by a grant from the Center for Research on Plurality in the Mekong Region (CERP), Faculty of Humanities and Social Sciences, Khon Kaen University, Thailand.
2 Manuel Castells, *The Rise of the Network Society,* 3 vols (Oxford: Blackwell, 1996), 412.
3 Ibid.
4 Ibid.
5 Interview with local people at Rom-Hoob Market (12 January 2007).
6 Sarah Wigglesworth and Jeremy Till, 'Table Manners' in *Architectural Design* 68, No. 7 (July 1998), 31–5.
7 Simon Unwin, 'Constructing Place on the Beach' in *Constructing Place: Mind and Matter*, ed. Sarah Menin (London and New York: Routledge, 2003), 77–86.
8 Ibid.
9 Arnold Berleant, 'The Aesthetic in Place' in *Constructing Place: Mind and Matter*, 41–54.

Part Two

Spaces of Flow

Chapter 8

Controlling Flow: On the Logistics of Distributive Space

Craig Martin

The struggle for control over time and space is a permanent feature of capitalism[1]

Introduction

Mangled shipping containers; bumper packs of nappies; high-end German motorbikes wheeled off into the night by looters; requisitioned tractors to pull ever more debris from the ocean. These images of flotsam punctuated the media following the grounding of the container ship the MSC *Napoli* in January 2007 at Branscombe on the Devon coast in the UK.[2] This incident was a stark but not entirely un-rare index of interruption in the logistics of global commodity movement. As the 'trash' of global commodity capital these deposits were an image of order gone wrong, order unordered. The essential spectacle of the Branscombe incident was the display of 'matter out of place', those objects (or dirt in Mary Douglas's argument) which do not conform to the classificatory system.[3] In this guise these commodities are errant products of an established system of ordering.

The immanent forces of error are ever-present. Flotsam is a mark of this process torn open, both literally and metaphorically; offering an insight into the ordering strategies that govern the distributive phase of commodity flow, a process that otherwise would have remained unseen.[4] The present discussion uses this event as a backdrop to some of my concerns – most notably, the effects of the ordering strategies of logistics and supply chain management on certain conceptions of time and space. The role of distributive space suggested in the title alludes to the position of logistics as a key component of distributive space – a space networked into production and consumption; a space that is the 'vehicle' of the wares of global capital. Following Nigel Thrift's notion of 'movement-space', distributive space covers both the transportation of raw materials for production, the transit of commodities, and the final transit of waste materials as well as the conceptual and material apparatus that supports this.[5]

The overarching aim of this text is to ascertain how the operation of logistics management is ultimately concerned with marshalling mobility, and in light

147

of this to consider the highly regulated and organized flows of commodities. At the heart of this concern is the complexity of the relationship between flow and control. The inherent dynamic of this relationship is at the root of my interests in these issues, elicited in part through the competing politics of flow as becoming, or flow as control.[6] Ultimately this text sets out to consider how competing forms of time and space are produced through the specific *construction* of logistical ordering that stands in contrast to the wider debates on spatiality, those which emphasize the multiplicitous, open, unpredictable and disruptive notions of time-space.[7]

With these opening points in mind, my aim is to argue that in the realm of global capitalism there is 'administration' of time-space through logistics: namely the practical, material realization of control and order. As a means to investigate how the logistical ordering and management of time-space works, I briefly consider the organization of shipping container movements through the port-space of London Thamesport in Kent, UK.[8] In doing so I will initially discuss the multiple and interlocking layers of logistical time-space, focussing firstly on the central function of infrastructure. Following this, the relationship between this organizational infrastructure and logistics is considered, primarily in terms of projected and distributed mechanisms of control and ordering. The production and continuation of flow is dependent upon the notion of control at a distance, manifested in practical terms through modes of regulation, filtration, coordination and routinization. I will also be addressing some of Manuel De Landa[9] and Paul Virilio's[10] work on military logistics and asserting that the military domination of time-space has clear analogies to the role of logistics in global capitalism, with specific emphasis on the management of efficiency in commercial logistics.

The Layering of Logistical Flow

For my argument concerning the material realization of control, Manuel Castells' description of the space of flows as 'the material form of support of dominant processes and functions in the informational society' demonstrates the centrality of material structures and devices that not only support but actively facilitate the production of flows.[11] He goes on to state that, 'the space of flows is the material organisation of time-sharing social practices that work through flows', clearly suggesting how the organizational aspects of producing flows are dependent on specific temporal and spatial dynamics.[12] In outlining the material conditioning of time-space Castells identifies a central facet of the space of flows: that of the *organizational infrastructure* which 'power' the flows of information, but also people, objects, waste, energy, etc., via temporal and spatial apparatuses. For flows to flow (so to speak) there has to be a substantial material infrastructure which facilitates the movement of these entities. Critical to these supposedly effortless flows is the efficient operation of infrastructure *below* visible flows: hence why the rhetoric of globalization instils images of unfettered flows.[13] Such mechanisms of control take substantive forms, be that the construction of intercity road networks in United States,[14] or the development of the British rail networks in the nineteenth century.[15] However, as Stephen Graham argues, examples of major infrastructure projects disguise the often mundane forms that infrastructure can take, be they road markings or light switches. Central to the organization of infrastructure is the apparently effortless ability to produce controlled, predictable and regularized forms of flow.

In particular, organization is extended through the repetitive and programmable quality of flows, a facet that Henri Lefebvre recognized in relation to space itself. He argued that, 'repetition reigns supreme'.[16] Its supremacy premised on the power to conceal repetitiveness through infrastructural domination. Repetition itself is a fundamental form of material organization, for it enables specific practices and procedures to be plotted and set within an interchangeable and universal spatio-temporal structure. Harari and Bell contend that repetition (in the context of method) implies certain forms of predictability, domination and closure, most readily in relation to types of repetition as routine.[17]

On this point specifically, repetition covers both the spatial configurations of repeat journeys and the temporality of scheduling. John Law maintains routinization is a form of stabilization that enables the efficacious functioning of repeat practices.[18] In doing so the intention is to normalize such practices to the extent that they become taken for granted and merge into the background. However, as Law points out, when these practices of routinization (and repetition) become overtly normalized, the specific mechanisms which initially produced them are hidden from view.[19] Graham identifies such processes of concealment as central to the operation of infrastructure, for these render infrastructure as fixed and 'embedded stably in place'.[20]

There is then a highly efficient infrastructural system that enacts, stabilizes and controls this repetitive form of time and space. Castells extends his outline of the space of flows by emphasizing the three layers of flow-space. For the purposes of the present discussion on infrastructural stability the first of these, the 'circuit of electronic impulses', accentuates the role of information technology in producing the most efficient flows.[21] The infrastructural armature of the first layer is concerned with the seamless movement of commodities, but simultaneously and crucially for my own interests, this has to be controlled and secured from outward 'disorder' through the 'reduction of uncertainty'.[22] If the material devices and practices that constitute the infrastructural organization of flows depend on the combined notions of repetition, routinization and concealment, then these are enacted and performed by the operations of logistics and supply chain management.

If we take a potential definition of logistics as 'a "science" of the efficient organization of movement within spatial systems that entails the design and management of supply chains' then we begin to posit the geographical nature of this.[23] As an apparatus, infrastructure facilitates the distribution of raw materials, commodities and waste via the strategic management of space and time. From an industry perspective, further mechanisms such as facilitation, coordination and long-term planning are all central to the organization of movement.[24] These suggest the centrality of ordering strategies to the operation of logistics and supply chain management. Further defined as 'the process of strategically managing the acquisition, movement, and storage of materials, parts and finished inventory (and the related information flows)', commercial logistics is primarily concerned with strategy and organization.[25] It represents 'a set of knowledges synonymous with movement, effectively the science of moving objects in an optimal fashion'.[26] In the language of logistics there is an overt emphasis on this scientific approach, a methodology that is premised on the facilitation and coordination of movement. Commercial logistics relies upon techniques of totalized systemic control, exemplified by the contemporary focus of logistics literature on the 'Total Logistics Concept' (TLC), which provides 'a complete working structure that enables the overall system to run at the optimum'.[27]

To focus this argument on total control, if we turn to Manuel De Landa's conception of logistics in *War in the Age of Intelligent Machines* as a 'distributed system of control', then it is evident that distribution per se is critical: this implies the spatial extensivity of control, a mode of networked seepage that projects methods of control via the infrastructural apparatus.[28] As Deborah Cowen has also argued, this clearly suggests the importance that a critical social science must ascribe to the spatial and temporal power of logistics and supply chains.[29]

It is immediately apparent why this is the case: for the history of commercial logistics and supply chain management stretches back to the role of logistics in military campaigns. One of the most pertinent definitions of military logistics and one that is plainly applicable to its commercial offspring is from Van Creveld. He states that, 'one arrives at a definition of logistics as "the practical art of moving armies and keeping them supplied".'[30] Such an explanation alludes to the specific qualities Castells discusses – from the *production* of movement through to the *continuation* of movement. There are again confluences between the practical art of military logistics and the layering of flow-space at the first level, notably in keeping the logistical apparatus 'lubricated' through effective management and servicing of the apparatus. The potentiality of movement is determined, as Van Creveld sees it, by the 'requirements, supplies available and expected, organisation and administration, transportation and arteries of communication'.[31] Again, this folds rather neatly back onto the critical importance of facilitation, coordination and long-term planning in the commercial sphere.

For De Landa, military logistics is premised on the control over operational processes *at a distance*. Similarly, Thrift contends that distance is a constitutive feature of logistical power: 'producing geopower involves the construction and distribution of objects at a distance, objects which must stay stable if they are to be projected.'[32] These modes of projection or distribution outline the connections between military, agricultural and commercial modes of supply, in particular the scalar relationships of military and commercial *distribution of means* through logistics. By this I contend that ideological intent is distributed through logistical circuits. Likewise, De Landa's overarching concerns are with the reach of the military-industrial complex where, for example, the 'management science' that emerged out of Cold War research paradigms transfers the methodology of military 'command and control structures' to the commercial, industrial context. This transference from the military to the industrial produces the commercial logistics we know today, but also the historical development of standardization and mass-production. The basis of mass-production and routinization of time, for example, developed out of the demand for standardized weapons in the nineteenth century with parts that could be interchanged. But this requirement for interchangeability was, in part, determined by logistical issues such as 'weapon repair, procurement and supply'.[33] This suggests just how central distribution and movement of raw materials has been to both industrial and military power. We see with logistics in the military-industrial context the continuous, ordered upkeep of movement through planning, organization and routinization. The relationship between military organization and industrial methods was a decisive one; in particular the control over operational processes at a distance was critical, as De Landa puts it, in the 'evolution of the American business community in the nineteenth century'.[34]

In strikingly similar terms we see in Virilio's work a parallel proposition of the obvious relationship between military and civilian logistics. In the discussion of movement and its role within the geographies of modernity his book *Speed and Politics* outlines the organization of movement, be it within military strategy, urbanism or the rise of the automobile. For Virilio 'modernity is *logistical*' it makes modernity possible; it produces and sustains acceleration.[35] Logistical organization provides a means to determine time-space. In the urban context, the city for Virilio is a moment in the trajectory of the channels of 'rapid communication', made up of river, road, coastline, railway. The city is a 'stopover', as he calls it. This is the key factor in his development of the term 'habitable circulation', which essentially reflects the role of movement in the urban context.[36] The city itself is organized through logistical moments or seams that regulate and filter movement, something that will be outlined below in relation to the example of London Thamesport.

In spatio-temporal terms, military logistics has dealt with this same problem of regulation through the creation of paths and schedules. Spatially a route is designed to secure the quickest path possible. Temporally these 'paths' are the schedules that determine moments of movement and intersections in order to eradicate any potential blockage. In relation to military space, Virilio notes the construction of military fortifications is not so much concerned with containment but rather with the control of movement. And this notion of the means to order and regulate movement is at the root of the State's political might; for there is an assumption that rational, social order is manifested through 'the control of traffic (of people, of goods)'.[37] He suggests that military power is predicated no longer on direct confrontational power but through the 'permanent verification of their dynamic efficiency'.[38] On this point it is important to stress that the root of commercial power now lies with the ability to produce movement through the most efficient means possible. The means by which this efficiency is demonstrated is through those 'organisational techniques able to control fairly vast spaces'.[39]

Impediment

Control of extensive territory has been both the remit of military power, but as the opening quotation suggested also for capitalist prowess. This is manifested in part by the means to eliminate hindrance, error or destabilizing influences more generally through a system of management and security.[40] De Landa sees this as the problem of *friction*, of the resistance to free, unimpeded movement. For him this was perhaps not so much an issue for early industrial logistics, but was for the military logisticians – 'friction becomes a factor which makes or breaks a logistic network'.[41] In rather more contemporary terms it is a permanent feature for commercial logistics, especially when we see the move toward a 'just-in-time' model of scheduling, due to the change in inventory stock levels that this system of organization elicited.

    The management of friction, as De Landa terms it, in the military situation takes a number of guises, but most obviously for him through the means of forecasting of demand or predicting moments of encounter with the enemy. In rather more dramatic terms Virilio discusses the means through which speed is guaranteed – not by methods of forward planning but rather through the erasure of territory. Just as De Landa talked of paths and routes, Virilio's paradigm is that of the armoured vehicle which eradicates impediment through sheer technical force. He sees these all-terrain vehicles as more akin to 'sans-terrain' vehicles, as they eliminate the inconsistencies of terrain.[42] Although there is an obvious relationship between military and commercial logistics it is clear that the *actual* flattening of space that Virilio's 'vehicle' carries out is not the case with commercial logistics; however, the efficiency of movement that constitutes this civilian progeny is a somewhat more representational flattening.

    To be sure, it could be argued that such processes of flattening out territorial impediment lie at the heart of the expansion of logistics as a conceptual field, particularly with the rise of the computational ability to manage time-space. This, however, is clearly not a solely contemporary situation, given the development of transport and communication technologies in the nineteenth century, which as De Landa highlights were fully exploited by military logisticians. This growing reliance on technology to overcome and delineate friction in logistics is embedded within the development of production techniques from the early twentieth century. David Hounshell has noted that the success of Fordist mass-production was not so much due to the scientific management principles associated with Taylorism but instead through Henry Ford's readiness to *dispense* with human labour, rather than attempting to turn human labour into an equivalent of the machine, as seen with time and motion studies: 'Taylor took production hardware as a given and sought revisions in labor processes and the organization of work; Ford engineers mechanized work processes and found workers to feed and tend their machines.'[43] Similarly in contemporary terms, logistics is largely a computational condition, but whilst immaterial in relation to operation it is highly material in terms of the sheer bulk and scale of the objects that are distributed.[44] Logistical techniques are concerned with the management of 'spaces and surfaces' from 'open oceans to shared spreadsheets' and it is through the technology of computation that control is made omnipotent.[45] Again, as with the concealment of infrastructural prowess, the omnipotent power logistics has within the serpentine constitution of global capital is premised in part on the hidden computational control of territory and temporality.[46]

    The concealed quality of control is important, as I wish to suggest that the totalizing effects of logistics might be rendered in the language of Virilio's other seminal text, *Pure War*.[47] Here he sees 'pure war' as the militarization of everyday life, and it is tempting to extend this from the space of the military to the space of the commercial and claim that 'pure logistics' is the organization of everyday life.[48] This totality of control, the 'veiled' presence of logistical domination, may indeed account for the lack of awareness of commodity movement illustrated through the opening example of Branscombe; it could be argued that there is an assumption on the part of consumers that commodities simply appear. There is an apparent lack of appreciation for *how* commodities are transported through time-space, the idea of effortless arrival being a result of the instantaneous qualities associated with hidden logistical control. This again highlights what Graham describes as the banality or ubiquity of infrastructural flows.[49] The speed and efficiency of commodity movement, the purported instantaneous appearance, seems to depend on the invisibility of commodities in transit. Because of this purported effortlessness of commodity movement, the power that logistics wields is the means to *shroud* the work that is involved in distributing commodities. Instead there is a routinization, a naturalization, or indeed an inevitability of movement.

London Thamesport and the Material Realization of Control

So as to illuminate some of these issues I now turn to a specific logistics space in order to briefly consider just how the routinization of movement is produced. In particular I attempt to highlight how the material realization of control is made manifest through attempts to produce forms of stability. As already attested to, the notion of stability and certainty is at odds with discussions of non-equilibrium processes, self-organization and, in particular, irreversible time. For Ilya Prigogine, 'classical science emphasized order and stability; now, in contrast, we see fluctuations, instability, multiple choices, and limited predictability at all levels of observation'.[50] The language and ideology of logistics is premised on time as routinized, with emphasis on order and stability. Clearly, time in logistics cannot actually be reversible but the routinization of contemporary distributive time-space emphasizes the role of spatial and temporal control. Further to this the 'architectural' notion of certainty is intended to refer to a broad conception of the material structures, devices and practices that produce these forms of certainty and stability.

Within global capitalism the control and flattening out of time-space is seen through a number of examples, including the early historical precedents of time-space compression seen with the development of the railway. One other key instance is the organization of movement instituted through the development of the shipping container, and containerization more broadly from the late 1950s onward.[51] As a way of considering the implications of Virilio's and De Landa's work on logistical time-space, a variety of scales of ordering could be looked at in relation to containerization, from security clearance documentation, through to the shipping agents who organize the global movement of containers. However, for the present discussion I would like to outline another potential 'scale' – that of the port-space of London Thamesport at the Isle of Grain, in Kent.

Owned by Hutchison Port Holdings, London Thamesport is the UK's only fully automated port. Given this there are important relationships back to the preceding discussions on both the use of technology as an organizational force but more specifically with regard to efficiency and the marshalling of mobility. The key area of interest with this port-space is the system of container movement, one that utilizes a number of the key characteristics already discussed, namely the flattening out of time-space within the port; the use of computational/technological means to control the movement; the reduction of uncertainty; but perhaps most tellingly for the consideration of controlled flow, the role of *interlocking*. By this I suggest the way in which the various nodes within the port-space come together through various spatio-material devices, including the entrance gates to the port, road layout, automated container stacks, warehousing, gantry cranes, etc.

London Thamesport – like all container ports and other logistics enclaves, such as distribution centres – is striking on a variety of levels, including scale, the hermetic qualities in relation to the surrounding locale, and high levels of securitization.[52] In particular, one is confronted by the sheer manifestation of efficiency, demonstrated most tellingly by the aesthetic qualities of the proliferation of minimalist containers.[53] The overarching impression produced by London Thamesport and its working environs is the control of blankness. It is precisely the standardized design of the shipping container that facilitates the efficient movement in the port-space itself and throughout the wider infrastructural network. Given the nature of the container design one is never privy to the contents of the box.[54] Everything is hidden from view, to the extent that all that is given to the eye is the spectacle of efficiency.[55] The facilitation and coordination of movement are testament to the systemic power of logistics and supply chain management in general. It could be argued that the port and its surroundings are a key example of the 'Total Logistics Concept', whereby the reach of logistics is far beyond the boundaries of the space itself. This, however, is not apparent when one is within the specific context of the port, for it appears to be a closed system of sorts that is premised on a highly mediated form of interlocking in order to facilitate optimal effectiveness. Again, there is a decisive quality to this aspect – the apparent autonomy of the space itself belies the projected methods of coordination that De Landa identifies.

As a system it is highly secure; only those lorry drivers with the correct documents are granted entry into the port-space. According to the Logistics Manager at Thamesport, such a system enables a level of security that relies on encrypted data, meaning that only a driver with the correct reference number will be able to enter the port space.[56] Once cleared to enter, the driver is provided with a pager that identifies both the driver and the container they are there to either collect or offload. This device is used by the driver to enter the space through a security-gate system, at which point a dedicated printout provides the information as to where, in the automated container stacks, the container is to be picked up from or dropped off at. Once this is carried out, for the driver their allotted role within this space is over and they drive off using the pager to exit the system, with an average turnaround time of 35 minutes.[57] Devices like the pager system produce a secured system within the port that attempts, at least, to develop a structure based on the elimination of 'uncertainty', or more prosaically, the refusal of entry to those individuals not cleared to enter.

As with the much earlier Fordist worker, on entering the system the driver of the truck becomes 'machinic' in their requirement to log into the system, be recognized, catalogued, the truck and container photographed, and carry out the simplest of tasks – to follow a predetermined path from security gate to container stacks.[58] It is clear that the system in place at London Thamesport, as with all other container ports, is intended to facilitate the quickest turnaround speeds as possible. Cowen points out that logistics is tasked with 'annihilating minutes or even seconds from transactions along supply chains': a situation that is clearly in operation at London Thamesport.[59] The Logistics Manager, for example, describes the procedure for transferring containers from the automated container stacks to the trucks through the quickest means possible:

> so what the driver will do, on this paper printout it'll tell him which stack he needs to go to, like this one is H. So the driver will [. . .] back into the one of four available bays. The driver then jumps out and goes to one of these little blue and grey boxes – again, puts his pager in a little holder. And that notifies the system that he's arrived at the bay. That will then task the crane to go and locate the container.[60]

In this scenario it is evident that the speed of transfer relies upon a series of multiple points of interlocking between various material devices – the driver follows the predetermined schedule to the specific stack, reverses into the allotted parking bay, places the pager in the holder which then instigates a further series of automated manoeuvres, finally depositing the allocated container on the truck bed. Although this is an over-simplification of the complexity of the day-to-day workings of the port, my key assertion with such an example is that even at this relatively small scale the organization and regulation of time-space is evident. There is the flattening out of the multiplicity of time-space and the attempted elimination of error through prior clearance of containers, the encryption of data and, in particular, with the pager system for the drivers. These are fundamental to the operation of this space of flows.

The operational activities and material devices at London Thamesport typify the rise of logistics spaces in general; these being 'spaces within which the precise and rapid shipment of goods, freight and people across the planet are coordinated, managed and synchronized'.[61] As Graham and Marvin suggest, the management of movement within these sites is critical for the continuing efficiency of the space of flows. As seem at London Thamesport the intention is to facilitate the 'interconnection' between the variety of nodes within the supply chain, shown in the present example, through the movement from one node to another as with lorry to container stack, or from ship to rail network. The control room itself is a decisive node that oversees the entire operation of the system. Given the importance of interlocking to this discussion, the use of the 'locking' suffix is intended to emphasize the attempt to control and so mediate the interrelations between these nodes. In order for the container to interlock with a truck or rail bed, a universal, standardized locking mechanism had to be developed so as to allow the *seamless* transferral between modes, demonstrating the emphasis on compatibility and interchangeability.[62]

Whilst the language of standardized systems proffers terms such as these, interlocking is a deliberate attempt to suggest a coming together of two mutually dependent factors within a system, a coupling of two elements, with 'lock' implying a means to stabilize and make semi-permanent the interaction, so that when permanence is required it is available, but when flexibility is the requisite, this too is accessible via a simple disengagement of the mechanism. This may be the case with an obvious 'lock-on' such as the container's twist lock mechanism, locking the container to the truck bed; it may also be seen with the larger scale lock-on systems such as the pager system at London Thamesport. Further to this, the interlocking function may be extended to a global scale – in the organization of customs clearance procedures as part of the operation of shipping lines, for example.

Whilst I suggest the lock as a means of thinking these temporal and spatial relations, Graham and Marvin propose that the interconnections between disconnected sites are provided by 'tunnel effects'. These are connected at a variety of hubs where the 'adjustment' occurs (major seaports, teleports, railway stations, e-commerce hubs, etc.).[63] The requirement, according to the authors, is that the switch between tunnels is 'as seamless an experience as possible'.[64] It is this *seamless* quality that is most critical I would argue, and is shown through the attempted simplification of movement within London Thamesport. The overarching quality of the seamless is the spatial dialectic of the edge, or perhaps more aptly the *boundary*: for in order to control impediment or error, where there is any raised edge, any obstruction is smoothed out. But simultaneously this also figures the edge of the space of London Thamesport as a boundary, a barrier to the system that may be raised or lowered according to requirements – once again, only if the driver has prior clearance can they enter the system. The consideration of the seam raises the role of interlock once more, for both the seam (closed) and the seamless (open) are necessary conditions of movement in logistics – the ordering processes of logistics are proprietary in terms of the ownership of specific types of movement.

Conclusion

As seen with the opening scenario – where impediment is made manifest in the form of an accident – or with other mundane hindrances such as physical breakdowns of machinery, computer malfunction or infrastructural failure, this is not always possible. As Easterling aptly notes, this essentially is an idealized scenario, for 'the quarantined territories of ports and [logistics] parks are, strangely, another iteration of the dream of optimized frictionless passage'.[65] Many factors have the potential to produce 'uncertainty'. Where logistics attempts to eradicate such uncertainties through modes of planning and coordination, this is not always possible and suggests the unwanted spectres of temporal and spatial multiplicity that haunt logisticians. The seamless efficiency of container distribution, for example, is often interrupted by the parasitic figure of the drug, people or cigarette smuggler. Alluding to Graham and Marvin's work, the breakdown of efficiency is tantamount to a blockage in the 'tunnel', and in order to alleviate the blockage a series of methods to secure free flow are in place, most notably in recent years through security provision.

These multifarious issues hopefully serve to briefly underline the scale of organization that pervades the flows of objects (people and information) within distributive space. As discussed, logistics utilizes ordering strategies on time-space;

it is used for the purpose of marshalling mobility, thereby creating a form of movement that is tantamount to being repetitive and programmable. The flattening out of time-space, as we have seen with the work of De Landa and Virilio, leads to a situation where the attempt is made to wipe out territory in the language of military logistics, or the eradication of uncertainty through scheduling and ordering in commercial logistics, with the latter, the aim being to produce seamless transferral. Overall it is clear that the projected methods of control, such as standardized, universal design solutions intended to facilitate interlocking, are distributed through and throughout the space of flows. In this sense stability is embedded both in terms of the material devices and practices, but also through their spatio-temporal distribution.

The brief example from London Thamesport was employed to illustrate just one manifestation of this material realization of control; although singled out for the purpose of the present work this type of space cannot be disassociated from the other scales of interlocking within the system of distribution, for it is obvious that the space of flows is an intricate, highly managed infrastructural apparatus made up of multiple spatio-material entities: from the twist locks of the container, through the overwhelming scale of contemporary container ships, to the turbulence of the global shipping lanes. All of which posits the decisive role that the power to harness and regulate movement now holds in political, military and commercial terms. As we have seen throughout this text, Virilio recognized this some time ago when he argued that power no longer resided in knowledge, in the Foucauldian sense. Instead he contended that this had shifted from power-knowledge to 'moving-power' – that is, 'the study of tendencies, [the study] of flows', be they highly controlled container movements or packs of washed-up nappies.[66]

Notes

1 Erica Schoenberger, 'Competition, Time and Space in Industrial Change' in *Commodity Chains and Global Capitalism*, ed. G. Gereffi and M. Korzeniewicz (Westport, CT: Praeger, 1994), 63.
2 See MAIB (Maritime Accident Investigation Branch), *Report on the Investigation of the Structural Failure of MSC Napoli, English Channel on 18 January 2007* (Southampton: MAIB, 2008).
3 Mary Douglas, *Purity and Danger* (London: Routledge, 2007), 44.
4 See Craig Martin, 'Re-securing and the "Ever-Presence" of the Accident'. Paper presented at *Securing Mobilities and Circulations* workshop, Keele University (27–8 November 2008).
5 Nigel Thrift, 'Movement-Space: The Changing Domain of Thinking Resulting from the Development of New Kinds of Spatial Awareness' in *Economy and Society* 33, No. 4 (2004).
6 Craig Martin, 'Legitimating Movement: The Organisational Forces of Contemporary Time-Space' in *Nonsite to Celebration Park: Essays on Art and the Politics of Space*, ed. E. Whittaker and A. Landrum (Bath: Bath Spa University, 2008).
7 Doreen Massey, *For Space* (London: Sage, 2005); J. Murdoch, *Post-Structuralist Geography* (London: Sage, 2006).
8 I would like to thank the staff of London Thamesport for their willingness to assist me in my research.
9 Manuel De Landa, *War in the Age of Intelligent Machines* (New York: Zone Books, 1991).
10 Paul Virilio, *Speed and Politics* (New York: Semiotext(e), 2006).
11 Manuel Castells, *The Rise of the Network Society* (Oxford: Blackwell, 1996), 412.
12 Ibid.

13. Cf. Anna Lowenhaupt Tsing, *Friction: An Ethnography of Global Connection* (Princeton, NJ: Princeton University Press, 2004).
14. Keller Easterling, *Organization Space: Landscapes, Highways, and Houses in America* (Cambridge, MA: MIT Press, 1999).
15. Wolfgang Schivelbusch, *The Railway Journey: The Industrialization of Time and Space in the 19th Century* (Leamington: Berg, 1986).
16. Henri Lefebvre, *The Production of Space* (Oxford: Blackwell, 1991), 75.
17. Josué Harari and David Bell, 'Introduction: Journal à Plusieurs Voies' in Michel Serres, *Hermes: Literature, Science, Philosophy* (Baltimore: Johns Hopkins University Press, 1982), xxxvi. Also see Nick Bingham and Nigel Thrift (2000), 'Some New Instructions for Travellers: The Geography of Bruno Latour and Michel Serres' in *Thinking Space*, ed. M. Crang and N. Thrift (London: Routledge, 2000), 293–4.
18. John Law, *Organizing Modernity* (Oxford: Blackwell, 1994), 35.
19. Ibid., 36.
20. Stephen Graham, 'When Infrastructures Fail' in *Disrupted Cities: When Infrastructure Fails*, ed. S. Graham (Abingdon: Routledge, 2010), 8.
21. Castells, op. cit., 412.
22. Ibid., 157–8.
23. Deborah Cowen, 'A Geography of Logistics: Market Authority and the Security of Supply Chains' in *Annals of the Association of American Geographers* 100, No. 3 (2010), 601.
24. Alan Rushton, Phil Croucher and Peter Baker, *The Handbook of Logistics and Distribution Management* (3rd edition), (London: Kogan Page, 2006), 15.
25. James Cooper, 'Introduction' in *Logistics and Distribution Planning*, ed. J. Cooper, no page number (London: Kogan Page, 1988).
26. Thrift, op. cit., 589.
27. Rushton, Croucher and Baker, op. cit., 15.
28. De Landa, op. cit., 123.
29. Cowen, op. cit., 602.
30. Martin Van Creveld, *Supplying War: Logistics from Wallenstein to Patton.* (Cambridge: Cambridge University Press, 1978), 1.
31. Ibid.
32. Nigel Thrift, 'It's the Little Things' in *Geopolitical Traditions: A Century of Geopolitical Thought*, ed. K. Dodds and D. Atkinson (London: Routledge, 2000), 381.
33. De Landa, op. cit., 31.
34. Ibid., 111.
35. Benjamin Bratton, 'Introduction: Logistics of Habitable Circulation' in Paul Virilio, *Speed and Politics* (New York: Semiotext(e), 2006), 7.
36. Virilio, op. cit., 31.
37. Ibid., 39.
38. Ibid., 62.
39. Ibid., 42.
40. See Deborah Cowen, 'Containing Insecurity: Logistic Space, U.S. Port Cities, and the "War on Terror"' in *Disrupted Cities: When Infrastructure Fails*, ed. Stephen Graham (Abingdon: Routledge, 2010), 69–83; K. Easterling, *Enduring Innocence: Global Architecture and its Political Masquerades* (Cambridge, MA: MIT Press, 2005).
41. De Landa, op. cit., 112.
42. Cf. Weizman's discussion of the strategy of 'walking through walls' used by the Israeli Defence Force in Eyal Weizman, *Hollow Land: Israel's Architecture of Occupation* (London: Verso, 2007), 185–218.

43 David Hounshell, *From the American System to Mass Production, 1800–1932: The Development of Manufacturing Technology in the United States* (Baltimore: Johns Hopkins University Press, 1984), 252.
44 Bratton, op. cit., 13.
45 Ibid., 8.
46 For a discussion of the relationship between calculation and territory, with specific regard to Foucault, see Elden (2007).
47 Paul Virilio and Sylvere Lotringer, *Pure War* (New York: Semiotext(e), 1997).
48 Cf. George Thorpe, *Pure Logistics: The Science of War Preparation* (Washington, DC: National Defense University Press, 1986 [1917]).
49 Graham, op. cit., 2.
50 Ilya Prigogine, *The End of Certainty: Time, Chaos, and the New Laws of Nature*. (New York: The Free Press, 1997), 4.
51 See Frank Broeze, 'The Globalization of the Oceans: Containerization from the 1950s to the Present' (St. John's, Newfoundland: International Maritime Economic History Association, 2002); Marc Levinson, *The Box: How the Shipping Container made the World Smaller and the World Economy Bigger* (Princeton, NJ: Princeton University Press, 2006).
52 See Easterling, *Enduring Innocence*; Joe Moran, 'Big-Shed Nation', www.newstatesman.com/uk-politics/2008/08/shed-goods-warehouses-near; Martin Pawley, *Terminal Architecture* (London: Reaktion, 1998), 182–8.
53 See Allan Sekula, *Fish Story* (Düsseldorf: Richter Verlag, 1996).
54 Fuller argues that 'each container is self-contained' in terms of its specific content. Whilst the container does have monadic qualities it is the interchangeable nature of the standardized design that makes it such an important material example of global exchange. See Matthew Fuller, *Media Ecologies: Materialist Energies in Art and Technoculture* (Cambridge, MA: MIT Press, 2005), 94.
55 There is an interesting comparison to be made with the spectatorial regimes present in other forms of mobility. Adey notes how the airport is not only a space of the authoritative gaze, it is also one where the passenger is often cajoled to gaze upon consumer items in the departure halls. By contrast there is a distinct closure of the consumer gaze with containerization, prior to the spectacle of retail. See Peter Adey, '"May I Have Your Attention": Airport Geographies of Spectatorship, Position, and (Im)mobility' in *Environment and Planning D: Society and Space* 25 (2007), 515–36.
56 Anonymous, interview with author, London Thamesport (29 March 2007).
57 Ibid.
58 Although outside the remit of this text, it is critical to identify the changes in labour relations that the onset of containerization caused. As with the earlier Fordist production practices, containerization dramatically reduced the workforce at ports throughout the world. See Edna Bonacich and Jake Wilson, *Getting the Goods: Ports, Labor and the Logistics Revolution* (Ithaca, NY: Cornell University Press, 2008) 15–22.
59 Cowen, 'A Geography of Logistics,' 602.
60 Anonymous, interview with author.
61 Stephen Graham and Simon Marvin, *Splintering Urbanism*. (London: Routledge, 2001), 358.
62 Levinson, *The Box*, 138–44.
63 Graham and Marvin, op. cit., 358.
64 Ibid.
65 Easterling, op. cit., 119.
66 Virilio, *Speed and Politics*, 71.

Chapter 9

Temporal Flows

Steve Basson

It is as a direct descendent of nineteenth-century historicist thought that architecture is still seen to traverse time along a linear course that both guides the orientation and momentum of its history progressively towards the present whilst also, via inverse lines of chronological trajectory, exposing the contents of its past to the comprehension and experiences of the present. In particular, these flows of temporal advancement and return enable us to conceive of architecture as a continuous and accessible subject of historical knowledge. Thus we can speak chronologically of recurrence and coherence; of heritage and exemplification; and of architecture's trans-historical properties of meaning, value and purpose. But to what extent do these meta-historical conventions portray architecture's actual conditions of chronological being, or fully describe the more complex, transitory and fragmentary interactions of time, built form and human space? And to what degree do these temporal flows of tradition comprise no innocent or positive dynamic of chronological transmission and immersion, but a ruthless instrument of subjugation for maintaining an illusory, fetishistic and conceited ideal of architecture by denial of all that is contextual and everyday to the historical possibilities of built and lived space? The following discussion will consider these questions critically around the concept of flows, historiography, and how to rethink our understanding of the temporal subject of architecture.

Introduction

'What is time?' Augustine asked, adding, 'Who can explain it easily and briefly, or even, when he wants to speak of it, comprehend it in his thought? Yet is there anything we mention in our talking that is so well known and familiar?'[1] On a similar question, J.M. McTaggart noted, 'I believe that nothing that exists can be temporal, and that therefore time is unreal', a point shared by Francis Bradley who observed, 'Time is so far from enduring the test of criticism, that at a touch it falls apart and proclaims itself illusory'.[2] Such an illusion was one that Ludwig Wittgenstein saw in relation to the passage of time, a non-existent state whose reality is confused for mechanical devices that mark out the arbitrary measure and course of seconds, minutes, hours, days, etc.: a substitute process that reflects not time, but abstract numerical and mechanistic rules of division.[3]

But whatever time may or may not be, the built environment seemingly reflects a terrain permeated with the signatures and flows of time that reflect what is individually and collectively known and familiar of its past, both distant and recent. Here through the conventions of historical discourse, there is little that is outwardly unreal, illusory or confusing. Indeed, our very occupation and perception of this realm testifies to the reality of temporal passage and being via the physical transitions of aging and decay; through memories of places once visited or lived in; or by way of established narratives and perspectives that expose the chronological and periodized specificity of forms and styles, of the heroic and monumental history of buildings, their designers, owners and the inspiring or dark deeds that took place within them. To be an actor within the built environment is to be a player in a theatre of diverse temporal encounters in which we can commune and interact within the lived space of prior buildings as promoted and informed by compelling narratives exposing the historical potential and mystery of earlier architectural possibility. In this realm, the subjects of architectural history become apparent through a built environment that speaks of chronological coherencies and connections, of shared national and cultural heritage, of common identities, and of a vision of time that encapsulates the meanings, experiences and values of those earlier worlds of form as continuous, immutable and participatory.

Ours is an age that still readily desires the attractions and promise of distant eras and, as a result, allows for conceptual connections and lines of chronological flow to convey us along a known span of time, to afford life and air to all manner of material and experiential encounters with the past, and to perpetuate the nuances of a temporal poetics and romance with time. But should we in fact be quite so eager to encompass such a participatory and trans-historical vision of time, so accommodating and uncritical of those conventional accounts of architecture's past that, from another viewpoint, might seem more reflective of flawed and artificial engagements with time and space, of a strained ideal that can never be realized but only ever fetishized? And if so, what does this say of our longstanding devotion to historicist dogma and deference towards those architectural idols of temporal possibility?

The continuing and shadowy presence of historicism, *zeitgeist* and progress still underpin pronouncements on what is deemed eternally true, of what expresses the universal and timeless spirit of peoples, cultures and artefacts, or of what across time is counted as freely available to contemporary experience and comprehension. And yet, as Michel Foucault reminds us, what permits such perceptions to persist is related to the 'curious sacralization' of history and retention of 'subjugated knowledges'.[4] Following this, Gilles Deleuze points us towards the problems of difference and repetition, whilst Friedrich Nietzsche confronts us with the dangers of conceiving the past as 'great and living', or of seeing time through the prism of a monumentalized history where the dead can only ever end up burying the living.[5] Walter Benjamin more brutally suggests that the very being and vitality of what we are, of how we conceive of ourselves in the world of today can only ever diminish and become drained by such an historical perspective born as it is from within the 'bordello of historicism' by the 'whore of once upon a time'.[6]

How far then do our traditional engagements, histories and celebration of prior architectural forms represent not any profound merging with the contextual being and rationalities of the past, but with a schema of time that relies on masking or erasure to ensure their timeless status as hallowed temples of historical exemplification and pilgrimage, and upon the illusion of those flows of temporal passage so devoutly upheld by historicism's high priests? And to what degree can it be said that the conventional horizons of architectural history still encourage a defective epic of contrived heroes and buildings of the great and good, or that our current yearnings for the temporal pleasures of the past rest on nothing more than a cheap fantasy of chronological continuity, coherency and familiarity? Thus, questions arise around how we perceptually interact with the prior conditions of architectural space in relation to the still active imperatives of subjugated knowledge and those myths of once upon a time.

What needs to be considered in respect to such concerns, as will be discussed, is how such flaws should be acknowledged; how to re-address our engagement with architecture's past in response to an indifference that is played out by conventional perceptions and their abuse of any critical will to historical knowledge, in order to promote a delusory sense of flow, connections and modes of shared experience with prior subjects of the built environment – to fulfil empty dreams and illusory desires of temporal perfection.

I

Philosophically, time may be said to exist nowhere other than on the periphery of imagination. But for architectural history there would seem to be no such ambiguity. On the contrary, time and chronological passage are deemed an inherent condition of its entire periodized and sequential organization of forms that span from the distant past to the world of today: a 'living continuity' that for David Watkin exposes an uninterrupted 3,000-year-old story of Western architecture and its recycling of classical form and language.[7] Also considered intrinsic to this constructed course of architectural eras, movements and typological recurrences are subjects conceived not as discontinuous or incommensurate, but as part of an accessible and unified order of meanings, values and purposes. As a result, what remains an endemic and conventional feature of Western architecture's conceptions and framing of historical space is a chronological horizon of equivalences, permanence and repetition and, from this, a historical field that is totally explicable within the terms and sensibilities of the now. Thus, interpretive possibilities of architectural history can still find resonance with such as Immanuel Kant, who spoke with abhorrence of time being a product of aimlessness and blind chance and closed to any 'natural plan' or 'guiding thread of reason', or of G.W.F. Hegel who, sharing Kant's distaste for discontinuity, saw history as expressive of unified, progressive and immutable systems of thought spanning thousands of years.[8]

Following a similar meta-historical vision of temporal unity, Arthur Schopenhauer advocated that the essential nature of things such as art represented truths equal for all time and thus closed to the vagaries of change, given that they impede the 'wheel of time' by virtue of remaining the same for all time.[9] Whilst part of nineteenth-century historical discourse, that ascendant era of historicism, it is the conceptual undercurrents of such as Kant, Hegel and Schopenhauer that has bequeathed the temporal constitution of architecture those ingrained channels of linear flow and universality that render unchallenged the ease by which we seamlessly invite the past to inform the nature and values of the present, or fluently converse and merge within the modes of rationality and contextual complexities of more distant moments in time. In particular, it is those presumed streams of interaction and connectivity, of trans-historical flows that empower the chronological space of architecture to act as a shared terrain of common identities and rational exchanges, and its subjects to appear as timeless and universal categories of historical knowledge.

But what does such an historical perspective serve? Certainly for architecture, it allows for an ordered, familiar and comprehensible chronology of subject as portrayed through those all too predictable linear journeys and objects of stylistic adoration demonstrated by such as Nikolaus Pevsner, Watkin or Spiro Kostof: those same deterministic frameworks and tired taxonomies of form interlaced with that most pernicious of contrivances, typology.[10] Also played out along these journeys, as observed by Andrew Ballantyne, is the belief that stylistic and aesthetic readings of form and obsession for buildings of the rich and powerful exhaust all that needs to be said or known of architecture's past.[11] Such then, at least in part, is how the conventional and myopic perspective of architectural history is served and perpetuated.

On the other hand, drawing from Nietzsche, such a form of history also serves 'the man of action' who 'fights a great fight and needs examples, teachers and comforters'.[12] And it is from this that a platform of exemplification facilitates the smooth entry of the past into the present. But its arrival should not be seen as any neutral emissary of what once was, but rather as an instrument of adjudication, improvement or emancipation; as a mechanism described by Benjamin as one of judgement and messianic redemption.[13] Such a view is by no means alien to the traditional scope of architectural history or the trans-historical licence granted its own elevated subjects of prior form and whose arrival is always most anticipated and desired by those who perceive a need for action when confronted by a contemporary architectural setting of seemingly lesser value, in decline or suffering beneath the weight of some imagined oppressor.

Unfolding here are signatures peculiar to an historical discourse of loss. And what is unleashed via such discourse and inclination for temporal lessons and prior models of perfection is an unremitting drive to manipulate, compel or humiliate. The weight of time as a rationalization of loss holds a strange fascination and authority for those who seek action and remedy to the extent that, as put by Foucault: 'Under the sign of the history cross, all discourse become a prayer to the god of just causes.'[14] But, by welcoming the overtures of earlier eras that, by definition, usurp the contextual identity of the now, is not the present submitted to the seductions and pleasures of that whore of once upon a time?

It was, in any case, against a constructed horizon of temporal flows, interventions and exemplars that empowered nineteenth-century revivalism and individuals such as Pugin, a man of action who saw his immediate present in a state of deep architectural, social and spiritual crisis and for whom the solution lay in reinstating the architectural language and associated religious purity of the so-called Gothic era. However, the idea of conceiving the truth of architectural possibility as an absolute product of a past always considered greater than the present did not end with the nineteenth century. Nor did the notion of the past conceived as a privileged repository of answers to the perceived problems of the present. What also did not cease was the capacity of what Nietzsche referred to as the 'tempting comparisons' of time to lead the 'brave to rashness, and the enthusiastic to fanaticism'.[15]

The recurrent theme of time as a resource for action, struggle and restitution by the brave and enthusiastic is one that can certainly be associated with the likes of Colin Rowe and Fred Koetter or with Hannah Arendt's and Richard Sennett's pronouncements on the imminent demise of public space.[16] The same, of course, can also be said of Alberto Perez-Gomez's and Dalibor Vesely's perceived crisis of architecture, representation and modern science when, as through a Husserlian/Heideggerian lens, they declared the pre-industrial world of architectural being as both a source of deliverance and model of an age whose forms were intimately at one with the essences of *lebenswelt*.[17] More recently, Nili Portugali has reiterated this same narrative of phenomenology, timeless essences, spiritual experience and a contemporary world of lost values and alienation.[18] But to seek a reawakening of the past as a means to combat the perceived evils of the present is to enter into an extreme alliance with the flows of time as a necessity for salvation. And yet, at the same time that one may look back in anger for messianic properties of deliverance, the cause of salvation has ever been a catalyst of rashness and of course, fanaticism.

And yet these temporal streams and signatures of the continuous and timeless also flow in a reverse direction and provide connective lines that pass from the present to past. What these channels serve, however, is not so much a cause for action as a participatory horizon of historical comprehension and experience. At one level, this converges around the very substance of normative historical practice in terms of analysing, investigating and recovering the meanings of past architecture. At another, this concerns how we interact and converse with the conditions of prior forms, how we inhabit and become familiar with those earlier manifestations of architecture. This brings into view the landscape of preserved and protected buildings of the great, good and powerful; of those picturesque and romantic icons of built form inclusive of examples such as Chatsworth House, Woburn Abbey or cities such as Bath. Set within a privileged geography of architectural heritage, sites such as these need no longer fear the forces of natural erosion, the caprice of modification, or suffer the indignity of destruction when no longer deemed necessary. And it is within the bounds of such security that time can be thought conquered and rendered tangible via a past materially retained and celebrated as an essential constituent of the present. Here the trans-historical flows of time are channelled through conceptions of shared national and cultural heritage, of common temporal identities and, as a result, a sense of architectural space that frames the meanings, experiences and values of the past as fully legible and experientially accessible. It is also here, as advocated for instance by Maurice Merleau-Ponty, that experience can transcend time and, as such, allow us to spatially reintegrate with the events of our memory, forebears and origins.[19]

Steve Basson

To the extent that heritage as an idea has presided over the persuasive rhetoric of recovered encounters and experiences of the past, such possibilities should not be considered unique to the physical qualities of prior architectural structures alone. Under the rubric of postmodernism, stylistic or aesthetic references have also been employed to raise the spectres of times gone by and equally entertain a chronological metaphysics of presence. Both Libeskind's Jewish Museum and Eisenman's Holocaust Memorial, by way of example, embrace the optimism of achieving an abstract or symbolic recovery of earlier events and experience through a complex play of form and spatial organization. Through such artifice, we are thrust into the respective presence of, amongst other things, the absence of Berlin's Jews or the destabilization of reason during the Nazi years of government. What is promoted here is an explicit dialogue with memory, experience and history and a touching, if naïve, faith in the possibility of temporal transportation and flow from one conceptual reality to another. The expectation that emerges from the undulating *stelae* of the Holocaust Memorial or the holocaust tower of the Jewish Museum is the belief that an individual will attain a degree of correspondence with each design's predetermined point of historical reference – as though each structure, as some kind of temporal transmitter, can attune its occupants towards the actualities of loss, pain, torture or mass execution; that for perhaps only a moment, it can transform each inhabitant into a real victim of history's greatest act of carnage and suffering. What is, therefore, implicit to such purpose-designed constructions, whether consciously or subconsciously, is the desire to invoke an intense relationship with history, to collapse the past and present into a space of the same and bring to mind and life a direct confrontation with events increasingly beyond memory and direct experience.

From a traditional viewpoint, time for architecture and urban space is suspended along a two-way corridor through which the past and present flow inextricably together into a singular realm of the known, familiar and same. Against this, the historical past transposes into a treasured endowment of ordered unities, periodized structures and progressive forces; of timeless objects of knowledge, inspiration for action, and revered conduit of return and reference. But it is also this desire for a fluid dynamic of time and obsession for those contrived promises of historicist intercourse, heritage and recovery that overcomes the problems of temporal discontinuity and instability, or those questions posed around the extent to which we can ever really achieve significant engagement with the rational horizons and contextual being of the past, of separating ourselves from all that we are now in order to embody the epistemological and ontological actualities of each earlier architectural event. To embrace history as a synchronic structure or realm of synonymous time is to preserve the orthodoxy of historicism's high priests, of stylistic adoration and linear succession, of fanatics and all those who march with an air of self-righteous purpose beneath the cross of architectural history. It is not possible, however, to avoid the irritation of such problems and questions forever. The wheel of time, or the treadmill of historical tradition, can indeed be stalled; not to facilitate the eternal in things as rather expose within the space of such inactivity those conventional desires of a temporal immersion and their privileged subjects of architecture's past as being, in the terms of Nietzsche, 'somewhat distorted, of being reinterpreted according to aesthetic criteria and so brought closer to fiction'.[20]

II

Virgil once warned of Greeks bearing gifts. As a result, we should be even more wary of historical discourse that promises the same. Lost golden ages, timeless truths and heritage-inspired journeys into the past do not derive from any contributions of historical rigour but from the offerings of nostalgia, myth and fiction. Such gifts have ever been sponsored by the high priests of architectural historicism, whether as prophets of doom preaching on the glories of prior ages to redeem us from the inadequacy of ourselves; as keepers of those conserved temples of iconic form to experience the life and being of past eras; or as metaphysicians extolling the sacred virtues of progress, universality, experience and meta-historical narratives. Such is the providence of historicist perception and presumption of temporal flows that preserve a continuous and coherent reading of time through which the built environment can act as chronological container, mirror and conduit.

But whilst time may never be conceptually absent from built space, neither is it ever materially present. And yet, such a distinction for those temporal desires so indebted to a conjoined sense of time and history can never be ultimately acknowledged, only ever transgressed and violated in order to preserve the symmetry and irreducible nature of time and human space. It was of course through the human – all too human – eyes of Zarathustra that the absurdity of such convergence was played out by Nietzsche within a parable that introduced a literal portrayal of time and being as part of a single continuum.[21] In particular, it was here, on either side of Nietzsche's metaphorical arch of 'this moment', that Zarathustra pronounced on the deceit of treating time and history as a pure, undeviating line stretching infinitely both into the past and future, or that the combination of such moments or slices of the 'now', equate to a knowable and interconnected whole.

For George Santayana, such a view of time was one that should be seen as belonging to either a supreme form of egotistical imagination or to the 'normal pathology of an animal mind'.[22] In any case, it was Zarathustra's partner, the dwarf, whose deformity testified not to the perfection of human evolution along some predetermined path of progress, but to such conceptions of time and temporal passage being only a construct of imagination and hindsight; that human ideas, events and biological development belong to broken and random strands of possibility and accident. The historical course of human or architectural affairs is not obvious, nor do they correspond with any smooth linear flow of time, whether characterized as succession, progression or determinism. Time is not about history, nor is history about time. The confusion of the two merely serves the simplistic convenience of architectural convention and those who would bend the past to meet the ends and mindset of the present.

And yet, like Sisyphus, we still labour in our absurd efforts to preserve the veneer of a perfectly functioning linear view of blended historical moments set along a successive and interlocked course of distinct stages of architectural development. Doing so also retains the paradoxical juxtaposition of defined architectural periods that are conceived on the one hand as representing stable, autonomous and insulated moments of architectural identity and on the other, expressions of continuous, unified and trans-historical qualities of architectural value, meaning and purpose. The conception that movement coincides with immobility was an idea described by Henri Bergson as absurd.[23] And yet, knowledge or suspicion of such absurdity does little to disturb the conventional course and wisdom of architecture's historical being. Nevertheless, through such totalizing and incongruous perspectives on architecture's past, each age is chronologically categorized and stamped indelibly with the imprimatur of its own unique distinctions of stylistic identity. We can speak therefore of the Gothic, Renaissance or Baroque as exclusively demarcated regions of architectural production imbued with the same array of values, significations and rationalization.

But what is in a name? For architecture, the possibility of an entire period's stylistic identity is captured through the descriptive power of designations such as Ancient Greece or the Renaissance. But how credible is it to assume that the so-called age of the Renaissance, for instance, was consumed by the singular passion of rebirth, that every facet of life, meaning and individuals from princes to butchers, bakers and candlestick-makers were animated and subsumed to this one principle? If we were to try and describe the totality of the present in one word or phrase, what would that be? Or would we realize only too quickly the futility of such an exercise, whether we extended this to a sentence, paragraph or entire book? And besides, would we not be just a little offended to see all that we are, or think we are, in the world of today condensed into the simplicity of a single word or statement? And yet this is precisely what traditional historical nomenclature has visited upon the past by categorizing and ordering the potential wealth and depth of architectural subjects within the narrow limits of stunted descriptions and inflexible periods of time. What is in a name when it holds the power to determine the temporal entirety of all things within neatly constructed boundaries, to reduce what can be seen, said or known of the architectural subjects confined within such artificially determined and branded moments of historical reference? What then indeed is in a name when, as George Orwell inscribed, 'Who controls the past – controls the future: who controls the present controls the past'?[24]

Through the imposed limits of language and chronological identity, the elegant and conventional sweep of a continuous, universal and participatory image of architectural history endures and, with it, connective lines of trans-historical flow. And yet, what has been propagated from this absurdity might ultimately be described as a cardboard cut-out history, a temporal narrative of forms that decreases the key features of architectural possibility down to a narrow set of visual traits that speak of style and of course, the heroic trials of those who produced them. Moreover, it is within this stage-scenery vision of architectural history that the complex relationships of society, culture, politics or economics play little or no part in why buildings were deemed necessary or rendered possible. Such questions are left instead to the hollow rationalization of aesthetic purpose, meaning and value to account for the production and significance of architecture in any given age.

Such segregation concerned what Foucault referred to as subjugated knowledges: specifically, what is historically subdued, masked or erased in order to perpetuate a particular dominant discourse or meta-narrative constitutes a subjugated knowledge, a strategy deployed consciously or subconsciously to favour certain relationships within history in order to privilege them in the present.[25] Foucault explored this question in terms of the pivotal role history played as a relationship of power in maintaining the myth of monarchical necessity. Drawing from this, what is at stake for architecture is retention of the established scope and periodized order of its conventionalized exemplars, heroes and imperatives of aesthetic necessity. As a result, what would reduce the purity of a designated stylistic era, disrupt the trans-historical status and flow of architectural knowledge, or dilute the primacy of aesthetic production is simply rendered consciously or subconsciously mediocre, irrelevant or invisible. Within this space of prescribed appearances, those palaces and religious structures so profusely represented in Western architecture's past, can act as models *par excellence* of stylistic intent and primary rationalization for the possibility of such forms.

Yet, by gazing beyond the veil of convention, it would soon be realized that such examples were never constructed to gratify some universal idea of architecture, but to fulfil the needs of their respective institutions. And to speak of the institutional objectives and rationale behind such forms is to undermine that aura of neutrality and innocence applied to the traditional subjects of architecture's historical discourse; to reveal structures reflective of ideological relationships of power imbued, like Nazi architecture, with the excesses of various monarchical and religious regimes and their systemic practices of intolerance, torture, war and genocide. From the conventional perspective of architecture's past, such knowledge remains subjugated. But in so doing, are not such instances left as contextually neutered from the conditions of their own social, cultural, political and economic possibilities? And as such, do they not leave architectural history as the last cheerleader of monarchical and religious institutions; as an apologist for what, like Nazi forms, should not be counted as impartial or simply picturesque spatial events?

The implicit pursuit of a reductionist agenda through historicist architectural discourse also brings with it what was seen by Deleuze as the subordination of difference to the rigidity of the identical.[26] Fundamentally, architectural history abhors diverse, disjointed or contradictory conceptions of architecture. What such relationships imply is a chronological nightmare of disparate, fragmentary and discontinuous subjects and destruction of all that has conventionally been invested within a perfectly interlinked and sequentially linear picture of history. Instead, what predominates for all that is habitual, indifferent or conceited, is the vision of a past founded upon what is shared by all built forms and thus, on what is presumed inherently common or essentially the same for any individual or periodized subject of architecture contained within this temporal structure. This is not to say that difference is absent – on the contrary. But from a perspective concerned with the historical whole and smooth flow and continuity of architecture as a trans-historical concept, such distinctions can only be limited to questions of stylistic variation and innovation; as secondary to what is identical in terms of those particular values, meanings or qualities assumed to repeat themselves eternally through all forms, whether Ancient Egyptian, Romanesque or Modernist.

Yet repetition, as Deluze emphasized, is not an historical fact.[27] More to the point, repetition, as the key constituent within any chronological matrix of the same, represents a pure product of retrospection, an illusory array of resemblances (as with the idea of typology) that artificially binds the historical subjects of architecture together into a space of contorted equivalences. In the end, retaining an inclination for the historically identical, repetitious or recurrent is to prolong a subsuming strategy based on nothing more than a *reducto ad adsurdum*; a strategy of convenience and tradition that denies what is contextually unique to architecture within any given moment of time in favour of meta-historical narratives, participatory encounters and those men of action who see the past as relevant to the present. But then, it is only within the bordello of historicism that it can still be believed that the same pleasures are to be both desired and gained by all.

And yet to speak of desire, seduction and those historicist prescriptions of subjugation and subordination is also to enter that overtly precious domain of conserved architectural monuments dedicated to the virtues of national identity and heritage. Within such an array of preserved sites, the citizens of the modern nation state see themselves directly connecting with the events of the past. But as these visitors navigate their way through the halls, corridors and apartments of such buildings and elevate them along with the banality of the dining room furniture, conjugal beds, kitchen utensils and water closets into sacred shrines of shared cultural heritage, exactly whose past is being expressed and experienced?

We may pronounce on the architectural refinement, exemplification and national heritage values of buildings in the UK like Blenheim Palace, Castle Howard or Longleat. But this is hardly the whole story. Are the aesthetic qualities of such architectural monuments all that are necessary to understand the complexities of their context and form? Certainly for the 1715 edition of *Vitruvius Britannicus*, it was also important that this same group of buildings be accredited, respectively, as the 'seats' of the Duke of Marlborough, Earl of Carlisle and Lord Viscount of Weymouth.[28] Such emphasis was intended to openly proclaim the privilege, personal power and inherited political and social rights of their owners. Such distinction also disclosed buildings that comprised a geographical network of architectural forms and sites that spoke not only of aristocratic class, wealth and prestige, but also of purposes and meanings that were exclusive to the nobility and gentry. As such, these were structures that were never designed for or anticipated as representing the national identity or common cultural heritage of the general population, but emerged as a selective range of non-participatory residences that constituted statements on the social elite and whose houses reinforced the segregation of a 'superior' social class. In this sense, the eighteenth-century architect Isaac Ware saw a clear distinction between houses and social class. On the one hand there were the residences of the nobility and gentry and on the other, those associated with 'the meaner sort of country people' and those of 'middling fortune' who were considered neither equal nor worthy of invitation into one's home.[29]

The lesson that unfolds from this for history is not one of exemplars and heroes, but that such architecture was conceived as an insular reflection of the great and good and not as some future collective expression of an entire people.

As a result, we have yet to acknowledge that most who visit these so-called icons of national heritage today played no part in that historical past and remain, as then, social outsiders, paying guests who are permitted to merely glimpse from behind rope barriers a world of individual privilege that they can still never fully share. Arising from this, is a need to accept that the history of such forms as part of a nationalized agenda of heritage is a sham, as much as the mannequins who inhabit the interiors of such realms in their period costumes and frozen tableaux. In the end, it is the singular heritage of the gentry and nobility that is expressed, celebrated and perpetuated by the obsequious presence of cultural tourists who come to praise and not to bury the great and good within their hallowed halls.

Heritage was ever a virtue and necessity of an aristocracy concerned with genetic lineage whilst for commoners, an idle curiosity. Today, all too readily, we live within the consensual illusion that all architectural forms by definition comprise an inventory of buildings that reflect a commonality of cultural background, social equivalence and chronological flows that satisfy conditioned desires for theatricalized modes of knowledge and experiences of times gone by. Such a perspective can only exist by denying the historicity of such forms and by ripping such structures out of their own contextual conditions of being, in order to maintain a fiction of once upon a time. Here there is subjugation, subordination and the construction of subjects who desire the artificial experiences of invented pasts. It is also here, as Nietzsche observed, that the 'free air' of history is 'darkened by the idolatrous' as we 'dance round the half-understood monuments of a great past'.[30]

There is then something rotten in the state of architectural history. It is also not chance but choice that has continued to drive an ongoing enthusiasm for spurious lines of trans-historical flow, messianic interventions and illusory experiences of the past. The embedded nature of such infatuations and their associated eccentricities of continuity, universality, and eternal veracities of architectural being and heritage is an outcome of actively sidestepping any considerations of caution, critical reflection or challenge. And the cost of such activity for the historical subjects of architecture is, on the one hand, to negate the historicity of events unique to their own moments of possibility and on the other, to fully endorse and celebrate the imperfections and obfuscations of a historicist past addicted to exemplars, heroes, labels, subjugation and repetition. It is thus here in the space of a bland chronological horizon of the same that architectural history has assiduously been deprived of what is contextual, epistemological or necessary in developing any critical will to historical knowledge. In return, architecture is afforded a sense of temporal engagement that rests on nothing more than a history of outward appearances, on a theogony of style or, if one prefers, a cargo cult of aesthetics.

It is those who follow the flows, cross and high priests of this history that emerge at one level as adherents of a myopic and exaggerated veneration of architectural objects and at another, as a 'restless, dilettante spectator', or as *flaneurs* of time – those who are indifferent to the actualities of the past and only open to self-referential perceptions and subjective experiences of prior forms and, as a result, are incapable of accommodating what is divergent or alien, what is discontinuous or ruptured, or of taking notice of what has always historically been there.[31]

One cannot travel to the past with the present in mind, nor treat it as a two-way street. Rather, we must rethink our engagement with the past as will be considered next. But whilst false desires of a temporal nature still lead us towards the tempting red-lit interiors of historicism's bordello and into the seductive arms of that whore of once upon a time, then we shall never breathe the free air of architectural history and will remain instead condemned to dance around the fetishized subjects of architecture's past with little or no understanding.

III

When Thomas Hobbes declared in *Leviathan* that humanity was possessed of a 'perpetual and restless desire of power after power, that ceaseth only in death', this could equally refer to the taste for power that permeates conventional conceptions of architecture.[32] For what unfolds from such a chronological ethos reflects an insatiable and uncompromising need to control the scope and manner by which prior subjects of architecture are recognized and understood; and to ruthlessly constrain the conceptual boundaries of this past around the deficient and limited rationalizations of continuity, subjection, repetition and style. It is also the practice and enthusiasm for such power that sustains for architecture the mystique and authority of the designer and, as a consequence, protection of a trans-historical hero whose command *par excellence* of the aesthetical and phenomenological determines how, across the temporal flows of time, all individuals will experience and comprehend the singular veracity of their built outcomes. And yet what is not explained through such limits and contradictions of chronological purpose and meaning are the actualities of architecture's historically contextual conditions of being, nor how architecture emerges as a complex response to varied social, cultural and political necessities. Instead we are left with the vainglorious and insular myth that architecture is a pure and trans-historical product of itself, of its own internalized and self-referential conditions of possibility. But such fictions, conceits and desires of power after power also cease in death.

It is time, therefore, to rethink our engagement with architecture's past and through this, render inert all connective flows of temporal exemplification, participation and return; eradicate all that is continuous, universal and deterministic; and consign to oblivion all the heroes, *flaneurs* and high priests of historical convention. Certainly, it is only via such disengagements and departures that a certain kind of death and corresponding cessation of power is to be found. More crucially, if one wishes to entertain the prospect of an historical horizon unfettered by those impossible flows of eternal truth, reinstatement or reconciliation, then such a mode of termination becomes something of a necessity.

What, therefore, needs to be considered here is a chronological landscape of architecture that is no longer condemned to act as an automatic cause, source of legitimacy or excuse for the present. Nor should any re-conceptualization of architecture's prior subjects be held hostage to any metaphysical or metahistorical deployment of justice, morality or aesthetics. The task is rather to uncouple the historicity of architecture from contemporary designations of right and wrong, superior and inferior, or hope and despair by stepping beyond present attributions of good and evil; by perceiving the past in terms specific to itself, unconstrained by the prejudices of the now. Here we must begin to conceive of history as a series of indefinite encounters where architecture appears as a contingent object of knowledge that is read and conceptualized in relation to each contextual moment of chronological being and not channelled by any rigid linear journey along some predetermined path of fixed periods, styles and trans-historical relationships. The challenge for architecture thus becomes one of embracing an historical realm, composed not from any singular subject, rationale or temporal course, but from the flux and collision of multiple subjects and chronological trajectories that reflect ruptured, fragmented and extinct strands of architectural possibility. It is also here that architectural identity, value and meaning, as immutable and trans-historical properties, finally die in the face of historical relationships that speak of transition and becoming, not of stability, uniformity or recurrence.

Let us then sweep away the wreckage of those once compelling flows of historical imagination, power and illusion by turning our attention towards more intimate and localized settings of historical engagement, and towards the identification of what contextually specific formations of thought, perception and action within such individuated arenas of the past informed the actuality of architectural possibility. Crucially, what is embodied here, as discussed by Ian Hacking, is the ability to analyse the manner by which the possibilities for choice and being occur in history; to understand how normality or preference are structures whose roles and power have been 'determined by specific histories' as opposed to grand abstractions or unified accounts of prior events.[33] The historical question of architectural production thus no longer needs to derive from asking how any given built form was constructed or designed within the insular and self-referential terms of tradition, but by considering what relations of discourse or social, cultural and political formations acted on the potential of its appearance in the first place. Such a realigned mode of temporal engagement, as further suggested by Hacking, would also defeat, for instance, any trans-historical claims of 'individual experience' via an emphasis on chronologically individual relationships of experience.

By vanquishing all that aspires to the eternal, universal and associated constraints of historical encounter and potential, architecture will be left free to rediscover itself around various temporally localized orders of rationality, veracity or even fear that rendered built forms not only possible, but necessary during particular and differentiated points of time. When Andrea Palladio saw the 'little temple' of the church as resembling the greater temple of the heavens and cosmos, he was speaking to an idea of church architecture divorced from those that preceded it in the era of Medieval thought or replaced it during the theatrical spatial environments of the Baroque.[34] By giving voice to the impact of concepts associated, for example, with the Reformation and Counter-Reformation, theology and liturgical practice; belief, faith and doubt; of humanity's relationship to the heavenly and earthly; or of similitude, ideology and power, the churches of the so-called Gothic, Renaissance and Baroque would collapse as expressions of the same essences or typological recurrences of form to recompose into structures reflective of their own individuated and transitional narratives on religious reality.

But in speaking of what is historically localized and architecturally individuated, there is no room for half measures. One must be committed. Thus when assessing what informs the specific historicity of architectural possibility and becoming, any valuation of such forms that draw from our own contemporary designations of rationality, truth or morality must be ruthlessly suppressed. It may seem obvious to count the past practice of burning of witches as contemptible. And yet, such practices comprised a rational, just and necessary solution to the fear of such entities in an era that believed in their existence, in spite of what we may think today. The past is owed an obligation not of deference or condemnation, but an uncovering of what degrees of discrimination were particular to its own sensibilities of good and evil, along with notions of architectural worth.

To historically play the role of judge, jury and executioner is to afford unquestioned support to universal or continuous orders of morality, admiration and error. Conventional historical space is infused with those false echoes of recurrence and the illusory elevation or relegation of architectural forms that stem from the imposition of contemporary verdicts of significance and value. Thus as Deleuze declared on behalf of history, repetition is a transgression.[35] The same offence invested what Hacking saw as a problem especial to any historical interpretation that assumes a rationale and logos equal to our own.[36] What is, of course, forged from all such presumptions is an iniquitous power to judge. And what Nietzsche saw as the single produce of such judgement was annihilation of the present and, it should be added by way of extension, the past's own individuated conditions of life and being.[37]

Transgression and annihilation are, then, all that can be expected of an inward-looking model of architectural history that subjects all prior forms to the same rules and rationalities of aesthetic and functionalist merit. It is by challenging such a self-limiting historical agenda that we can, for instance, question the built form of the house as a container that has always been designed and spatially organized to meet the standards and moral ideals of family life and domestic values of comfort, care and privacy. The Englishman's home may well be his castle. But within the same domain during the eighteenth and nineteenth centuries, their wives could be legally raped, generally abused and have their activities constrained. Moral anxieties around child welfare and incest led over the course of the nineteenth century to the introduction of separate bedrooms to accommodate the gender division of male and female children, and the parental duties of the conjugal couple. Before this, a large proportion of families slept together in a single room: not everyone lived as characters out of a Jane Austin novel.

Between the present and the past, the house represents no historically static entity as rather, a transformative arena that has responded to chronologically divergent and localized rationalities of family and ideas of home that can be found, for example, around the competing values and presumed benefits or fears of privacy, sexuality and gender relations and roles. The task for any reconsidered mode of historical analysis is overcome the transgression of repetition, and the annihilation of all that is particular to each differentiated, lived and everyday moment of architectural possibility. In short, we must open up Pandora's box and release what our age may well consider the evils of the past, but which constituted from earlier perspectives their own distinct sense of spatial morality, truth and being.

What lies then beyond those historical traditions of once upon a time; of heroes and high priests, of timeless exemplars, experiences and aesthetic objectification; and of those infinitudes of rationality, identity and flow is a mode of historical engagement that suggests another idea of architectural history. Detached from any totalizing visions of convention, this reflects the potential of a history dedicated to what actually rendered architecture possible within particular temporal contexts and drives of social and cultural organization, economic and political imperatives; formations of ideology, normality and rationality; and how built forms were inhabited, used and perceived. What is conceived of here is an architectural history of the everyday, of human and lived space deployed within historical settings born of their own discursive conditions of being, transition and becoming. This is a history, therefore, that should be seen, as described by Foucault, as composed from not a single span of time, but a 'multiplicity of time spans that entangle and envelope one another'.[38] The architectural past that unfolds from this, is one that belongs to a field of multiple subjects, identities and values; of multiple relationships, possibilities and moments of formation and termination. To speak, furthermore, of finite, intimate and truncated strands of architectural possibility and becoming, is also to counter and bring to and end those restless desires of power to oversee a colonized terrain of architectural subjects that live or die on the whims of the present.

Conclusion

Beginning with the problem of time, the focus of this chapter centred on a particular and conventional way of historically viewing architectural form in respect to the two-way street of trans-historical flows. Discussing why such implied and perceptual flows are problematic, the chapter then turned, if briefly, to a possible alternative to the analysis and understanding of prior architectural production. What was considered within this chapter via the idea of flows was, more especially, another means to comprehend the historiographical relationships and chronological complexities of architecture. What was also posed by this discussion was a question of choice. We can, therefore, choose, for instance, to maintain what Nietzsche described as a 'belief in the affinity and continuity of the great in all ages'.[39] But at what cost? For such a desire would necessitate, as Nietzsche added, a 'protest against the change of generations and transitoriness'.[40]

The cost of such protest, of course, extends further than this. It invites the power to control, deny and annihilate and, as a consequence, maintain the graveyard of architecture's past, a necropolis of cold stone forms generated through the Medusa-like stare of an historical perspective unconcerned with what gave everyday life, meaning and purpose to those prior and multiple worlds of architectural possibility. On the other hand, we can decide to challenge what Derrida described as the 'classical categories of history', and lay to rest all that is subjugating, subsuming and that subscribes to those destructive flows of time.[41]

In the end, what was invoked by this discussion on the flows of history is a need to pause and reassess what has for too long been treated as self-evident. Against this, the task for any critical will to historical knowledge must ultimately be to counter those old powers of time and space so as to arrive at another and more temporally contextual sense of architectural being that is responsive to localized horizons of possibility and the transformative energies of becoming, life and demise.

Notes

1 Augustine, *Augustine* (London: Routledge, 1991), 179.
2 J.M.E. McTaggart, 'J.M.E. McTaggart: Time' in *Metaphysics: Contemporary Readings*, ed. Michael J. Loux, (London: Routledge, 2001), 260; Francis Bradley, *Appearance and Reality: A Metaphysical Essay* (London: Adamant Media Corporation, 2005), 207.
3 Ludwig Wittgenstein, *Tractatus: Logico-Philosophicus* (London: Routledge & Kegan Paul, 1971), 141.
4 Michel Foucault, *Aesthetics, Method, and Epistemology* (New York: New Press, 1998), 280; Michel Foucault, *Society Must Be Defended: Lectures at the College De France 1975–1976* (New York: Picador, 2003), 7.
5 Gilles Deleuze, *Difference and Repetition* (London: Continuum, 2007); Friedrich Nietzsche, *The Use and Abuse of History* (Indianapolis: Bobb-Merrill Company Inc., 1976), 13, 17.
6 Walter Benjamin, *Illuminations* (New York: Schocken Books, 1973), 262.
7 David Watkin, *A History of Western Architecture* (London: Laurence King Publishing, 2005), 7.
8 Immanuel Kant, 'Idea for a Universal History from a Cosmopolitan Point of View' in *Classical Readings in Culture and Civilization*, ed. Stephen Mennell and John Rundell (London: Routledge, 1998), 40; G.W.F. Hegel, *Philosophy of Mind (Hegel's Encyclopaedia of the Philosophical Sciences)* (Oxford: Oxford University Press, 1971), 13.
9 Arthur Schopenhauer, *The World as Will and Representation* (New York: Dover Publications, 1969), 184–5.
10 Nikolaus Pevsner, *An Outline of European Architecture* (Harmondsworth: Pelican, 1976); Watkin, A., op. cit.; Spiro Kostof, *A History of Architecture: Settings and Rituals* (New York: Oxford University Press, 1995).
11 Andrew Ballantyne, 'Architecture as Evidence' in *Rethinking Architectural Historiography*, ed. Dana Arnold, 40 (London: Routledge, 2006).
12 Nietzsche, op. cit., 12.
13 Benjamin, op. cit., 254.
14 Foucault, *Aesthetics, Method, and Epistemology*, 280.
15 Nietzsche, op. cit., 16.
16 Colin Rowe and Fred Koetter, *Collage City* (Cambridge, MA: MIT Press, 1976); Hannah Arendt, *The Human Condition* (Chicago: University of Chicago Press, 1998); Richard Sennett, *The Fall of Public Man* (London: Faber & Faber, 1993).
17 Alberto Perez-Gomez, *Architecture and the Crisis of Modern Science* (Cambridge, MA: MIT Press, 1983); Alberto Perez-Gomez, 'Hermeneutics as Discourse in Design' in *Design Issues* 15, No. 2 (1999); Dalibor Vesely, 'Architecture and the Conflict of Representation' in *AA Files*, 8 (1985).
18 Nili Portugali, *The Act of Creation and the Spirit of a Place: A Holistic-Phenomenological Approach to Architecture* (London: Edition Axel Menges, 2006).
19 Maurice Merleau-Ponty, *Phenomenology of Perception* (London: Routledge & Kegan Paul, 1962), 70.
20 Friedrich Neitzsche, *On the Advantage and Disadvantage of History for Life*, (Indianapolis: Hackett Publishing Company Inc, 1980), 17.

21. Friedrich Nietzsche, *Thus Spake Zarathustra* (Hertfordshire: Wordsworth Editions, 1997), 154–6.
22. Santayana, George, 'Sentimental Time' in *The Human Experience of Time: The Development of its Philosophical Meaning*, ed. Charles M Sherover (Evanston, IL: Northwestern University Press, 2001), 408.
23. Henri Bergson, *Creative Evolution* (New York: Barnes and Noble Books, 2005), 255.
24. George Orwell, *Nineteen Eighty Four* (London: Penguin Books, 1989), 37.
25. Foucault, *Society Must be Defended*, 7–9.
26. Gilles Deleuze, op. cit., xvii, 2, 112–13.
27. Ibid., 113.
28. Colen Campbell, *Vitruvius Britannicus* (New York: Dover Publications, 2007), Vol. 1, p. 5, Vol. 2, p. 3.
29. Isaac Ware, *A Complete Body of Architecture* (London, 1768), 96.
30. Nietzsche, *The Use and Abuse of Power*, 16.
31. Ibid., 29.
32. Thomas Hobbes, 'Leviathan: Part 1' in *Classics of Moral and Political Theory*, ed. Michael L Morgan, 583 (Indianapolis: Hackett Publishing, 2005).
33. Ian Hacking, *Historical Ontology* (Cambridge, MA: Harvard University Press, 2004), 23, 53.
34. Andrea Palladio, *The Four Books of Architecture* (New York: Dover Publications, 1965), 79.
35. Deleuze, op. cit., 3.
36. Hacking, op. cit., 92.
37. Nietzsche, *On the Advantage and Disadvantage of History for Life*, 38.
38. Foucault, *Aesthetics, Method, and Epistemology*, 430.
39. Nietzsche, *On the Advantage and Disadvantage of History for Life*, 16.
40. Ibid.
41. Derrida, Jacques, *Of Grammatology* (Baltimore, MD: Johns Hopkins University Press, 1997), lxxxix.

Chapter 10

Navigating Flow: Architecture of the Blogosphere

Wael Salah Fahmi

Introduction

According to Castells, the city is not just a physical space, but also an informational system made of structural domination of the space of flows,[1] with various technological, geographical and spatial layers. Mobile interactions and communications represent an ongoing flow of social dynamics regulated by the digital mobility in the physical space of places:

> The space of flows links up electronically separate locations in an interactive network that connects activities and people in distinct geographical contexts. The space of places organizes experience and activity around the confines of locality.[2]
>
> We carry flows and move across places.[3]

While the space of places is enriched and elevated in its meaning as an important node – a hub of several networks: synchronous and asynchronous, in presence and in telepresence – space of flows achieves new meanings through social network interaction enhanced by online communication, digital mobility and pervasive or ubiquitous computing systems. This is related to actor network theory, which suggests multiple, contingent worlds of social action and heterogeneous networks, with telecommunications and information technologies being closely enrolled with human actors and socio-technical relations across space.[4]

All the evidence today suggests that, whilst there may be some substitution of routine face-to-face exchanges by ICT-mediated flow today, at every geographical scale the explosion of digital mobility is going hand in hand with a parallel explosion of physical mobility.[5] Cities do not disappear in the virtual networks. But they are transformed by the interface between electronic communication and physical interaction, by the combination of networks and places.[6]

Rheingold recognized spaces of flows regarding a complex social network of agents, media communication and mediated interaction.[7] Consequently public spaces are transformed into interfaces for new smart mobs' social actions with ubiquitous access to mobile communication networks, with such performative media being connected to real and mediated spaces of flows.[8] This will be examined here in terms of navigating spaces of flows from the blogosphere to street protest actions.

Such network connections (digital communication and social interaction) within the space of flows are directly related to Egyptian bloggers' social usage of ICT in terms of cyber activism and socio-spatial street protests. This study indicates that the network affects and modifies 'real space' and gives a new dimension to human communication interactions – synchronous or asynchronous, face-to-face or mediated.[9] This refers to 'hypermobility', which opens up to a symbolic kind of interaction between humans actors, 'real space', and network connections and relations.[10]

The space of flows within the blogosphere is characterized here by a network of electronic exchanges, connections, links and hubs. This is related to street blogging, also known as moblogging or mobile blogging.[11] This chapter explores this phenomenon, which brings blogging into the street as a new form of personal and social interaction of the space of flows in real public places. Such moblogging, as noted in the case study, is a new social practice with the ability to post and publish images, text and video clips within the flow of network. This is relevant to Kopomaa's idea of a condensed city, where mobile interaction within private and public spaces generates modern forms of public engagement and urban social interaction.[12] The emergence of new media and information technology has therefore put people into a space of 'total flow', whilst creating virtual spaces for identity construction and self-representation as well as for political action. The efficacy of techno-culture and media-reform initiatives have led to the creation of 'virtual public spheres' with cultural content of flows and information intensity, and, in turn, to new forms of cyber activists and empowered identities (bloggers). In a territory where non-place and space of flow prevail, a new category of 'blogosphere landscape' is experienced by online users of the net as they cross these 'in-between' boundaries of reality and virtuality.

The empirical study undertaken adopted a qualitative ethnographic analysis of Egyptian bloggers' real and virtual experiences in terms of political activism and civil participation. This considered the electronic repertoire of contention for Egyptian bloggers as represented online through the blogosphere, whilst their offline actions continue to evolve and (re)claim Cairo's real public spaces. The author's informal discussions with various bloggers focused on their opinions regarding cyber activism and the blogosphere as spaces of flows. Anecdotal records of bloggers' sit-ins and street demonstrations for democratic reforms over a period of six months (March–August 2006) highlighted the social dimension of blogosphere as spaces of freedom. Digital images (photoblogs) and video stills (vlogs) created a symbolic representation of bloggers' street actions, unravelling different layers of Cairo's contested spatiality.

Blogging was very much related to and intertwined with bloggers' practical 'offline' everyday experiences, as they navigated into a space of flows between the virtuality of the blogosphere where they practised their online activism, and the reality of Cairo's (downtown) public spaces, where they regularly expressed political dissent and a repertoire of contention in the form of street rallies, demonstrations and sit-ins. Whereas their cyber activism determined how collective identity boundaries extended through spaces of flows to include a broader (virtual) community of 'hacktivists' (hackers and activists) who perceived themselves as part of wider online global social movement, the study confirmed that blogosphere became inextricably interpolated into practices of social spaces and places in offline environments.

The Blogosphere in the Space of Flows

As a new communication system radically transforms space and time, localities become disembodied from their cultural, historical and geographical meaning, reintegrating into functional networks, inducing a space of flows that substitutes for a space of places.[13] The proliferation of virtuality through technologies of communication and computation, real-time connectivity and interface, has transformed the experience of place identity, wherein the global and local become inextricably intertwined, operating in topographies between actual and digital spaces.[14]

The synchronous and playful environments of IRC (Internet Relay Chat) and MUDs (Multi-User Domains), the role-playing and use of pseudonymous names, lead to online or virtual identities as performative, fragmented, multiple and often subversive.[15] With the active role of the blogosphere[16] within global computer mediated communication (CMC)-based virtual space, bloggers become part of a virtual transnational community, encouraging civil participation and online political activism whilst continuing to produce unimaginable quantities of indexed, archived and hyperlinked material created by the mass ceremony of instant publishing. According to Packwood:

> The blogosphere is made up of blogs and bloggers. These elements that make up the blogosphere as a system of blogs are often functionally interchangeable categories. Where bloggers can and do interact with little if any expectation of meeting one another directly and in the flesh, that is to say unmediated by the Internet, the voice of the blogger and its textual articulation as blog are placeholders for each other. It is important to note the blog is not only a signifier for the blogger as signified. Indeed, the non-local presence of the blog as sign allows the blogger to be inferred as a connotative signified of the blog as denotative sign. The blog is concrete where the blogger is an hypothetical reification of the blog as an enactment, an 'actually existing' sign. We can interact directly with blogs but find it more difficult to materialize each other as bloggers. There is a metaphysics of presence at play where we pretend other bloggers are in some sense there actually (and there and there) but our system of exchange is confined largely to text and hypertext.[17]

However, postmodern notions of identity on the web have represented the bloggers as fragmented, networked and fluid.[18] The bloggers' 'fluid identity', which is fostered and negotiated, elaborates the metaphor of virtual space, eliding the distinction between the screen and viewer, signifier and signified, real and representation. With cyberspace putting people into a 'space of total flow' as they overcome spatial barriers, under time-space compression, the 'as if you are there' is truncated to a 'you are there'. The fluidity of social roles and discursive practices of identity, enabled by the primacy of the blog over the blogger, produces blogging as a communicative practice transcending many offline barriers and global–local borders.

Therefore weblogs (blogs) have been heralded as a new space for collaborative creativity, allowing writers greater access to flexible publishing methods.[19] RSS (Really Simple Syndication), which allows users to subscribe to feeds from blogs and other websites, is the most obvious example of technology that allows internet users to tailor the content they want to read. Blogs offer online interactions between bloggers and readers, through bloggers' updates, audience comments and the number of 'hits' or visits to their blog sites.[20] Representations of the author-function, narrative coherence or brand identity of a blog demonstrates the continuing importance of local particularities and identities that make weblogs relevant in global and local contexts.[21] Blanchard argues that at least some blogs could be virtual settlements.[22] Whilst blogs with active comments can have public space for many-to-many communication, interactive blogrolls between blogs authors create a social network within the blogosphere whilst modifying the CMC technology to meet their needs in developing a vibrant virtual community.[23] Blog readers become involved in the expression of difference in particular places and social spaces, articulated and communicated by people from other parts of the 'real world'. The textual internet offers a sense of anonymity and pseudonymity, where one presents a persona or a character, constructing any imaginable identity with any sort of virtual embodiment.[24]

The conceptualization of the blogosphere as 'virtual' sets it up as a radically different space and obscures the importance of the everyday social and cultural practices in which online interaction and presentation of the self is embedded. There are organizing metaphors which make the blogosphere's virtual environments places to be, concerned with being elsewhere and being 'other' in an evolutionary, powerful conflation of real space and simulation of real life and virtuality.[25] The presentation of self on lifelogs with an 'about me' page, happens primarily through the articulation of mundane, everyday qualities and categorizations, with regular updates much more embedded in the everyday offline and online life of the blogger.

The blogosphere is used as a medium for manifesting abstract ideas into the realm of virtual place so that they can be kinesthetically explored and bodily lived in real events, suggesting alternative ways of seeing and being in the world. The blogosphere promises to occupy the coterminous territories of real and virtual spaces, calling into play the possibility of merging a physical city of bricks with a conceptually experienced 'city of bits'.[26] Today's intertwined real-virtual worlds are more democratically shared across cyberspace and between online communities, as we experience a world no longer divided by virtuality, but one made rich with spaces of animated potentials and realities.[27]

With the rapid development of mobile technology, blogging from a portable device (mobile blogging, moblogging, photo blogging, video blogging) has affected many users' personal communications, as images became an increasingly common element within the blogosphere.[28] Such visual blogs reveal how images operate online and how they interact with text, representing the unadorned evidence of everyday events.[29] Visual blogs may be thought of as nodal points within the broader system of spatial flow that makes up the blogosphere, moving beyond the metaphor of maps and cartographies into metaphors that better encompass systems and relationships. The emphasis in visual blogs is less on individual photos and more on serial images, which read like a time-lapse sequence. It is the space between images where the viewer constructs bridges between one image and the next, filling the gaps, making the connections.[30]

Networked Social Movements and Cyber Activism

The age of communications and its associated transnational public spheres have witnessed the emergence of new social movements represented through loosely organized and open networks.[31] These 'resistant networks' are regarded as a defence 'against the placeless logic of the space of flows characterizing social domination in the Information Age'.[32] Flows of people, information, images easily cross borders with a greater degree of flexibility than ever before.

With the emergence of 'Notopia' (no-topos, no-place, no-location, no-maps) the internet has become inhabited by global cyber 'hacktivists' who are also mobile flaneur activists.[33] These hacktivists mobilize and organize massive anti-globalization rallies via the internet, constantly travelling and reassembling for street demonstrations in various cities around the globe – a shift from the immobility of old urban movements of the working class. New social movements, with their do-it-yourself approach to information and communication technologies, have nevertheless mixed old and new technologies, merging virtual and physical spaces into 'networks of alternative communication'.[34]

These networks are linked to 'social centres' which shelter transnational networks in unoccupied buildings and abandoned urban spaces, where innumerable media groups work with WiFi, video streaming, satellite wireless connections, websites and the non-commercial open-source operating system Linux.[35] From the national 'print publics' that informed movements to the 'electronic sit-in' by activists blocking the World Trade Organization's website in 1999, information tends to outrun institutional networks, flowing along more invisible spaces and 'submerged networks'.[36] The spaces of resistance constituted within these hybrid physical and virtual worlds have created new geographies of protest. On the one hand, global networks are often described as extremely fluid in form, with the ability to 'reterritorialize' their geographic mobility, loose organizational models, and access to communications, thus shifting their campaigns and resources to alternative virtual venues.[37] On the other hand, as events are reported through websites, blogs and streams in a collaborative social process, a means of navigation is provided for street protestors.[38] Media activism no longer means just making and editing images/texts or viewing video or audio clips, but also uses the internet as a work space, social center or project workshop, so that virtual and physical spaces are experienced almost as a single space of communication. The expansion of the communication space and creation of public spheres for political organization and network formation have contributed to holding together the diversity of the anti-globalization movement,[39] mainly through public access points regarded as hubs of information exchange.[40]

What happens behind the scenes of video images of protest, which, in fact, largely still adhere to thoroughly traditional patterns in terms of form, modes of production and discourse? What is going on in the virtual and physical workshop spaces of the globally networked movements? How does the virtual space of the internet relate to geographically definable, 'real' locations? Can they still be clearly distinguished and how do they merge? How is the understanding of space and communication changing within the relatively small, relatively privileged group of those active in alternative media with the rapid appropriation of information technology?[41] Since the 1999 protests in Seattle against the World Trade Organization talks, the process of reclaiming the streets and producing emancipatory globalized public spheres has taken different forms of expression and practice, with the launching of Indymedia (the internet-based network of Independent Media Centres – IMCs), which emerged as the backbone of communication for the broad coalition of anti-capitalism movement activists.

> Those on the streets could get messages from friends via SMS about what was happening where. The permanent presence of portable, mobile, transportable media equipment on the street, whether in the form of buses or public access terminals, satellite dishes or camera and mini-disc recording devices, affects more than reporting – it changes the form of political articulation, can become part of interventions, contribute to the permanent production of the public sphere, a public sphere no longer has to distinguish between "real" and "virtual". It is thus only logical when parts of the global protest movement increasingly demand not only "free movement", but also "free communication" while skillfully connecting virtual and physical space.[42]

> Reports were coming in from video makers, radio journalists, reports with mobiles around the city. We knew the precise scale of the clampdown against the anti-WTO protestors, who was injured, who was arrested. The tension was rising and the IMC was stuck right in the middle of the "no-protest zone" where all constitutional rights were suspended.[43]

> Imperfect, insurgent, sleepless and beautiful, we directly experienced the success of the first IMC in Seattle and saw the common dream of "a world in which many worlds fit" is possible – step by step, piece by

piece, space by space, pdf by pdf, word by word, over the net on pirate broadcast, in the streets, streaming live, and most importantly – face to face.[44]

Indymedia has linked decentralized actions and networks with familiar forms of struggle such as mass marches, rallies and reclaims of spaces, challenging the boundaries between reporter and activist, documentation and spectacle, expert and amateur, techie and content producer, cyberspace and real space.[45] In an interview, Jeff Perlstein of Media Alliance stated:

> We linked high and low technologies, old and new technologies. So the internet and the website was the backbone of our distribution. For example we posted audio, video, text and photos to the site [which were] easy to download. Then community radio stations, cable access stations, even community-based organizations internationally could download and distribute them to those with no internet.[46]

> Although we are all linked now by this website Indymedia.org there's a real emphasis on the physical spaces because one of the whole points is to reclaim space for ourselves for people to interact and to come together and dialogue and exchange, and that can happen in the virtual realm, but most powerfully happens when we're face to face. So these physical locations are linked by this virtual connection.[47]

It has become common to think not of a single movement,[48] but of a 'movement of movements',[49] lacking a centre, difficult to control, monitor and police, and not conducive to the formation of hierarchies, leaders and centralization of power. The use of affinity groups sharing common goals and areas at a human scale has been common with alternative and independent media, such as Indymedia, which have developed non-hierarchical techniques for communication.[50] Such techniques as collaborative webpages used by social forums allow wide participation and discussion on visions and practical alternatives. In 1996 the Critical Art Ensemble (CAE) called for a strategic move away from the streets, declaring that the new geography is a virtual geography and the core of political and cultural resistance must assert itself in electronic space, thus bringing a new model of resistant practice into action.[51]

The Egyptian Blogosphere[52] and Spaces of Flows

The qualitative study reported here explored the Egyptian bloggers' movement, looking at their experiences with cyber political activism and street actions for democratic reforms. In addition to drawing on alternative media online publications posted on the Egyptian blogosphere, the author conducted informal discussions and unstructured interviews with various bloggers, and was an observer at sit-ins and street demonstrations over a period of six months (March–August 2006), including the 2006 spring demonstrations in downtown Cairo's European Quarter. The study indicates the importance of participant observation (as opposed to purely quantitative research methods) in examining the social dimension of the blogosphere, given the complexity of its literal and metaphorical construction, and its interconnectedness in terms of social space.

Confronted by an emergency law since 1981, which restricts the organization of public rallies and distribution of posters in the streets, the Egyptian blogosphere has developed into a virtual platform for socio-political expression, as bloggers navigate between online activism and social spaces for protest.[53] Since 2005 Egyptian bloggers have created spaces of protest within hybrid physical and virtual worlds, with their extensive use of information and communication technologies being appropriated through collaborative content management systems (Wikis) and media streams, in convergence with various forms of street protest. Despite showing similar tactics, Egyptian bloggers' street actions were not initially connected to anti-globalization movements. These bloggers started to experiment with the internet as an additional space to articulate political dissent, organizing their repertoire of contention through web-based campaigns, and were only later influenced by practices of transnational movements against neoliberal globalization.

Recent figures (July 2007) LISTED a total of 1,481 blogs on THE EGYPTIAN BLOG RING.[54] All new posts on any of these blogs are aggregated at the Egyptian blog aggregator (http://www.omraneya.net/) with an index enabling readers to follow new posts minutes after the bloggers have published them. This multi-faceted web hub provides open source web development.

> We offer Drupal-based[55] free hosting space and free aid developing a website for any cause we find worthy or interesting, and for any speech that is censored or prosecuted in Egypt. The blog has posts in both Arabic and English, and the site includes an Egyptian blog aggregator – also in both languages – photo galleries, a database and video documentaries. (informal discussion with a blogger)

Bloggers are part of a loose network not affiliated with a particular political group, although some are active members of the Egyptian Movement for Change (Kefaya – Enough).[56] After government supporters assaulted protesters during a 25 May 2005 demonstration against the presidential referendum,[57] despite facing hostility when filming during actions and demonstrations, bloggers posted reports, with several photoblogs and vlogs of police attacks and arrests, which spread throughout the Egyptian press, Arabic satellite television stations and the internet.

> I never heard the word blogger until May 2005. But now I know them well because of all the amazing coverage they gave of the protests. I followed what happened through the blogs, because they have more credibility than the mainstream media. Activists in Egypt rely on blogs to find out the time and place of future demonstrations, to learn who has been arrested and where they have been taken, and to debate the effectiveness of opposition strategies. The Egyptian blogosphere is marked by its

diversity, enshrining the principles of free speech, which is an essential pillar for a healthy civil society. I like their proactive attitude and their readiness to join support campaigns when in most of the cases they do not know each other. (an opposition activist)

Internet access is subsidized by the Egyptian government, with widespread internet cafes and 4.2 million users. However, the recent establishment of the General Administration for Information and Documentation and the Department for Confronting Computer and Internet Crime – two security units within the Ministry of Interior, in charge of online surveillance and monitoring – has led to the detention of some bloggers and the blocking of their blogs by authorities. Bloggers were among the 300 protesters jailed during the April–May 2006 suppression of pro-judiciary reform demonstrations. 'Blogging is a new but growing phenomenon. The government is monitoring, and it does not like what it sees', said the director of the Arabic Network for Human Rights Information.

Under Egypt's emergency laws, which have been in place for nearly 25 years, bloggers can be jailed indefinitely. A special court reviews such detentions every 15 days, applying article 80(d) of the penal code which criminalizes 'harming Egypt's image'. Officials announced:

> They could be punished for what they are writing according to the law, because it is libel . . . If they think that what they are doing is an expression of their freedom, they should remember who gave them this chance, and who is insisting on its continuity.[58]

Nevertheless, such security reactions have only strengthened the networks of alternative communication, resulting in technical improvements and new connections between bloggers and advocacy groups and civil liberty organizations.[59]

Bloggers' Narratives

Most Egyptian bloggers use pseudonyms, as they feel this gives them more freedom to write about politics without being detained. Given the recent detainment of some bloggers and the blocking of their blogs by security authorities, the author has agreed not to reveal the names of those bloggers who do not use pseudonyms, nor the names of blogs referred to.

> 'The Internet, and the rise of blogs in particular have afforded Egyptians an unprecedented opportunity to make their voices heard, to exchange ideas, and to communicate across borders. Where the press is tightly controlled, human rights activists, journalists, and opinionated citizens can now set up their own blogs free of charge. Pro-democracy and human-rights activists, shut out from the mainstream media, have taken to the Web to disseminate information. When it comes to the influence of Internet online activism, pro-reform blogs might indirectly inform public policy insofar as blogs connect with journalists abroad.'

'I believe blogging is an empowering medium but we don't have that many Internet users and most of those who do use it, don't check out blogs. Information about blogs spreads through word of mouth and seems to be restricted to certain groups: some activists, people who are interested in politics in general and some random Egyptians – mostly middle or upper class Egyptians. Blogs are being read by the elite who have access to computers and high-speed Internet and have the luxury of time to sit around and talk about these things. Most bloggers have been infused by politics rather than having driven the political movement. Maybe in few years when we see thousands of blogs we can claim that blogs affected politics. Right now I think it's the other way around: The political climate has affected bloggers.'

'Blogging, is mainly about freedom of speech – a chance to express yourself in any way you like. I am particularly excited about how the new tool is changing people's attitudes and teaching them to accept the "other". Generally, I blog when I read about violations of human rights. I'm talking about stories that receive little media coverage or ideas and events that are misrepresented by mainstream media. I reject the idea of referring to the blogosphere as a purely political community or a united movement. True that most of our writing is about politics due to the current circumstances but the Egyptian blogosphere has many more things to say. I don't believe that blogging or Internet activism will have a direct effect on real life. But it will do the most important thing in the whole operation: encourage people to speak their minds after ages of silence.'

'I think there is disagreement about political activism through blogging. Most bloggers simply express their political views, but only some of them are also activists. They need to preserve their individuality which makes many bloggers averse to locking themselves in a certain organizational mould. Some have been politicized by the blogs and have become part of the Egyptian Movement for Change. Practically, there are many similarities between the activism of some bloggers and the political actions of the reform movement. What they all have in common is a call for more democracy, freedom and respect for human rights. They interact with the movement on both fronts: the intellectual (through analysis and criticism); and the practical (by physically joining demonstrations). This is why they are attracted to the Egyptian Movement for Change: the movement itself is open. It's more of a coordinating framework than an actual organization or group.'

'Declaring one's identity on the blog and being politically active at the same time could be dangerous. What we're betting on is that more people will overcome the fear barrier and begin to express their opinions. This is the only thing that will guarantee safety for everyone. I am convinced that blogging will eventually influence pro-democracy reform initiatives in Egypt, but that doesn't necessarily mean taking to the streets. Activism, though it could be fuelled by bloggers, remains a supremely personal choice.'

'I think activist bloggers are forming an interactive popular electronic journalism with their coverage of recent political events in Egypt, being more truthful, reliable and revealing than the coverage of any other form of mainstream media. The good thing about blogs is that they're an independent sources of information. This kind of effective activism is informative whilst creating a new kind of awareness among Internet users. Internet activism contributes substantially to initiatives of reform. Before the recent detention and unlawful arrest of some Egyptian bloggers, I would have said that cyber activism would have little effect. But now I believe that detaining activist bloggers exposed security measures used against Egyptians in general if they tried to express themselves. The detentions drew the attention of most human rights organizations in Egypt and abroad and raised so many questions about the seriousness of the reform process in Egypt.'

'Blogging is the best way to make your voice heard. The best thing a blogger can do is record demonstrations and events by taking pictures and publishing them. This is the most fulfilling aspect of blogging for me. I believe in the power of blogging and internet activism in general. You only need to look at how much media attention was given to the arrest of bloggers to see how effective this new tool is becoming. Who organized the sit-in of Midan al Tahrir? The bloggers. Many magazines and papers are now publishing pictures taken by these bloggers.'

'Blogs have been a good means in providing accounts of recent street protests, and yes, they are much better than mainstream media. On the one hand usually mainstream media would report a protest through a short clip on TV or a photo in a newspaper. On the other hand bloggers give a very detailed description of street protests, with many photos, and personal side of stories as compared to the official media. They are not regulated by censorship nor by any political affiliations. Each blogger just captures his or her experience. Mailing lists, online forums, e-mails and SMS messages could provide forms of citizen journalism and are effective ways of delivering information and mobilising people who already belong to your network. I think we gained more than an extra 100 youth activists through blogs and other forms of citizen journalism.'

'As a freelancer I coordinated the production of a short documentary tracing democracy in Egypt. After the official filming was over, I continued taking photos during demonstrations. Every time I would go home and archive the photos with no specific plan on what to do next! The people who were absolutely unknown to me became very familiar contacts and friends later on. At this point, a blogger helped me design my web page and later encouraged me to turn it into a blog This was the start. The most attractive feature of blogging is the passion with which bloggers express themselves. Freedom to post. Freedom to comment. Engaging readers in your news items is just so reforming, refreshing and challenging to both writer and reader. I believe in the power of Internet activism if the number of users continues to grow without state control.'

'Blogging is an extension of my activism. It has always been my dream to speak freely, to let the whole world hear what I want to say without restrictions, to unveil the truth without borders. Bloggers are increasing in Egypt, their voice is heard and they are influencing reform initiatives in the country. Sometimes I find myself drawn to covering an issue as a journalist. I try to be as objective as possible to satisfy my own curiosity but without hiding my biases. I would like to see actual democracy where citizens enjoy absolute political freedom and civil society has more authority, so that various social classes and communities can lobby for their demands to achieve justice.'

The Flâneur Activist and Bloggers' Street Actions

Bloggers' alternative news websites are probably the most important sites through which networks of critical and informed constituencies are formed; yet the extent and efficacy of these new virtual spaces of contention remain limited. Public spaces remain the most vital locus for the audible expression of collective identities.[60] Bloggers developed new means of reclaiming public spaces, articulating dissent, political campaigns and protest art with innovations in mobilization, styles of communication and organizational flexibility in terms of cyber activism. As they used their laptops, mobile phones and digital cameras to form temporary (virtual) social centres within Cairo's public spaces, high-tech encrypting lent the bloggers' strategies a further sophistication. They created an internet hub to encourage other activists to engage in 'citizen journalism' by sending accounts of demonstrations and street rallies, through short message service (SMS) and Twitter,[61] posting pictures of police abuses on their blogs as a contemporary archive of Egypt's battle for democracy and becoming increasingly employed in directing political campaigns and mobilizing people for rallies and demonstrations.

At the 2006 World Social Forum meeting, the anti-global movement prepared a Charter for the 'Right to the City',[62] challenging the neoliberal attack on public spaces.[63] According to its preamble, the Charter '. . . is an instrument intended as a contribution to the urban struggle and as an aid in the process of recognition of the right to the city in the international human rights system.'[64] Social movements' street actions are related to the concept of the 'right to the city', which implies the right 'to freedom, to individualization in socialization . . . to participation and appropriation', and also includes 'the right to the use of the [city] center.'[65] This has highlighted people's right to participate in the public sphere, spatializing this right and associating it with everyday urban life. In this case, the urban experience, the social encounter in the street, becomes a political event.

A classic repertoire of contention used by social movement actors is to flood into public spaces, fill them with a special kind of active presence, and stop other kinds of flows.[66] Literal flows of people (and blockages) are crucial to social movements,[67] from the barricades in Paris in 1848[68] to the 'Reclaim the Streets' (RTS) events organized by anti-roads protesters in the 1990s. These actions of appropriating space have made visible the latent power of state authority to exercise coercion at the most personal level by stopping freedom of movement and by incarcerating people.

In Paris, Haussmann's wide boulevards and grand squares provided a perfect urban venue for massive demonstrations.[69] A similar relationship between space and politics was evident during the spring 2006 pro-democracy street rallies and sit-ins organized by urban youth and blogger activists within Cairo's European Quarter, this part of the city being regarded as a contested site for collective action and as a symbolic space for urban youth's political participation and spatial appropriation.[70]

During the spring of 2006 a group of bloggers (calling themselves the '30th February group') organized a two-day sit-in in downtown Cairo's main public square, Midan Al Tahrir (Liberation Square). The square was flooded with protestors calling for democracy, political changes and judiciary reforms (figures 10.1 and 10.2), with the central garden resembling a venue for social interaction and political debates and exchanges. This was complemented by hundreds of candles that lit the square once the sun had set. A month later in April, there was another sit-in in Unions' Street (Abdel-Khaleq Tharwat Street) on the pavement in front of the Press

Figure 10.1 Photoblogs of street demonstrations – Midan al Tahrir.

Wael Salah Fahmi

Figure 10.2 Video stills (vlogs) of street demonstrations – Midan al Tahrir.

Syndicate and Judges' Club (figure 10.3). For five days urban youth activists and bloggers transformed the street into heterotopian zones (social centres) for public protest, employing urban installations and street graffiti, prompting the construction of Spaces of Freedom, a significant site of urban resistance and spatial contestation. Both sit-ins were part of a series of civil society solidarity, with judges demanding

Figure 10.3 Photoblogs of sit-in – Union Street.

judiciary reforms and independence from the state-appointed Ministry of Justice, which directly influences any elections.

In the face of all obstacles that the state presents to collective action – particularly an emergency law which 'renders illegal even a meeting of five people in open spaces such as the boulevards and streets in the city without government permission' – Midan al Tahrir and Unions' Street represented contested Spaces of Freedom for urban youth activists and bloggers. There are already areas within downtown Cairo's European Quarter and close to Midan al Tahrir which have undergone urban gentrification, with the introduction of security surveillance to provide policing powers to physically remove young activists and bloggers from cafes. This was noted in the pedestrianization of the Stock Exchange Sector, with its coffee shops regarded as temporary social centres where bloggers gather and exchange information.

By 2008 the government proposed a decree prohibiting demonstrations without prior permission from the Ministry of Interior. The law, which would oblige protestors to define the location and time of demonstrations, effectively prohibits any criticism of the regime and any calls for democratic and political reforms. Despite such measures, a broad coalition of civil society representatives and Facebook[71] online activists called for a general strike on 6 April 2008 to demand decent living conditions and to protest against corruption, nepotism, inflation, torture, poverty and police brutality. The plan was to stay at home and not report to work or school, or alternatively to join protestors in street processions converging on main city squares.

As the April 6th general strike gained local popularity and international exposure through SMS, emails, blogs, Facebook, YouTube and Twitter, riots erupted in Mehalla al Kobra City, resulting in confrontation between workers and police security. Simultaneously a number of bloggers and internet activists were detained, particularly those 'Facebookers' involved in initiating the online mobilization for the general strike. Although the call for the general strike coincided with the Mehalla al Kobra textile workers' strike, no direct coordination was noted between the 'Facebookers' virtual actions and the workers' physical mobilization.[72]

Conclusion – Emerging Hybrid Spaces of Freedom

According to Hamm[73] the social construction of geographies of protest is characterized by 'deterritorialization', where events are reported through websites, blogs and streams in a collaborative social process, changing the subjective experience of online activists whilst providing a navigation for street protestors. 'Deterritorialization' through geographies of protest also affects notions of identity as emotional and embodied responses adjust to the online environment, with gender, age, class and ethnicity being less relevant in cyberspace. Simultaneously, new boundaries are reterritorializing the emerging hybrid space, with real-time online tools creating a sense of immediacy and urgency. During socio-political events, opening up spaces of resistance with temporary autonomous zones as well as ongoing technical infrastructure has created socially constructed and temporary geographies of protest within virtual and physical worlds. As spatial metaphors are used to evoke a vision of future communication practices, social movements with their do-it-yourself approach to information and communication technologies are competently mixing old and new technologies, merging virtual and physical spaces into 'networks of alternative communication'. This could be noted within the worldwide network of Independent Media Centers (Indymedia), where transnational movements against neoliberal globalization have created their own mobilization platform on the internet.[74]

Similarly, Egyptian bloggers have created temporary geographies of protests that have changed the spatial and temporal construction of space. Their extensive use of information and communication technologies was appropriated through collaborative content management systems (Wikis) and media streams, in convergence with various forms of street protest. As virtual and physical spaces occurred in close proximity, Egyptian bloggers started to experiment with the internet as an additional space to articulate political dissent. Through online and offline discourses and practices, they organized their repertoire of contention through street demonstrations and sit-ins, and through web-based campaigns, whilst being influenced by practices of transnational movements against neoliberal globalization, with its globally synchronized activities.

Nowadays the Egyptian blogosphere provides more than a news resource, representing an alternative urban hub and acting as an interface between events in the streets and the internet. The commitment to openness and a participatory, consensus-based style of collaboration resonates both with the free software movement and the 1990s grassroots movements,[75] as reflected in the Zapatista's 1996 call for 'networks of alternative communication':[76]

Let's make a network of communication among all our struggles and resistances. An intercontinental network of alternative communication against neoliberalism . . . [and] for humanity. This intercontinental network of alternative communication will search to weave the channels so that words may travel all the roads that resist . . . [it] will be the medium by which distinct resistances communicate with one another. This intercontinental network of alternative communication is not an organizing structure, nor has a central head or decision maker, nor does it have a central command or hierarchies. We are the network, all of us who speak and listen.

Notes

1 Manuel Castells, *The Information Age: Economy, Society and Culture: Volume 1: The Rise of the Network Society* (Oxford: Blackwell, 1996).
2 Manuel Castells, 'Space of Flows, Space of Place: Materials for a Theory of Urbanism in the Information Age' in *Cybercities Reader,* ed. Stephen Graham (London: Routledge, 2004), 82–93.
3 Ibid., 88.
4 Stephen Graham, op. cit.
5 Ibid., 154.
6 Castells, 'Space of Flows, Space of Place', 85.
7 Howard Rheingold, *Smart Mobs: The Next Social Revolution* (Cambridge, MA: Perseus Books Group, 2002).
8 Rheingold coined the term 'smart mobs', a concept that describes a group of people who cooperate with each other by using information and communication technologies to organize activism. Smart mobs include '[p]eer-to-peer collectives, pervasive computing, social networks, and mobile communications', Rheingold, op.cit., 66.
9 William Mitchell, *Me++: The Cyborg Self and the Networked City* (Cambridge, MA: MIT Press, 2003).
10 Gianni Corino, *Spatial Issues and Performative Media in Digital Mobility: A Network Perspective*, Digital Futures (final dissertation, University of Plymouth, 2004).
11 Rheingold, op. cit., *passim.*
12 Timo Kopomaa, 'Speaking Mobile: Intensified Everyday Life, Condensed City' in *Cybercities Reader,* ed. Stephen Graham, 267–72 (London: Routledge, 2004).
13 Castells, *The Rise of the Network Society.*
14 Frances Dyson, 'Space, Being, and Other Fictions in the Domain of the Virtual' in *The Virtual Dimension: Architecture, Representation and Crash Culture*, ed. John Beckmann (New York: Princeton Architectural Press, 1998), 27–45.
15 Elizabeth Reid, 'Cultural Formations in Text-Based Virtual Realities' (masters thesis, University of Melbourne, 1994). http://www.aluluei.com/cult-form.htm (accessed 15 November 2007).
16 A blog is an interactive webpage, regarded as an online journal which is published on the World Wide Web. Blog articles or blog entries are called posts, which appear in reverse chronological order, with the most recent appearing first. Old posts which are categorized by topics or by dates are accessed through sidebar links. A blogosphere is a collection of related blogs which can cover a particular topic, current events or personal thoughts, with each post having a comment section for readers' interaction with the blog author and with other readers. To read blogs and news via RSS XML format, an account needs to be created to use any of the freely available online blogs and news feed syndicators. Blogs have links to various websites and homepages and to lists of other blogs (blogrolls). Some of the popular hosting services are https://www.blogger.com/ and http://www.blogsome.com/
17 Nicholas Packwood, 'Geography of the Blogosphere: Representing the Culture, Ecology and

Community of Weblogs' in *Into the Blogosphere*, ed. Laura Gurak, Smiljana Antonijevic, Laurie Johnson, Clancy Ratliff and Jessica Reyman (2005), http://blog.lib.umn.edu/blogosphere/geography_of_the_blogosphere.html (accessed 10 November 2007).
18 Sherry Turkle, *Life on the Screen: Identity in the Age of the Internet* (London: Phoenix, 1995); Eleanor Wynn and James E. Katz, 'Hyperbole over Cyberspace. Self-Presentation and Social Boundaries in Internet Home Pages and Discourse' in *The Information Society,* 13, No. 4 (1997), 297–329.
19 Rebecca Blood, 'Weblogs: A History and Perspective' in *Rebecca's Pocket*, 2000, http://www.rebeccablood.net/essays/weblog_history.html (accessed 11 November 2007); Graham Lampa, 'Imagining the Blogosphere: An Introduction to the Imagined Community of Instant Publishing' in *Into the Blogosphere*, eds. Laura Gurak, Smiljana Antonijevic, Laurie Johnson, Clancy Ratliff and Jessica Reyman (2005), http://blog.lib.umn.edu/blogosphere/imagining_the_blogosphere.html (accessed 17 November 2007).
20 Anita Blanchard, 'Blogs as Virtual Communities: Identifying a Sense of Community in the Julie/Julia Project' in *Into the Blogosphere*, ed. Laura Gurak, Smiljana Antonijevic, Laurie Johnson, Clancy Ratliff and Jessica Reyman, 2005. http://blog.lib.umn.edu/blogosphere/blogs_as_virtual.html (accessed 11 November 2007).
21 Blood, op. cit.
22 Blanchard, op. cit.
23 Ibid.
24 Frank Schaap, *The Words That Took Us There: Ethnography In a Virtual Reality* (Amsterdam: Aksant Academic Publishers, 2002), 41–2.
25 Char Davies, 'Virtual Reality as an Arena of Embodied Being' in *The Virtual Dimension: Architecture, Representation and Crash Culture*, ed. John Beckmann, 145–55 (New York: Princeton Architectural Press, 1998).
26 William Mitchell, *City of Bits: Space, Place and Infobahn* (Cambridge, MA: The MIT Press, 1996).
27 Wael Fahmi, 'Reading of Post Modern Public Spaces As Layers Of Virtual Images and Real Events,' paper presented at *ISoCaRP 37th International Planning Congress, 'Honey, I Shrunk The Space' Planning in the Information Age*, Utrecht, the Netherlands (16–20 September 2001), http://www.unesco.org/most/isocarp/proceedings2001/cases/cs01_0234/utrechtisocarpfinale.pdf (accessed 2 December 2007).
28 Hsiu-Chuan Wang, Yi-Shin Deng and Sean Chiu, 'Beyond Photoblogging: New Directions of Mobile Communication', paper presented at the 7th international conference on human computer interaction with mobile devices and services, Salzburg, Austria (19–22 September 2005), and published in *ACM (Association for Computing Machiner) International Conference Proceeding Series*, 11 (New York, 2005), 341–2.
29 Meredith Badger, 'Visual Blogs' in *Into the Blogosphere*, ed. Laura Gurak, Smiljana Antonijevic, Laurie Johnson, Clancy Ratliff and Jessica Reyman, 2005 http://blog.lib.umn.edu/blogosphere/visual_blogs.html (accessed 11 November 2007).
30 Ibid.
31 Lila Leontidou, 'Urban Social Movements: From the "right to the city" to Transnational Spatialities and Flâneur Activists' in *City* 10, No. 3 (2006), 259–68; Alberto Melucci, *Challenging Codes: Collective Action in the Information Age* (Cambridge: Cambridge University Press, 1996).
32 Manuel Castells, *The Power of Identity* (Oxford: Blackwell, 1997); Melucci, op. cit.
33 Fivos Papadimitriou, 'A geography of "Notopia". Hackers et al., hacktivism, urban cyber-groups/cyber-cultures and digital social movements,' *City* 10, No. 3 (2006), 317–26; Leontidou, op. cit.; Walter Benjamin, *Charles Baudelaire: A Lyric Poet in the Era of High Capitalism* (London and New York: Verso, 1983).

34 Marion Hamm, 'A r/c tivism in Physical and Virtual Spaces' in *republicart.net,* 2003, http://republicart.net/disc/realpublicspaces/hamm02_en.htm (accessed 10 December 2007).
35 Notes from Nowhere, 'Indymedia "Precursors and Birth"' in *We Are Everywhere: The Irresistible Rise of Global Anticapitalism*, eds. Notes from Nowhere (London and New York: Verso, 2003), 230–44.
36 Benedict Anderson, *Imagined Communities* (London and New York: Verso, 1988).
37 Sidney Tarrow. *Power in Movement: Social Movements and Contentious Politics* (Cambridge: Cambridge University Press, 1998).
38 Marion Hamm, 'Reclaiming Virtual and Physical Spaces. Indymedia London at the Halloween Critical Mass' in *Open* 11 (*Hybrid Space – How wireless media mobilize public space*, NAi Publishers SKOR, 2006): 96–111.
39 Hamm, 'A r/c tivism in Physical and Virtual Spaces'.
40 Notes from Nowhere, 'Indymedia', 241.
41 Hamm, op. cit.
42 Ibid.
43 Notes from Nowhere, 'Indymedia', 241.
44 Hamm, op. cit.
45 Notes from Nowhere, 'Indymedia', 241.
46 Ibid., 232.
47 Ibid., 234.
48 Jenny Pickerill and Paul Chatterton, 'Notes Towards Autonomous Geographies: Creation, Resistance and Self-Management as Survival Tactics' in *Progress in Human Geography* 30, No. 6 (2006), 730–46.
49 Tom Mertes, *The Movement of Movements: A Reader* (London and New York: Verso, 2004).
50 Dorothy Kidd, 'Indymedia.org: A New Communications Commons' in *Cyberactivism: Online Activism in Theory and Practice*, ed. Martha McCaughey and Michael Ayers (London: Routledge, 2003), 47–70.
51 Hamm, 'Reclaiming Virtual and Physical Spaces.'
52 The term 'Egyptian blogosphere' usually refers to blogs written by Egyptians or by non-Egyptians living in Egypt. See http://www.egyptsites.com/dir/egypt-blogs
53 Asef Bayat, 'The "street" and the Politics of Dissent in the Arab World', *MERIP* 226 (2003), http://www.merip.org/mer/mer226/226_bayat.html (accessed 11 October 2007).
54 59% in Arabic language; 47.5% personal blogs and 21.6% political blogs.
55 Drupal is a free and open-source modular framework and content management system (CMS), which allows the system administrator to create and organize content, customize the presentation, automate administrative tasks, and manage site visitors and contributors. Drupal is described as a 'web application framework', with the ability to accomplish most tasks with little or no programming, extending from content management to enabling a wide range of services and transactions (http://drupal.org/).
56 Kefaya was formed in 2004, when intellectuals and public figures signed a founding statement demanding real political changes and an end to economic inequality and corruption. Between 2004 and 2005, Kefaya transformed from an umbrella organization binding various groups, ideologies and visions into a protest street movement. Kefaya's 'strategic vision for change' aimed at the transformation from one-man state to multi-party democracy, the adjustment of legal and judicial situations, and respect for public liberties and basic human rights.
57 The 2005 referendum was mainly focused on amending the Constitutional Article 76, which allows the nomination of more than one candidate for presidential elections.
58 Arabic Network for Human Rights Information 2007.
59 Reporters without Borders have released a handbook on blogging, with detailed information on

how to set up a blog, ethics of blogging, blogging anonymously, censorship and personal accounts of bloggers from different countries. http://www.rsf.org/rubrique.php3?id_rubrique=542
60 Bayat, op. cit.
61 Twitter is a free social networking and micro-blogging service that allows users to send updates (or 'tweets'; text-based posts, up to 140 characters long) to the Twitter website, via short message service (on a cell phone), RSS or a third-party application such as Twitterrific or Facebook. Updates are displayed on the user's profile page and instantly delivered to other users who have signed up to receive them. http://twitter.com/
62 Eleni Portaliou, 'Anti-Global Movements Reclaim the City' in *City* 11, No. 2 (2007), 165–75.
63 Manuel Castells, *The City and the Grassroots* (London: Edward Arnold, 1983).
64 World Charter on the Right to the City, see http://www.urbanreinventors.net/3/wsf.pdf
65 Henri Lefebvre, *Writings on Cities, Part II: Right to the City,* transl. and ed. E. Kofman and E. Lebas (Oxford: Blackwell, 1996).
66 Mimi Sheller, 'The Mechanisms of Mobility and Liquidity: Re-thinking the Movement in Social Movements', working paper (Lancaster: Lancaster University, 2003).
67 John Jordan, 'The Art of Necessity: The Subversive Imagination of Anti-Road Protest and Reclaim the Streets' in *DiY Culture: Party and Protest in Nineties Britain*, ed. George McKay (London and New York: Verso, 1998), 129–251.
68 Roger Gould, *Insurgent Identities: Class, Community and Protest in Paris from 1848 to the Commune* (Chicago: Chicago University Press, 1995).
69 Leontidou, op. cit., noted that the city barricades of the Paris Commune in 1871 and the students' uprising in May 1968, took place within Boulevard St Germain in Quartier Latin. Both the 'NO' demonstrations against the EU Constitutional Treaty in May 2005, and the victory of the protest movement against employment legislation in April 2006, were celebrated around Bastille and the Arc de Triomphe.
70 Karen Malone, 'Street life: Youth, Culture and Competing Uses of Public Space' in *Environment and Urbanization* 14, No. 2 (2002), 157–68; Bülent Batuman, 'Imagination as Appropriation: Student Riots and the (Re)Claiming of Public Space' in *Space and Culture* 6, No. 3 (2003), 261–75.
71 Facebook is a social networking website, which provides various ways for people to interact – through chat rooms, messages, emails, videostreaming, file sharing, blogging and discussion groups. http://www.facebook.com/
72 An Egyptian blogger wrote, in a blog post criticizing what he described as a call 'coming from the cyberspace by bloggers, Facebook activists', that 'We, the Egyptian bloggers, have always prided ourselves on the fact that we have one foot on the ground and the other in the cyberspace . . . But this time, it seems some have thrown both their feet as well as brains in the cyberspace and are living some virtual reality, mistakenly believing (helped by the media sensationalist coverage of the "Facebook activism") that they are the ones behind the events in Mehalla . . .'
73 Hamm, 'Reclaiming Virtual and Physical Spaces'.
74 Ibid.
75 Pickerill and Chatterton, op. cit.
76 Greg Ruggiero, *Microradio and Democracy: (Low) Power to the People* (New York: Seven Stories Press, 1999), 43.

Chapter 11

The (Not So) Smooth Flow Between Architecture and Life

Stephen Loo

> Recently sitting in yet another panel about globalization, I listened to the Dutchman to my right metaphorize world culture as a huge ocean wave and offer – as an architectural strategy for dealing with it – the figure of a surfer, riding the crest. Although this image has certain détourning charm, the 'wave' model is all wet, camouflaging the reality of a constructed culture as a force of nature. Confronted by the massive sameness of sprawl – the urbanism of global capital – my colleague chose not to resist it but to go with the flow, to invent it as the inevitable substrate of the whole world. (Michael Sorkin, *Some Assembly Required*)[1]

This analysis commences with yet another account of flows within the smooth space of the contemporary city that summons the already overexposed urban research of Rem Koolhaas. Granted, the following analysis may perpetuate what Sorkin sees as the 'canny resignation of agency, hence responsibility' of urban subjects,[2] and more specifically the ambivalence inherent within the ethical function of architecture in the age of globalization in not resisting the generic aesthetics of neoliberal capitalism in the shadow of the post-industrial sublime. Sorkin's critique indicates a wariness that such analyses – as the one which follows – may exacerbate what it aestheticizes, namely the fundamental deterritorialization of human subjects holding on to world of precarious representations and moving existential territories.[3]

Can such architecture of resistance find footholds in the socius that Koolhaas shows us, made up of continuous movements whose trajectories generate and provide access to fields of events with indeterminate boundaries? What does it mean for architecture to enact certain freedoms, or be immanent to the type of freedom, implicit within the contemporary urban condition augured by free-flowing and mobile logics of the Deleuzian 'society of control',[4] as opposed to one which stems from the molar structures of disciplinary control?

Stephen Loo

Koolhaas's architecture dissolves strict functional programming to facilitate the multiplicity of chance encounters and a fluidity of spatial movement. Think his system of ramping floors that intersect in the Kunsthal in Rotterdam, where the continuous surface elicits circulation flows that destroy the status of floors in a building and makes ambivalent the possibilities of 'above' or 'below'. Or the competition entry for Paris's Très Grande Bibliothèque, where communal or public spaces are scooped out of the stacked floor plates of library accommodation floors, leading to swirling vortices of programming flowing uncontrollably from stable functional floors into public spaces that suddenly appear in their midst. Or in the Congrexpo building at Euralille, which is nothing more than a hub of transportation infrastructure that intersects multimodal pedestrian and vehicular flows. And lastly, the looping tower form of the CCTV Headquarters in Beijing, uniting while confronting – and confounding – building functions at the top and the bottom in a continuous flow.

However, the freedom espoused by Koolhaasian architecture does not merely concern a programmatic openness, but a deliberately differential conflagration of systems and infrastructure that cause the eruption of events that are not wholly predictable, nor wholly unpredictable. There are certainly concrete forms, rigid structures, and spatial and temporal delineations in functional programming, but it is around these that unprogrammed actions precipitate, reaching into and opening up the potential for the new to emerge in both architecture and the social.

Koolhaas's architecture is an architecture of flows imbricated in the flow of society: it seems that architectural *action*, in its systematic engagement with flows, enacts a connection with *potential* in the social realm. But this connection is far from a straightforward teleology between action and potential. The Koolhaasian imaginary relies upon the irreducibility of movement within the smooth space of neoliberal capitalism. Such movement is not so much geometrically definable by coordinates, as it is vectorially definable by field relations, fuelled by the compulsions neoliberal capital, namely repetitions of obsolescence and renewal, of limit and return, of aggregation and disaggregation, of material and immaterial entities. But it is becoming clear that these repetitions are neither cyclic nor linear, occur in no particular direction, and do not clearly subscribe to imposed power relations or prescribed sovereign models. These repetitions rely upon continuous variations, whose constantly changing directionality and proliferation depend upon the actions of participants negotiating the field themselves, resulting in what is seemingly an emergent simultaneity between cause and effect. That is to say, the flows associated with Koolhaas's architecture in the generic city, which are linked to globally networked information processing systems, fluid economic assemblages and slippery significations, are augured by material spaces and spaces of subjectivity that anticipate – and can only anticipate – in a self-organizing fashion, their own appearance, decline and subsequent return, all within a moving and relational field.

For me, the potential for an architecture of resistance through Koolhaas relies upon coming upon movement in a radically different way, one that necessitates a reworking of the concept of flow. Through reading a diagram of the contemporary city as provided by Koolhaas, namely the biopolitics of 'subjectivation' or becoming-subject within the condition of the multitude, and the interplay between constituted power and constituent power, this chapter problematizes the teleology between potential and act underlying the space of flows that connects architecture and life. I demonstrate that the space between architecture and life, said to be organized by the successions past and present, and of potential and actual, is not as smooth as is conventionally assumed.

Resistance to the effects of neoliberal capitalism on subjectivation, and therefore the possibilities in life itself, can only be effective if the *smoothness* of flow of power within the capitalist network is problematized. This chapter investigates the ontology of flows implicit in the concept of the multitude in Koolhaas research of generic cities, through a reading of the flow between potential and act in Deleuze and Guattari's frequently cited concept in architecture, namely the smooth space of the 'plane of immanence'. The chapter then rehearses the ontological primacy of either potential and act in the debate between philosophers Giorgio Agamben and Antonio Negri, before turning to the work of Gilbert Simondon on individuation, to which the Deleuzo-Guattarian concept of the plane is indebted. Attention is drawn to the processes of abstraction that effectuate and make material urban concepts such as the multitude, to emphasize the partially concretized consistency of flows across codified boundaries of geography and citizenship, and equally within the self-organizational capacity of urban subjects. Such a move is important because it reworks the ethical function of a profession like architecture, which relies heavily on concretization or material effectuation as a mark of production.

Not Quite Flowing Urbanism

The scene is a stationary interstate train in a sea of teeming human beings going about their daily routine. Local trading occurs everywhere and in no fixed place: through train windows, in the spaces between moving cars within the 'go slow' lane, in the interstices of buildings. Merchants make excellent use of the traffic problem: commuters are able to buy everything from groceries and drugs to a new DVD player while sitting in their cars, stuck on a freeway. The train moves, and the multitude, in a random and improvised way and without breaking trade, moves to fill the gap on the track. This is a 'culture of congestion' whereby traffic jams are such an overwhelming feature of the city that they have become a key marketplace. Lulled in congestion, and captive to the road's breadth, the traffic jam thrives with entrepreneurial activity.[5]

Lagos, Nigeria, is for Koolhaas a case in point for a neoliberal capitalist generic city. Koolhaas thinks the urbanism in Lagos is not lagging behind the globalizing modernity that is led by the West, but that it is the West who is catching up with Lagos. We could say that on one hand Koolhaas uses the African city's ineluctable disorder to diagram the limited condition of Western urban modernity. On the other, Lagos is for Koolhaas an unprecedented opportunity to observe a city's continual process of coming into being that defies, or perhaps overestimates, the normative constraints put in place by the hegemony of capital. The concern of the Lagos exercise – undertaken by Koolhaas under the auspices of a Harvard Design School project, alongside one on China's Pearl River Delta and another on Shopping[6] – does not merely lie in the understanding of flows from a formal urban sense, but in demonstrating the flows associated with the behaviour of seemingly individual but anonymous beings within the collective. The Lagosian multitude survives by a self-organizing capacity that has magically arisen from total chaos, but which interestingly remains within a capitalist context that is somehow disassociated from the flow of the global network. As Koolhaas says in a documentary by Dutch filmmaker Bregtje van der Haak, *Lagos/Koolhaas* (2002),[7] in which she documents her friend Koolhaas, documenting Lagos,

> While it seems that Lagos is much less organized than the typical city in the West, there are incredible self-organizing entities, for example the Alaba market, where through the sheer intelligence of self-organization, has made itself into a very powerful entity, as it is now the largest importer of electronics in West Africa.[8]

Lagos may be aestheticized as the paradigmatic city of smooth flows, where there is an indistinction between its inhabitants, their social orders, their urban activity and their buildings, public spaces and urban infrastructure. Certainly, from the planner's eye-view, Lagos is one glorious complex system of circulation, with a seamless, smooth consistency of movement akin to that of a swarm. However, on closer inspection, Lagos's circulation system – and let's concentrate on the traffic system here – is full of blockages and dead ends, very slow lanes with constant traffic jams that cannot be unravelled. 'Lagos's "street" is inadequately described by throwaway terms like "channel", or "communication artifact", "flow space" or "arena for social expression".'[9] These blockages on one hand disrupt the smooth flows of the city, with negative impacts for urban economics owing to the collapse of planning and bottlenecks to the flow of capital, and for the quality of life owing to the immense amount of time spent on the roads. On the other hand, rampant entrepreneurialism and improvisational skills transform these blockages, through the creation of detours, diversions, short circuits and momentary opportunities for exchange that break the street's linearity, turning it into a whole series of bifurcation points for further and novel action, and therefore new possibilities of urban life.

Koolhaas's project on Lagos engages with the space of flows, not as documentation which bears witness to the novel urbanities playing out as action drawn from human potential within third world populations, but as urban diagrammings that firstly undermine commonly held assumptions about the relations between cause and effect, or more accurately potential and action, within an ontology of flows in urban space; and secondly enact an incommensurability between potential and action that cannot be dialectically resolved. Lagos is always and simultaneously inside and outside of the systems of social and capital flows as defined by the West.

This reading of the Lagos project eschews the unproblematic appropriation of the space of flows and validates the view that the production of what Koolhaas famously calls 'junkspace'[10] is concomitant with neoliberal capitalism. The study of Lagos – and similarly Singapore's overwhelming *tabula rasa* approach to socio-urban development, and the unrepresentable morphogeneses of cities such as Shenzen, China – Koolhaas provides us with a diagram of contemporary urban life flows that in fact breaks the simplistic synonymy of generic cities with smoothness, speed and indistinction. The not so smooth flows in the contemporary city then throw new light onto the emancipatory role of architecture, and what Koolhaas means when he says an architect is simultaneously 'impotent and omnipotent'.

Smooth Space vs. Space of Flows in Architecture

The concept of flows, and the possibility of a space of flows, appears with some regularity in contemporary architectural thinking. The concept of flows is structured by the notion of evental continuity and consistency that also underlies the Deleuzo-Guattarian notion of 'smooth space' introduced in their *A Thousand Plateaus*. Smooth space with the nomad as its native inhabitant, and the concept of flows, are frequently paired in architectural theory. Defined as the surface of potential for free associations, smooth space has fuelled theorizations of urban and architectural experiences orchestrated between discrete entities with no predetermined conditions of relations, and the possibilities for 'life' that result from such topological connections between these entities. Think for example of Michel de Certeau's 'spatial tactics'. Smoothness is therefore resistance to metricized striated space that is characterized by constancy and eternity.

Non-linear relations between entities in smooth spaces are often conflated with unpredictable flows between entities. Smooth flow, however, does not always mean smooth space. The flow that occurs between entities in smooth space is deemed irreducible not because its vectors cannot be pre-empted, but because the flow is a movement between entities that are assumed to posses an undifferentiated molecularity. That is, a flow between one entity and the next assumes an immediacy and translatability, at every moment in time, of one entity into another, because the flow is a movement between like and like. And in the context of the relations between potential and action, the flow that is between an entity in a state of potentiality, and the actualization of that potential as action, assumes that potential and action are ontologically similar beings, where one can be unproblematically transformed into the other.

This condition is also set up by a temporal conviction, viz. there is a smooth flow between the past and the present. In terms of a common everyday understanding of time, flow occurs when the past comes into actuality as the present, and that present, in its occurrence, converts an event into the past; which is to say that when the present is exhausted of its current force, it flows smoothly into the past where it is stored as history or memory. It follows that the flow between undifferentiable entities, whether between potential and action, or past and present, within a homogeneous substratum cannot itself be differentiated.

But it needs to be qualified that in Deleuze and Guattari's work, entities in smooth space are not homogenous but amorphous or non-formal, with the capacity to juxtapose themselves alongside others without attachment, in a condition akin to pure patchwork.[11] In fact to Deleuze and Guattari, these juxtapositions result in space being 'striated' and resulting in what they call 'segmentation' – spatio-temporal divisions and lines of connection or lineages.[12] Segmentarity, on the one hand, allows forms (of life) to emerge. On the other, because they proliferate equally in all directions, space is demarcated into smaller and smaller measurable bits. The proliferation and the subsequent rigidity of segmentarity, usually as recourse to the anxiety arising from the uncontained flows of relations, paradoxically result in an indistinction and general homogeneity of the entities in relation.

Flow Problems in the (In)Distinctions Between Potential and Action

In Koolhaas's theorizations of a contemporary generic city such as Lagos, the indistinction between entities at play can be discussed through the relations between constituted and constituent power, that is, power imposed from above by the State, and power emergent of the public from below. The extraterritoriality of global economics in the Koolhaasian city make difficult the formation of communal life, traditionally defined as 'territorial' and 'place-specific'. It seems that the individuality of the citizen and their locatedness within the space of the nation are no longer essential ingredients for democratic constitution of State power. Mobile forms of surveillance, un-mappable knowledge relations resulting from immensely complex information flows and the hybrid nature of education, family and commerce, blur inside/outside and private/public distinctions. The constituent/constituted power distinction that politics holds as the ground for the practice of governmentality is similarly blurred. We can say that in the generic city, geographical and functional space is no longer the precondition for subjectivist agency. Architecture becomes porous, and the effectuation of its citizenship is concomitant to urban functions flowing between internal subjectivity organized by constituent power, and external sovereignty enacted as constituted power.

The productiveness of theorizations such as Koolhaas's generic city relies upon an equivalence that can be made between generic public space and the potentiality of undifferentiated life. The ability of cities and the multitudes within them to remain formally unqualified by withholding their actualizations into specific social, cultural or individual identities becomes their constitutive power.

The relations between constituted power and constituent power within generic urban space, if the latter is accepted as the material actualization of undifferentiated and non-communal life, interrupts in two different and philosophically irreconcilable ways – the ontology of the space of flows, and in corollary, the efficacy of resistance in architectural research and practice serious about the potentiality of undifferentiated forms of social life for new expressions and actualizations of the 'public' within current institutional settings.

Firstly, if the undifferentiated citizenship of place is a symptom of the flow of capital, then we may agree with Giorgio Agamben that there is an indistinction between constituent power of the many and constituted power of the sovereign life under State government within the generic city.[13] This is because the undifferentiated life that plays out in homogeneous public spaces – which is at once a symptom of and occurring as a 'state of exception' within the highly striated space of capitalism – has actually become the rule. Theorists like Lieven de Cauter draw the now familiar parallel between the extraterritorial nature of the generic city with its residual spaces used for unprogrammed public gatherings, and the Agambenian reading of concentration camps as spaces where the system cannot transform extant life into lawful sense.[14] And if we continue along the lines of Agamben's argument, it can be said that the spatial indistinction between sovereign and unmediated life spreads throughout the city by way of the urban subject itself as a site of indetermination between inclusion and exclusion from political mediation:

> When its [political system] borders begin to be blurred, the bare life that dwelt there [camp] frees itself in the city and becomes both subject and object of the conflicts of political order, the one place for both organisation of State power and emancipation from it.[15]

Life then exists as the excluded inclusion within the striated space of capitalism, creating a threshold zone that is both simultaneously inside and outside of the juridical order from which it cannot escape. That is to say, an ontological equivalence exists between the actualization of subjectivity in citizens of a place following the lawful norms of the State, and the potentiality inherent in the undifferentiated subjectivity of the generic multitude that is non-identifiable in relation to the norms of citizenship. This is because the latter's effectuation is inherently tied to the condition of exception to State power as the normative condition of actualization. Life is seen to flow, but it is a circular flow between potentiality of the multitude and the actualization of constituted power, because the former cannot be seen other than through relations with the latter as a form of actuality. The reverse must also be true: the production of the undifferentiated generic public is immanent to, and can never be free from, design of cities as the process of striating space through codification and identification. What this means for architecture is radical, if it is indeed the practice of actualization *par excellence* through its role in place making and subjectivation, as the processes of actualization would contain no alterity to the potentiality of the generic multitude that is not, and cannot, be actualized by design.

Secondly, in contradistinction, we can argue that the potentiality of the multitude, as forms of undifferentiated life in the generic city, cannot be predicted and is not in any way attached to the constituted power of the State that provides the norms of citizenship. Such is the revolutionary potential of the multitude, which Antonio Negri theorizes as totally intensive to its being, and is of an altogether different ontology to the extensivity of the sovereign State.[16] Also to Negri, the undifferentiated life that Agamben defined is actually highly productive and should not be reduced to barely human or animalistic precipitations of constituted power. The productive intensive capacity of the multitude is secured by the fact that value in capitalist modernity is no longer located in surpluses of industry but in human life itself: 'the excess of value is determined today in the affects, in the bodies crisscrossed by knowledge, in the intelligence of the mind, and in the sheer power to act.'[17] Negri and Michael Hardt are chiefly concerned with the connections between potential of singular bodies within the organizational structure that is the multitude, and their 'general intellect', a concept reworked from Marx, which is loosely defined as collective social intelligence that does not necessarily have its baseline measures in organic human bodies, but in its existence as a collection of knowledges and techniques.[18]

If the vitality of the multitude cannot be determined in dialectic with constituted power, can there then be a space of flows between potentiality and actualization in the multitude? Here, the space of flows is found neither in liminality, being inside *and* outside of juridical laws as it is for Agamben, nor pure intensity, within the vitalism of the multitude that creates irreducible possibilities within its own machinic logic as it is for Hardt and Negri. The constituting processes of the multitude, as self-organizing and self-affirming ontological transformations giving rise to possibilities beyond the measure of the originary entities, therefore enact a gap in the teleology of potential and action.

The Ins and Outs of Flows

For architecture to take up Koolhaas's challenge to ride the flows of the modern generic city, and for Koolhaas's own theorization of a multitude such as Lagos to be a productive critique of neoliberal capitalism, there must be an assumption of an ontological consistency between potentiality and action for the space of flows to exist; to ensure that the wave underneath is perceptibly secure enough to hold the architect surfer. However, the ontological consistency that promulgates the flow of relations between potential and action in the very analytical surfaces on which Koolhaas bases his work is beginning to show signs of strain. Theorizations of the multitude need to reconcile two seemingly contradicting positions on how the potential of the multitude is related to its actual material effectuation and performative action; that is, whether the flow between potential and action is an intensivity with its own productive logic, or is inseparable from the extensive force of juridical power owing to an ontological indistinction between that power and its states of exception.

Conventionally speaking, architecture as a practice of creative production is said to transform potential into action. As such, it instates action within a teleological framework that connects it to potentiality. If the multitude is creative in its own self-effectuation and configures itself as a *telos*, or that it is inseparable from the striated space of sovereign constituted power, then the place for architecture as a practice already highly inscribed by actual codes and norms has to be revised. Architecture in this situation may be positioned outside the possibility of resistance, owing to the assumption of *smooth* flows between potentiality and action provided by certain philosophical relations, which obfuscates the complexity of relations between constituent and constituted power, between potential and action. On the surface, it does seem like Agamben's indistinction between potential and act, and Hardt and Negri's virtual productivity of the multitude, where there is an immanence of the action of the multitude and their potential power (but absolutely no-flow between the potential of the multitude and action of the State), promulgates a kind of smoothness, a wavelike to-ing and fro-ing between potential and act that attests to a consistency between the two realms to allow constant cross-overs.

Architecture here risks being relegated to unqualified, and perhaps unqualifiable, repetitions of preconditioned relations between the potentiality and actuality.

Furthermore, the relations between potentiality and action continue to remain unproblematized because of a transparency afforded by the habitual synonymy of 'flow' with 'smoothness' and with 'potential' itself, in contradistinction to the stasis of actuality. Such transparency is also promulgated by a hierarchical bias towards potentiality as the origin of the multitude's power, and that its actualization as spatially and qualitatively different to the metricized space of already formed 'communities' or 'places' remain that which comes *after* some sense of transformation *from* potential. This temporal distinction between potential and action relegates the relations between them to a simplistic chronology of potential as a future storehouse of possibilities which comes to pass when transformed into action.

But while the extensive realm is often considered as further from, and therefore possessing less access to, ontological meaning than the intensive realm, the differential relations between potential and action are paradoxically only ever viewed from the extensive realm, the world of the present. The present is resolutely organized by a thinking of the world rooted in fully formed and fully differentiated actual entities. In the case of the multitude in architectural theory such as that promulgated by Koolhaas, it is the multitude's extensity – its dispersed form, patterns of behaviour, and what can be gleaned as its self-organizational capacity – as presence, that provides the frame for its ontological origins. To Miguel de Beistegui, such an understanding of ontology is restrictive because the thinking of genesis and the source of potentiality begin from the present alone. It is difficult then for thought to rise above identifying potentiality with already individuated beings and entities that make up the horizon of the present.[19] Potentiality framed by already individuated forms shortchanges the thinking of being as absolute difference, away from that based on identity.

Architecture as a space of flows, if it is to inform theorizations of the multitudinal citizenship of space, and the possibilities of resistance to neoliberal capitalist forces therein, entails a reworking of the extensive realm or material plane of life that does not succumb immediately to the metaphysics of presence, in order to explicate a potentiality immanent to the materialism of entities that is not pre-emptive and cannot be pre-empted. To say it in another way, it is a call for a systemic basis to reconceptualize intensive agency as emergent in the concrete empirical domain of extensity, where production of potential is as a result of extensive action, but one that does not necessarily entail a smooth flow between action and potential. In the same light, architecture must cease to be propositional or a pre-established realm of potential from which action flows. Potential does not precede, and thus flows smoothly into, action. Neither should the actual, as presence, restrict potential.

This process in the genesis of the multitude and the human individuals that make it up is far from indeterminate. It is a cumulative process of various local re-combinations in symbiotic becomings, organized by what Gilles Deleuze sees as the potential or 'internal resonance'[20] of an evolutionary process, a term which he appropriated from French philosopher Gilbert Simondon. Deleuze's (and Guattari's) transformation of the organism as individuated systems to epiphenomenal and autonomous molecular and hence non-formal processes – classically in the concept of the 'body without organs' where the disaggregated organism is an attribute of the transcendental intensity of being – may provide a model with which to proceed. Perhaps more architecturally relevant within this transcendental empiricism is Deleuze's proposition of the *plane of immanence*, whose geometry is a convenient way to configure the spatio-temporal relations between domain of potentiality made up of pre-individual singularities and their ongoing process of individuation, replete with flows but which are, as we shall see, not necessarily stable but metastable, and the extensive domain of molecular actualization.

Life On/As the Plane

How can we consider the multitude, on one hand, as a fully actualized state of things, but on the other, maintain the absolute potentiality of its being as a body with no beginning or end, consisting of infinite movements of partially formed entities connecting transversally between categories? On the plane of immanence, the geometry at the crux of Deleuzian ontology, forces, bodies, connections, relations, affects and becomings, in actuality and potentiality, are immanent. The only thing that can be demanded by a thinking concerned with this plane is an infinite movement: flow.

As a geometry, the plane of immanence is not a mentalistic construct like a mathematical theorem. The entities of the plane in constant movement are actual, aggregating into, and disaggregating from, each other to form new bodies and new assemblages. But yet the plane itself remains a virtual abstraction, and it possesses potentiality precisely because of its actual abstractive processes. Therefore, ontologically speaking, the plane remains formless as the self-organization of its entities in qualitatively and continuously differentiating from each other. As Deleuze says in a late essay,

> what we can call virtual is not something that lacks reality but something that is engaged in a process of actualization following the plane that gives it its particular reality. The immanent event is actualized in a state of things and of the lived that make it happen.[21]

On this plane, the concept of the multitude is a set of a molecular becomings between concepts and bodies, set free from specific confines of the organic and the social body. To Deleuze, the specific yet impersonal 'life' – '*a* life . . .'[22] – is discovered in the real singularity of events, that is, the virtual/potential can only be traced from the material empirical plane of the actual. The potential of any event is recognized by what has already happened in actuality: the phenomenon perceived, the language used, the drawing drawn, the action enacted. Deleuze has the ontological horizon stretch from the plane of the actual to the virtual being. The challenge put forward by the plane of immanence is not to see the actualities of spaces, bodies and concepts, as an extension, attribute or exteriority to any definition of multitude. It is to consider extensity or the actual world as the positive emanation of the multitude continuously in the process of becoming, without having to revert to pre-established notions of sociality or the body.

Therefore the task of architectural research and practice of resistance is to attempt to apprehend the event of the multitude and its becoming in all its inseparable variations,[23] not by arresting the space of flows between potential and action for 'scientific' circumspection, but acting in and on multitude as actuality, whereby every action determined increases its potentiality, its virtual power. The chiasmus of potential and act can only be unravelled or effectuated at local specific instances of engagement, where each unravelling creates further potentialities through counter-effectuations.

Intensive Flows

While Deleuzian ontology moves from the plane of the actual to the virtual, it seems there is an overarching, some might say transcendental, force that organizes the plane itself. What is it that holds together and drives the productive organization of the multitude on the plane of immanence, if it is something other than that which flows from an actually constituted sovereign power, or emergent of the virtual potential constitutive of the actual behaviour of a multitude?

On the plane of immanence, Deleuze dissolves everything – actual or potential-virtual – into a molecular level, a realm of constant individuation of particles. As immanent, these particles are more specifically ontologically partial but consistent. That is, they are pre-individuated entities within the system, whether they are forms, objects, bodies, concepts or information that remain always becoming, the force of which is the internal resonance belonging to the plane or system. And the entities are organized by the given fact of their potentiality, akin to the potential of an entropic viral system.

Owing to the consistency of all particles being epiphenomenal and autonomous on/as the plane, given by the fact that they are all attributes of the one intensity, such virology does not make a place within the ontological schema for the possibility of pre-established molar organization, such as individuated organisms or pre-established laws and codes of life. So that the entities on the plane do not rehearse the unities of already individuated organisms as their ontology of becoming, Deleuze shifts the locus of the ontology onto the other side of the fold, into the pre-individual realm whereby 'every differentiation presupposes a prior intense field of individuation'.[24] This structure installs an equivalence between the pre-individual state and a zone of becoming, that which is not differentiated but are made up of ontologically generic attributes of the one intensity.

Deleuze and Guattari's plane of immanence is thus compelled to be a transcendental domain of intensity, owing to the absence of any division between levels of organization 'within' the empirical extensity, as for Deleuze especially, it is all ontologically speaking attributes of a univocal being. On the plane is a unity of substance that bars anything that lands upon it or in it access to ontological equivocity. In many ways this is a convenient way of theorizing away the problems of *a priori* forms, agential subjects and real structures – as Deleuze and Guattari say in *A Thousand Plateaus*: 'Here, there are no longer any forms or developments of forms; nor are there subjects or the formation of subjects. There is no structure, any more than there is genesis.'[25]

To theorize this pre-individual realm as the intensity inherent within all actuality, Deleuze draws on the work of Gilbert Simondon,[26] who attempts to understand the individual not from the perspective of the already constituted individual, but rather from the processes of individuation or ontogenesis. Deleuze uses Simondon's concept of pre-individual singularities in an ongoing process of individuation to postulate an autonomous domain of molecular becoming. Interestingly, an analysis of Simondon's own theory of individuation shows that Deleuze's reading of the latter is perhaps more limiting than the possibilities offered therein for a materialist philosophy of the multitude.

In-Formation in Life-Flows

A closer look at Simondon's process of individuation shows a foregrounding of the empirical plane in the form of the body as central to a systematic ontogenetic process. On the surface this seems consistent with the Deleuzian flow on the plane of immanence from the actual to the virtual. However, while Deleuze uses (pre)individuation to maintain the intensity of being which then is determined (through the process of individuation) in extensive form, Simondon, contrary to Deleuze, introduces an intensity which simply cannot be separated from the specific processes informing the emergence at the concrete empirical or extensive field, which is where complexity emerges, including the processes of morphogenesis that govern the creation of organisms like the human being. There is no ontologically unified substance, form or matter outside individuation. To Simondon, the *process* of individuation is primordial to any substance that undergoes individuation, so we grasp the entire unfolding ontogenesis with all its variety without restricting it to the production of individuals as a movement from a primordial to material state, nor eschewing the role of wholly formed individuals – or the form of individuated subjects – in the process of individuation.[27]

To Mark Hansen, it is location of *information* within the process of individuation which radically differentiates Deleuze's notion of internal resonance from that of Simondon's.[28] To explain the role of information in human individuation, allow me, following Hansen, a biological explication. Bacteria participate in horizontal gene transfer that is non-linear and without a genealogical line of descent. They share their genetic information and reprogram their collective genome in response to certain conditions surrounding their host while activating genetic mutations in those colonies that enter into contact with them. The passage of information from one bacterial colony to another is by means of genetic mutation, that is information is carried by the transformations of their biological form. Therefore bacterial colonies do not constitute a homogeneous genus, but they are all connected by common strains of DNA organized in an uncommon interconnectedness that precipitates collective behaviour changing under certain circumstances.[29] In bacterial endosymbiosis, it is no longer the theory of form which provides the parameters for transformation, but it is information which potentiality informs matter.

Reflecting on endosymbiotic generation and the role of information within that process, it becomes clear that there is no smooth transfer of genetic information because each transference effectuates as a mutation of the organismic form. This is the problem when the Deleuze's univocal virtuality of being meets Simondon's process of individuation: the process of individuation does not rely on a wholeness but radical instability promulgated by the transduction of information. To quote Simondon:

> Individuation may be thought of as temporary resolutions taking place in the heart of a *metastable* system rich in potential. The system harbours a certain incompatibility with itself, an incompatibility due to the impossibility of interaction between incommensurable terms of extremely disparate dimensions.[30]

Simondon's theory highlights the empirical determinism in the philosophy of human behaviour. In the multitude, the body is not reduced to a pre-individual singularities, it is a living being which acts as 'a node of information, transmitted inside itself'.[31] There is a flow of information between one body and the next, but this flow is inseparable from specific physical, biological, mental or social informational process, propagating within a given group of bodies, through a structure. Each structure then serves to constitute the next one. And at the very time this structuration is effected, there is a progressive modification taking place in tandem with it.

But what is significant to note here is that information is not part of a cybernetic function, whose flow completes the circles of transformation of the individual. Information in the transduction process functions differently, as 'noise' immanent to the system being out of step with itself.[32] In its transmission, information causes the system to fall over at each step it takes and thus continuously reinvents itself, creating metastabilities that maintain the potential energy of, and the sources of becoming in, the individuating system. Information therefore provides the individual with its power of ontogenesis.

Theoretical Production and the Metastable Multitude

Through transduction of information in Simondon's process of individuation, creative acts such as design or design research are no longer unified by the transcendental existence of potentiality, nor do they actualize the unified virtuality of the multitude as the theoretical subject matter. It can be argued therefore that theoretical productions and informational transfers within the realm of epistemology, say the work by Koolhaas on Lagos, are co-extensive with process of individuation as a condition for ontology. What I mean here is that the potentiality of the Lagosian multitude is itself immanent to the urban diagrams that Koolhaas draws in the name of theoretical production. In this model there cannot be a total intensive being called the multitude because the actualization of the theoretical project raises in the existence of the multitude, other unactualizable potentialities.

What this demonstrates is that there is an irreducible ontological incommensurability between the potential and the actual because there is no immediately causal (therefore a spatial adjacency) or temporal flow that occurs between them. The difference is between the potentiality of the system, and potential that is implicated in the movements of its explication, or that which is organized by its actualization (say by the theoretical project). So it is the appearance of action, the actual, that belies a transformation of potential variations and encounters of the surface, not so much the sameness of the entities that underlies a flow from one ontological state to another.

What is also important to note is that the entities are not traditional nodes that remain stable, and that what characterizes the flow is movement from one entity to another, differentiated only by degree. Entities in the space of flows are also different in kind. To Felix Stalder, 'as flows change in the direction and volume, the nodes/entities change their characteristics. The characteristics of each entity are less dependent on their internal quality than on their relationship with others, which are created by flows.'[33] In a theoretical project on the multitude that investigates the relationships created by flows, the object of study itself becomes incomplete. The shape of this object cannot be fully known until it is placed into a specific intersection of flows, and its composite entities become equivocal under conditions that are not fully predictable.

Theoretical articulation of a system and the articulated system participate irreducibly in each other. This participation is not just as organized by representation, but by information as a form with minimal energy, somewhat as affect rather than directive, or what Brian Massumi would call an 'affective fact',[34] which in entering a system generates greater energy, thus deriving potentiality. Theoretical information is actualized (it becomes matter) as a force that is to come, a kind of pre-emptive power that generates in the present an affectual condition (an overwhelming dread, mood, aura, sense or composition that feeds on vibrational, a-temporal, a-modal, trans-sensory resonances), which informs itself as matter. Felt through the abstract, matter informs itself.

So Koolhaas's theoretical act in the study of Lagos is one of diagramming, a drawing that informs, which opens up the potential in the system not in causal. Koolhaas is not showing the West's future, but it is a diagramming which affectually brings the future into the economy of the present. It is theoretical articulation that makes the capitalist system fall over itself by a feeling its excesses.

Conclusion

In the space of flows, which is made up by flows of space, architecture needs to be able to bring generic abstractions as actual and highly localized practices to the forefront, to afford it a shape, or visibility in other ways than that which are necessitated by the smoothness in the space of flows. Abstractions such as the 'multitude', 'public', 'space' or 'flow' itself will always be the ground for architecture. However, these abstractions as actualizations become creative leaps into potentiality, whereby the definition of potentiality is not subservient to the presence of the act, but the act is a durational event that is temporally coincident and spatially adjacent with a point of intensity within the realm of potential. These are specific evental sites that may give rise to situation-transforming 'truth procedures' that build conviction and fidelity of future judgments on space and the public. Architectural abstractions as transformative acts are absolutely contingent, and cannot be explained by correspondence:

they appeal to the generic inarticulable category of truth. This means that we cannot assume that the space of flows in architecture is always smooth. Space in its flow, or ontogenesis, is necessarily lumpy, intensive and highly localized in its ontology.

The power in Koolhaas's theorizations in architecture, as we have seen from this analysis, which commenced with his work on the Lagosian multitude, lies in its taking charge of many concrete heterogeneous enduring shapes of value. These are repetitive, banal, ambivalent actualities of constituent power that have been coagulated by systems of economics and the state. But this is precisely the site of phased, controlled emergence of the multitude. Architecture, by acting to fold back these phases of emergence, creates patterns of interruption that open up to other, always partially grasping, productions of life. Resistance in architecture is not an oppositional practice, but the condensation of the vital powers of emergence, a pragmatics of intensified ontogenesis, at life's edge.

Notes

1 Michael Sorkin, *Some Assembly Required* (Minneapolis: University of Minnesota Press, 2001), vii.
2 Ibid.
3 I am borrowing a description from Felix Guattari, 'Ecosophical Practices and the Reinstating of the Subjective City' in Hyperurban, *Quaderns* (Col-legi d'Arquitectes de Catalunya, 2003), 48.
4 Gilles Deleuze, 'Postscript on the Societies of Control' in *October* 59, Winter 1992 (Cambridge, MA: MIT Press), 3–7.
5 *Lagos/Koolhaas* synopsis, First Run/Icarus Films, 2002.
6 Rem Koolhaas, Stefano Boeri, Sanford Kwinter, Nadia Tazi and Daniela Fabricius, *Mutations* (Barcelona: Actar, 2000); Rem Koolhaas and Sze Tseung Leong, *Great Leap Forward: Harvard Design Scoohool Project on the City* (Koln: Taschen, 2001); and Judy Chung Chuhua, Jeffrey Inaba, Rem Koolhaas, Sze Tsung Leong, *Harvard Design School Guide to Shopping: Project on the City 2* (Koln: Taschen, 2001).
7 *Lagos/Koolhaas* synopsis, First Run/Icarus Films, 2002 at http://www.frif.com/new2003/lag.html
8 Rem Koolhaas, quoted in Bregtje van der Haak (dir.) *Lagos/Koolhaas* (55 mins.) (First Run/Icarus Films, 2002).
9 Koolhaas, et al., *Mutations*, 686.
10 See Rem Koolhaas, 'Junkspace' in Chuhua, et al., op. cit., 408–21.
11 Gilles Deleuze, *Pourparlers*, transl. Martin Joughin, *Negotiations* (New York: Columbia University Press, 1995), 124.
12 Gilles Deleuze and Felix Guattari, transl. Brian Massumi, *A Thousand Plateaus: Capitalism and Schizophrenia* (London: Athlone Press, 1988), 208.
13 Giorgio Agamben, transl. Kevin Attell, *State of Exception* (Chicago: University of Chicago Press, 2005).
14 See Lieven de Cauter, 'The Flight Forward of Rem Koolhaas' in Ghent Urban Studies Team (GUST), *The Urban Condition: Space, Community and Self in the Contemporary Metropolis* (Rotterdam: 010 Publishers, 1999).
15 Giorgio Agamben, transl. Daniel Heller-Roazen, *Homo Sacer: Sovereign Power and Bare Life* (Stanford, CA: Stanford University Press, 1998), 9.
16 Antonio Negri, transl. Maurizia Boscagli, *Insurgencies: Constituent Power and the Modern State*, (Minneapolis: University of Minnesota Press,1999), 20–1.
17 Michael Hardt and Antonio Negri, *Empire* (Cambridge, MA: Harvard University Press, 2000), 365–6.

18 Ibid., 368.
19 Miguel de Beistegui, *Genesis and Truth: Philosophy as Differential Ontology* (Bloomington and Indianapolis: Indiana University Press, 2004), 316–17.
20 Mark Hansen, 'Internal Resonance, or Three Steps towards a Non-Viral Becoming' in *Culture Machine*, Vol. 3, 2001, at http://culturemachine.tees.ac.uk/Cmach/Backissues/j003/Articles/Hansen.htm, p.2.
21 Gilles Deleuze, transl. Anne Boyman, *Pure Immanence: Essays on a Life* (New York: Zone Books, 2001), 31.
22 Ibid., 25–34.
23 Deleuze and Guattari, *What is Philosophy?* (London: Verso, 1994),158.
24 Gilles Deleuze, transl. Paul Patton, *Difference and Repetition* (London: Athlone, 1994), 307
25 Deleuze and Guattari, *A Thousand Plateaus*, 266.
26 See Deleuze, *Difference and Repetition*, 162, 307–8, and Deleuze, transl. Mark Lester, *The Logic of Sense* (London and New York: Continuum, 1990), 119, 226.
27 Simondon calls for us to 'understand the individual from the perspective of the process of individuation rather than the process of individuation by means of the individual.' Gilbert Simondon, 'The Genesis of the Individual' in *Incorporations, Zone 6*, ed. Jonathon Crary and Sanford Kwinter (New York: Urzone, 1992), 299–300.
28 Hansen, op. cit., 2.
29 Lynn Margulis and Dorion Sagan, *Microcosmos: Four Billion Years of Microbial Evolution* (Berkeley, CA: University of Berkeley Press, 1986), 94–5.
30 Simondon, op. cit., 300.
31 Simondon's full quote reads 'The living being can be considered to be a node of information that is being transmitted inside itself – it is a system within a system, containing *within itself* a mediation between two different orders of magnitude.' Simondon, op. cit., 306.
32 The dynamism of the transductive process 'derives from the primitive tensions of the heterogeneous being's system, which moves out of step with itself and develops further dimensions upon which it bases its structure.' Transduction therefore furnishes a principle unity as 'nonidentity of the being with itself'. Simondon, op. cit., 312–13.
33 Felix Stalder, 'Space of Flows: Characteristics and Strategies' in *Doors of Perception 7 Conference*, Amsterdam (14–16 November 2002), at http://flow.doorsofperception.com/content/stalder_trans.html.
34 See Brian Massumi, 'The Future Birth of the Affective Fact' in *The Ethics and Politics of Virtuality and Indexicality*, ed. Griselda Pollock and Antony Bryan (Cambridge: Cambridge University Press, 2007), at http://www.litsciarts.org/slsa07/slsa07-500.pdf.

Part Three

Envoi

Chapter 12

Limits of Fluxion

Michael Tawa

Fluxions of Sense

> The Arcadia of dangerous hunts and lost shadows will become the name of an artificial landscape lived like the policed counterpart of the city and like the appeased memory of a shivering and otherwise dangerous excess (*démesure*) . . .[1]

Following Foucault's classification of prisons, asylums, the panopticon, schools, confessionals, factories, disciplines, juridical measures and architecture, Giorgio Agamben counts language (together with writing, literature, philosophy, agriculture, cigarettes, navigation, computers and mobile phones) as perhaps the most ancient apparatus, device or *dispositif*.[2] The apparatus is not merely a tool available to a subject, but a means of producing subjects, subjectivations and subjugations by creating a scission between living being, self and *milieu*. Experience of this scission, which Heidegger names the receptor-disinhibitor cycle, leads to profound boredom (*Langeweile*, the 'lengthening of the while') and to the Open, or to being 'open in captivation'.[3] For Heidegger, this opening constitutes 'the possibility of knowing the being as being, to construct a world, and with this possibility, the possibility of apparatuses which populate the Open with instruments, objects, gadgets, things and technologies of all kinds.' Agamben notes that such *dispositifs* make available to common usage, but also profane things, places, animals or people by liquidizing the boundaries that once enabled their consecration into a separate sphere.[4]

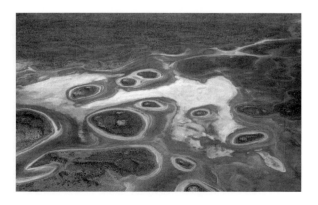

Figure 12.1

What is normally expected of an apparatus is precision, but the precision of language does not rest in the accuracy of what it communicates. Rather, it rests in its incommunicability, in the interminable dislocation of what it is given to say. In Heraclitus' fragment on the Delphic oracle 'the master to whom belongs the oracle of Delphi neither reveals (*legei*) nor conceals (*krupthei*) but signals (*semainei*)'.[5] Jean-Christophe Bailly identifies this signaletic character of the revealed or said with the possibility of the human, and concealment with that of nature (*phusis*), which is its permanent manifestation – *phusis krupthestai philei*; nature likes to hide itself.[6]

> The opposition is therefore that of speech and silence, of a proposition and a negation (*derobade*): it is the normal game of speculation which opens here. But the third mode, which belongs to the god, is different, and it is as if he transcended speculation to inscribe himself in a proposition tainted with obscurity and silence: it is still a case of speech, but blurry (*floue*), and this blurriness – constitutive of the oracle – is not an added value, it is the very mode of the constitution of the truth: we can raise the veil, but in veiling again . . .' – that is, it is not artifice, but 'of the order of provenance, which comes with the oracle, and is not a resolution, but an opening to the open of the enigma.[7]

This is the apparatus of language to which we are all destined – the fluxion and exfoliation of sense, the interminable enigmatic reflux of semantic mobility. If Hermogenes believed in the rectitude or truth value of names and Cratylus in the theory of the perpetual flux of sense,[8] for Deleuze, language is a system, an apparatus in perpetual disequilibrium. Its normative mode is stammering and babbling (*bégayer, balbutier*), according to which language struggles with its own limit[9] – a struggle the rhythm of which folds and unfolds to produce sense as weaving and hemming (*ourlant*), and where the hem is a fold that prevents the borders of sense from fraying and the weave from unravelling.[10] In this rhythm, sense ravels and unravels, arrives and departs in the same gesture. Words don't concretize or crystallize meaning. Rather, they are traces and waves of its interminable disappearance. They do

Figure 12.2

not capture sense but captivate it into a withdrawal that is the presentiment and presence of an un-evadable, fleeting evanescence.

Exfoliation

> Now to unfold signifies that I develop, that I undo the infinitely small folds that never cease to agitate the depths, but in order to trace a large fold on the face of which forms appear . . . I project the world on the surface of a fold.[11]

Sense flows; meaning and means are in states of constant fluctuation. Such wavering depends on contested boundaries and limits. Both space and flow are liminal words. They preserve the sense of an expansion to the brink, to a moment just before the breach, to a condition of excess where the limit threatens to burst. 'Space' is from the etymon *SPA = to expand, span, draw out, have room, prosper, accomplish, reach satiation. 'Flow' is from *PLEU, in the sense of an excessive pluvial outpouring, and *BHLEU = to swell up, in the sense of a pullulating thriving, blooming and flowering. The etymon *PLE gives ply, peel, flay, unfold. Flux inheres because of the fold, because of being the folding-unfolding reflux of becoming. The fold is involved and involving, it harbours a flux of implications. In it, something implicit and implied is hidden in replete profusion; an implicit exfoliation and application, a tactic or strategy of emplotment, a ploy or play, a scheming plot.

There are five senses implied in the word fold – a five-fold rhythm of articulation and exfoliation: weave, play, flat, full and flow.

Weave: pleat, fold, bend, bind, join; French: *plier* = fold, plait, pleat, bend, bow, turn; Latin: *plico/plicare* = fold, *applicare* = join, attach, turn or direct towards (*appliqué*, apply, application); Middle English: *aplien* = apply; Greek: *plekein* = weave; German: *flechten* = braid, plait, twist, entwine; Compare pliable = to accept continued working (like moulding wax); plastic = ability to be moulded, bent, formed; pliability, flexibility – from *PLEK/FLEH = to plait, weave, fold together;

Figure 12.3

Michael Tawa

Greek: *plekein/ploke*, Latin: *plectere* = to plait, *plicare* = to fold; Anglosaxon: *fleax* = flax. Another sense derives from *LEG = join; cf. obligation, from Latin: *ob-* = to, towards + *ligare* = to bind – hence, obligatory, obliging (there is something here of a giving, an offering, an oblation; oblique = bent or leaning towards, tendency, compearance;[12] flag(stone) = thin slice of turf or stone (as flaking-off, or split); flog, flail, flaw (all Scandanavian – e.g. Swedish: *flaga* = flaw, crack, breach; *flagna* = peel off); flexible = easily bent, supple – from Latin: *flectere* = bend (flexus, flexion, circumflex, deflect, inflect, reflect).

Play: Anglosaxon: *plega* = play, game, sport; stroke, blow, fight, skirmish, battle; to play an instrument by striking it; *plega* = stroke, blow; German: *pflege* = care, plight, to be busy with; to work at steadily, to urge; to toil (to ply a task, to ply an oar). Compare Greek: *polemos, pelomai* = warfare; Anglosaxon: *pliht* = risk, danger; Latin: *periculum* (cf. peri- = limit); Anglosaxon: *pleon* = risk, imperil; *pleoh* = danger; *plegen* = to be accustomed, experiment, try; Old High German: *plegan* = to promise or engage to do (cf. play); Middle English: *plyte* = state, condition, manner of being, situation; plot = conspiracy, stratagem – abbreviated from plotform/platform = plan, map or sketch of a place, purpose or territory.[13]

Flat: from *PLAT = spread out; Greek: *platus* = broad, spread-out flat, *platos* = breadth, plate = blade of an oar, plate, *platanos* = plane tree (as spreading out), *plax* = moulding board, flat surface, table, *plateia* = place, open square, street; Latin: *planta* = sole of the foot, spreading shoot, plant (to plant one's foot); Sanscrit: *prath* = spread out, *prthu* = broad, *prthivi* = earth; Anglosaxon: *plek* = a place; cf. plough; cf. floor – Middle English and Anglosaxon: *flor*, German: *flur*, Indogermanic: *pla-*, Latin: *planus* = plain, spread out. Compare *PLAQ/FLOK = strike (down, flat); Greek: *plakos* = flat surface, *plege* = stroke, *plakinos* = made of boards; Latin: *placenta* = flat cake, *planca* = plank; German: *flach* = flat (flay: to skin, strip-off; flag, flap, flop, flutter, flicker).

Full: from *PLE = fill; Sanscrit: *purna* = filled, *puru* = much; Greek: *pleros* = full, *pletho* = I am full, *polus* = much, *pleres* = replete, covered over, complete, *pleroo* = make replete, cram, furnish, finish, accomplish, perfect, *pleroma* = fills – what fills or is filled (a space, a time, a performance, a container); Latin: *plere* = fill, *plenus* = full, *plenarius* = entire, *plenitudo* = fullness, abundance, *plebes*

Figure 12.4

= throng, *plus* = more; *populus* = people, *manipulus* = handful; Anglosaxon: full; French: *plein* = full (plethora, polygon, plenary, plebeian, plural, popular, implement, complete, replete, full, fill, felt, felting (to full or thicken cloth by beating and pounding).

Flow: from *PLEU/FLEU = swim, float, flow; Sanscrit: *plu* = swim, fly; *plauaya* = innundate; Greek: *pleein* = sail, float, ploion = vessel, ship, *plunein* = wash; Latin: *pluuia* = rain, *flere* = weep; Anglosaxon: *flowan* = flow, *flod* = flood, *fleot* = that which floats (stream, bay), *fleotan* = float, *fleot* = ship, fleet (pluvial, flow, flue, fluid, float, fleet, flux, flotilla, fly).

The lexicon that flows from this fairly pullulates at the limit of sense:

> ply, apply, imply, reply, comply, explicit, explicate, implicit, implicate; play, deploy, display, employ; plastic; simple, complex; duplicate, duplicity; triple; multiple; plait, pleat, fold, field, plight; felt; floor, place; splay, supple, supplicate; oblique, obligation, obliging, oblation; flag, flake, flog, flail, flaw, flexion, circumflex, deflect, inflect, reflect; flax, complex, simple, duplex, triplicate, explicate, supplicate, supple, pleach; pluvial, flow, flue, fluid, float, fleet, flux, flotilla, fly.

Incontinent Nature

The city conceives and constructs itself as an ordered and geometric clearing in the midst of a forest of branching and fleeing signs which continue to carry a dimension of dread. The end of dispersion and the open spaces that structure it constitute at best an enclave that loses its efficacy the further away from it one is. Greek religion can be understood in its ensemble and in its contrasts as the effort to render compatible these two distinct universes, that of the city entirely given to measure, and that of a world sensed as immense, dangerous and unmapped (*inarpenté*).[14]

Bailly investigates the propensity in Greek thought to fix and arrest flux, to counter chaos and hubris and answer the *horror vacuui* – this terror that emptiness might be subject to pure and unimpeded manifestation; to the flooding excess and

Figure 12.5

interminable profusion of natural, aesthetic and semantic production. Flux is the wayward, unpredictable vector of dispersion, of everything that the city and civic virtue establish as counterpoints and safeguards against the troubling and pullulating incontinence of nature:

> The choral dimension of the city is also a rhythmic space: it answers to the violence of flux by measure, and to the distracting character of the void by an accentuated disposition. Confronting savage nature where entanglement and the shapeless dominate, the city imposes on itself the law of a choreia, it is rhythm or rhythmic enclave within the dangerous arrhythmia of hills and woods, and it is so only in the open space that it allows itself.[15]

This propensity to bring the threat of unregulated flow to a standstill is implemented by technologies, apparatuses and machines that organize and regulate the production of predictable order. All that the polis is symbolically, politically, economically, culturally, environmentally and architectonically conspires to keep unfettered abundance at bay, to safeguard the *politeia* from excess.[16] The city is a *dispositif* for a *techne* of limitation, boundary setting and exclusion. In this context, architecture becomes an apparatus and typology of control: *agora*, *acropolis*, *temenos*, *theos*, *oikos*, *oikonomia*, *templum*, *sanctum*, *deus*, *intervallum*, *impluvium* . . .

In mathematics and geometry, the control aims at countering the incommensurable by way of the orthogonal; in the natural sciences, the surfeit of production by way of classification; in music, discord by way of modulated harmony; in philosophy, linguistic and semantic ambiguity by the determination of fixed meaning; in architectural siting, nature by way of grounded appropriation, installation, orientation and survey.

This standstill and stabilization of flow has a negative and excluding function – the prevention, closure and shutting-down of potential; the stabilization of flux and the exclusion of altereity in favour of the planned, the predictable, the calculable and the exclusive admission of the same and homogeneous. And yet the stabilization of flow is not necessarily a gesture applied from without. Flow always-already

Figure 12.6

includes a condition of restraint. It is always-already an alternating flexion, a double gesture of retreat and advance, withdrawal and presence that constrains and affords. The apparatus of this double gesture, which brings fluxion to the brink, is rhythm.

(Re)flexion: Rhythm

> Even with Heraclitus, who is entirely on the side of flux, rhythm appears as what holds contraries together, like a sort of outrigger of becoming, and with Plato, who as we know condemned the unfurling effects of *mousike* and dreaded the Heraclitean perspective of a perpetual flux, is opposed to the dangers of arrhythmia. As Pierre Sauvanet shows, *choreia* is what counters *mania* and rhythm is a power at once syntactical and political, a sort of regulator of assemblages (*agencements*), a figure of *nomos*. No doubt rhythm is ambivalent and comports a potential *derive*, a capacity for flight, just as melody does: in truth, none of the three axes of representation – rhythm, melody and language – is exempt from this possibility of overflowing . . .[17]

The word rhythm (Greek: *ruthmos*) combines two etymons – *RH = flow (Greek: *rheo* = flow; river, rave) and *TH = stop, stand (step, station, install).[18] This complex of roots yields words associated with the general idea of measuring and organizing – for example order, art, articulation, repartition, radiation, ritual, rite, right, correct, orthogonal. Rhythm is the standing and reiteration of flow – not its elimination or closure, but a momentary poise, which brings flow back into itself; back into a knot that both gathers and propels it into the open. The pulse of rhythm is a kind of reflux – an interminable forwarding-return. This push-pull cuts and modulates, articulates and joins an apparently continuous trajectory. The standing of flow is poised or hinged on a point that represents the locus of a turning – not an alternation between contraries or a change of direction, but a change of phase or flexion in the material texture of a selfsame entity, undergoing alteration by a rhythmic transport (a body, a space, a geometric form, a phrase, an idea, a mood . . .).

Figure 12.7

Michael Tawa

For example in geometry, polygons (Greek: *poly* = many + *gonu* = knee, joint – from *GEN = generation, production) are not x-sided, but x-*jointed*; and the joint is not a point of fixity but primarily a site of articulation and production, a generative moment in the fluid commodulation of space. Yet contour and envelopment – or the delineating lineaments that mark contour – do not only have a distantiating function. The parts they articulate or dispose[19] are not separated elements but 'repartitioned intensities' and differentiations, oscillating phases or rhythmic pulsations, which liberate space rather than confine it:

> This line of contour which turns on itself, which, as a consequence, ceases to be a purely separative line in order to in some way vanish around the figure it traces, one must not make of it a contrary to the held line, it is rather its relief. At the extremity of the *tenuitas*, there is the quasi-erasure, the line of contour is no more than an almost, which enunciates the subtlety of the limit. Enveloped by the line, the figure announces itself by this limit even as something that is neither simply cut-out nor on the contrary embedded, but which floats into the depth and, one could say, into space.[20]

The line vanishes as it builds contour and relief, it relieves and is relieved of its work. This 'turning contour'[21] and tenuous dilation, leavens or interleaves a foliate, exfoliated and exfoliating space. This is less perspectival space than the space of *sfumato*, in which line and contour as elements of closure are dissolved, thereby constituting space as atmosphere rather than arrangement or shape. It is the space of pure formal evanescence, or of the undecidability between figure and ground, agent and support, form (*schema*) and flux or rhythm (*rheo*).[22] The interminable play and deferment of these two weave the tenuous texture and fluxion of a constitutive field or grain of appearance.

For Plato, *ruthmos* is a central condition of the archetype. It is the actualizing or manifesting phase of the formal idea (*eidos*)[23] – not as immutable paradigm in a state of *stasis*, but as *dunameis*: the manner in which *eidos* is deployed as formal and configurational pattern (*taxis*) in a moving (*kinesis*) and dynamic fluid or

Figure 12.8

substance.[24] Forms (*schema*) are configurative, recognizable shapes – but they are above all flexure maps, traces of confluent rhythmic organization, of trajectory and gesture, tendency and destiny.[25] They are in some way akin to de Certeau's 'intersections of mobile elements' that characterize a space of vectors, velocities and time variables;[26] and Deleuze's cinematic notion of the 'mobile section of duration' developed out of Bergson's idea of the indivisibility of existential movement and concrete duration.[27] The immobility of architecture is terminal, but architecture can also be considered as receptive to the flux of the movements it harbours – from the movement of ideas in its intellectual constitution, to the literal flow of processes, systems, bodies and substances that traverse it. In that sense the immobility is only part of a story – a cross-section that needs to be animated by embodied and continuous, indivisible spatial experience.

There are musical parallels. Every tone has a distinctive frequency, but the sound we hear is an approximation. A tone is in fact the sound of difference, of altereity, of the interval that separates two notes – for example, the sound of the space between two stops on a monochord. This difference is animated by rhythm, which is the vibrational character of tonality. Likewise tones and the modes or scales in which they are set, are not fixed formal configurations but rhythmic milieus with particular dynamics, tendencies, impulsions and combinational potential. In Deleuzian terms, music is an *agencement*, an assemblage of relational dynamics constituting an apparatus that can achieve specific effects[28] – for example of consonance or closure (the octave), compulsion (the third), restlessness or dissonance (the tritone or *diabolus in musica*). In Greek music, rhythm is *kineseo stasis*,[29] the standing of movement. It orders the flow (*reo*) of sound by bringing dynamic flux (*kinesis*) to rest (*stasis*).[30] It does this as an alternation 'first opposed, then accorded'[31] between the Same (*homoios*) and the Different (*heteros*)[32] about points of rest or pause called *chronoi kenoi* – literally 'empty times'. Rhythm is the mobilizing and mobilized vitality of difference, articulated around such empty times. It differentiates relational fields in traces drawn from altereity in alternation. It expresses the incommensurable discrepancies between limit-extremes whose spaces and tensions it traverses, convokes and weaves.

Figure 12.9

Standstill

> Behold, the present time, which alone we found could be called long, is abridged to the space scarcely of one day. But let us discuss even that, for there is not one day present as a whole. For it is made up of four-and-twenty hours of night and day, whereof the first hath the rest future, the last hath them past, but any one of the intervening hath those before it past, those after it future. And that one hour passeth away in fleeting particles. Whatever of it hath flown away is past, whatever remaineth is future. If any portion of time be conceived which cannot now be divided into even the minutest particles of moments, this only is that which may be called present; which, however, flies so rapidly from future to past, that it cannot be extended by any delay. For if it be extended, it is divided into the past and future; but the present hath no space.[33]

In Book 11 of the Confessions, St Augustine agonizes over the three-fold nature of time. None of the three – future, past or present – seem to exist, and yet we have a palpable sense of them. The future is not yet, the past is no longer, and the present is not yet past. Neither not-yet nor no longer – temporally unlocatable because always passing – the present is this fugitive existent that cannot-not be lived. As such it stands as the centre of time, belonging to neither past nor future, yet conditioning both as the hinge on which they turn and return one into (and out of) the other.

Here, the summer solstice has just passed – the moment at midday on June 21 when the sun appears to stand still at the limit of its ascending course, before descending once again towards its winter station. At that moment without duration, its poise is neither pause nor rest, but contraflexure, inflexion or limit of inversion. Likewise the gloaming of twilight, in which day and night become indistinguishable; the slack sea at high tide, when waters appear to swell and become heavy; the moment before a torrential storm; sweat in sweltering heat; flushed cheeks; laughter; the instant tears well up. Each one of these is a limit condition, which threatens to breach a boundary. But each is also an opportunity, a threshold between worlds, an opportune time (*kairos*) rather than a moment in time (*chronos*), or else *wu wei* – action without action.[34] In these moments, time and space are taken to a limit of

Figure 12.10

potentiality and undecidability. The dimensions of space compress; past and future withdraw into their common presence and hinge in the instant of time, leaving only ubiquitous presence – everything, everywhere, all at once, forever.

If rhythm articulates time – by diurnal, seasonal and annual cycles, the precession of the equinoxes, physiological phases, geomorphological eras, climatic shifts – it does not do so by cutting and subdividing a pre-existent time-matter of homogenous extent, but by articulating temporal densifications and rarefactions to creating time-zones of variable texture, speed, pace and pulse; of times tied to potentialities of life events like the compressed times of work, the dilated times of rest and the circuitous times of 'play':

> Time appears most generally under its 'fluvial' form, but it also belongs to it to be able to spread itself and to appear, from that moment, as an extended present. Of this immobilisation of what physicists, all children of Heraclitus, call the 'arrow of time', the shadow is one of the vectors, and according to this perspective the image always comes to inscribe itself as a shadow, that is to say as a *caesura* in the course of time. Every image (except of course in cinema) is arrest on image, arrest of time. It is as arrested that the image transits time, and every glance upon it triggers again the *caesura* that it opened.[35]

This *caesura* or incommensurable discrepancy at the heart of time is the instant, the hinge of time around which its rhythms and revolutions turn. Like the empty felly of a wheel or the eye of a storm, the instant has no substance and suffers no change – yet it constitutes the strength of the wheel and the pivot of movement. In the mythic dance of Siva Nataraja, the god is imaged poised as a mobile section through the whirl and the whorl of a cosmic dance, which produces, preserves and destroys the world. Siva's stance is a manifestation of *shakti* – his consort and the potential that is not actualized but preserved in his gesture, in his body's flexion as an articulated topography. Siva appears at a standstill. But what is stilled in this everpresent readiness to act is the full force of production maintained in the instant of an absent

Figure 12.11

Michael Tawa

presence. The arrest of flow and its suspended fluxion is a collected intensification, which wells up to a limit of potential and mass. In its evident groundedness, the figure is heavy and grave – and yet it gathers the telluric into an aerial promise. Siva is shown not at the moment of action, but just before it – like an offbeat that holds his rhythmic transport on just this side of a calamitous or felicitous rift.

In the Space of Flows

> The labyrinth, in all of its possible states, is in any case the place where one is led astray, the very place in which and by which space is scrambled and where all possibility of orientation is destroyed. Elsewhere it is also, in the Cretan case which interests us, the dwelling of a monster, intended and conceived for it. Now the city, all that it will become, all that it is in its earliest phase, is entirely directed by the effort of separating itself from the monstrous, and that is why we can say that the genesis of the city (*poléogenèse*) is essentially anti-labyrinthine; because it dispenses with the monstrous and what originally has to do with the monstrous, but also because it dispenses with space without measure or landmarks, seeking rather to establish by way of spacings and voids the clarity of a visible and legible harmony: the city that Greece seeks to give consistency to is drawn within a confused and tousled universe as the space where one does not get lost, where one cannot feel lost. It is as such opposed to the labyrinth, which, as we know, often serves as reflexive image of today's metropolis or of the great city in general.[36]

The space of flows would then constitute a place and condition of potential rupture, which is just about to, but has not yet taken place. This 'not yet' is not a moment that has yet to arrive. Rather, it is a moment of contraflexure between two coexistent and interpenetrate phases or states, each of which is defined by the advancing-withdrawal of the other. In that sense, the space of flows is a space of

Figure 12.12

Limits of Fluxion

forgetfulness, of oblivion and erasure, of avoidance and evasion. Yet, in a strange contradiction, in the midst of our passionate engagement with irremediable fluxion (everything is moving, intensifying, dispersing; growing, decaying, proliferating), there is the palpable sense of a still and grave presence, threatening one excess with a wholly and indiscernible other. Any architecture that seeks a place in the space of flows must encounter this difficult and expropriating condition that is its proper limit and opportunity.

Clearly there are several registers for engaging with the notion of flows in architecture: literal flows; metaphorical flows such as flows of capital across territories, settlements, identities and nations; virtual and vital flows of the kind foregrounded by Deleuze and Guattari, which haunt several texts in this volume; material and libidinal flows, flows of agency and assemblage which put desire into fluxion; milieus of flows and the frames and apparatuses that enable, register and mobilize them; flows of emergent conditions which crystallize intensities, adjacencies and coagulations of the milieu; flows of engagement which seek to sustain that milieu, render it operative and make it pullulate and produce. Ultimately, it is flows and nothing else that make buildings *work* – flows of desire, flows of capital and political power, flows of aesthetic and formal predilection, flows of activity and usage; flows across established boundaries between cultures, ideas, places and environments, communities and selves, multiplicities and singularities, cities, people and buildings. These fluxions constitute the uncertain, unpredictable and disruptive milieu out of which architecture can be provisionally thought, designed and produced.

A fluxional approach to architecture might potentially counter formalist ways of thinking and practising design by valuing trajectories of indeterminacy and emergence over volumetric coordination and formalization of concepts, data or any other pre-given conditions. It might value non-centralized and non-definitive transactional processes of deferral and networking, functioning within conflictual liminal zones, which enable decisiveness to emerge out of recognizing evolving, contingent, provisional and discursive conditions, rather than being imposed as pre-cognized decisions or triggered by crisis. Here, design is not a matter of control

Figure 12.13

but of strategically managing negotiable opportunity; and architecture is not the modernist cliché of judicious articulation of forms in light but the liquidizing, diffraction and unravelling of form that remains subject to constant mobilized fluxion. The space of such architecture (and the space in which such architecture is thought and produced) would make possible the means by which meanings transit and undergo fluxion; by which configurations, orders and forms are interminably unregulated, contaminated and displaced; in which the urban subject undergoes constant fluxion, proliferation and deterritorialization into the virtual identities and avatars that populate and constitute the political space as such.

What might such architecture look like? This is possibly not a very useful question since the issue is not about determining a look or appearance but about a process and condition in which what appears is not a predicated deliverable, more or less striking in its formal characteristics and lineage, but an emergent complex whose lineaments are produced in and by the interactive conditions of a milieu. It is a question of setting up enabling conditions, not of configuring fantastical form. Literal manifestations, crystallizations or monumentalization of the gestural, the dynamic, the fluxion of ideas, the flows of information, the vectors of deterritorialization, the trace of indeterminacy or the general restlessness that conditions the present time may have currency in recent architecture, and they allude to familiar types and shadows: science fiction, aliens, slugs, assemblages of holes,[37] woven substances subject to torsional force, soft rigidity, soft architecture, blob, fold, mobius strip, arabesque, forms and structures of the blur (*la structure du flou*) and the out-of-focus:

> The humid grid of Frei Ottto is a formation in which movement is structurally absorbed by the system: it is a combination of intensive and extensive movements, of flexibility and displacements . . . We should replace the passive flexibility of neutrality by the active flexibility of the blurry . . . of a soft constructivism . . . The blurry operates in differentiated fields of vectors, of tendencies, which articulate clearly defined habits or goals and actions as yet undetermined.[38]

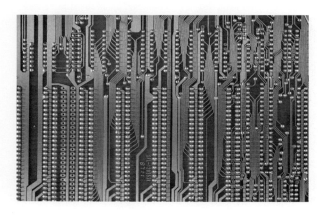

Figure 12.14

Yet with its claims of valorizing non-Euclidean geometries and of contesting classical orthogonal and hierarchical formalism, these projects prolong the other face of modernity – the non-rational tendencies that have never ceased to haunt it. The direct lineage of this work was made explicit in the 2003 Beaubourg exhibition 'Architectures Non-Standard'. It is traceable to at least late nineteenth-century experiments in diagramming corporeal movement and fluid dynamics, the development of harmonic imagery and chronophotography, the biomorphism of D'Arcy Wentworth Thompson, the advent of cinema, and the technologies and practices of force and fluid diagramming as a basis for artistic and architectural expression. The parallel neo-spiritualist and esotericist predilections of the times (Theosophy, Anthroposophy) constitute a critically related phenomenon. In 'Notes on Gesture', Giorgio Agamben achieves a lucid reading of Gilles de la Tourette and Eadweard Muybridge's work of 1886 on the animated imaging of human gesture. Agamben concludes:

> By the end of the nineteenth century the gestures of the Western bourgeoisie were irretrievably lost . . . In the cinema, a society that has lost its gestures seeks to reappropriate what it has lost while simultaneously recording that loss.[39]

The striking effect of 'Architectures Non-Standard' was the decidedly rearguard character of such contemporary attempts to formalize the dynamic. Might it be that the current fascination and motivation for formal representation of gestural, dynamic and fluxional processes and systems, mobilized by the potential of digital technologies developed in tandem with the motive, represent a further phase of this reappropriational archiving and memorialization of the lost art of gesture? In turn, might a different, contestational and necessary architecture of resistance be articulated? Such an architecture might be one founded on poise, on that instant of circumflexion, on the still and uneasy moment before a storm – an architecture that gathers and preserves the unrealized but indefinitely available potential of the limit to touch its own and overburdening excess; an architecture whose power rests not in more or less fantastical fluxional or flowing form, but in a kind of erasure or

Figure 12.15

withdrawal of form in favour of receptive environments which afford experiences of the slow and measured, of the troubling and uncanny indiscernability of the gloaming, of a stuttering convocation of the unpronounceable and the evanescent, of the unprogrammed and the unprogrammable, of the makeshift, and of the fugitive lineaments and boundaries that waver and flex like uncertain outlines of a shimmering form whose legibility hovers in forgetfulness.

Notes

1. Jean-Christophe Bailly, *Le Champ Mimétique* (Paris: Editions du Seuil, 2005), 268–9.
2. 'I call *dispositif* everything that has, in one way or another, the capacity to capture, to orient, to determine, to intercept, to model, to control and to assure the gestures, conducts, opinions and speech of living beings.' Giorgio Agamben, *Qu'est-ce qu'un Dispositif*, trans. Martin Rueff (Paris: Rivages, 2007), 31.
3. Martin Heidegger, *The Fundamental Concepts of Metaphysics*, trans. William McNeill and Nicholas Walker (Indianapolis: Indiana University Press, 1995), 59–273.
4. Giorgio Agamben, *Profanations*, trans. Jeff Fort (New York: Zone, 2007).
5. Heraclitus, Fragment 93.
6. Ibid., Fragment 123.
7. Bailly, op. cit., 256.
8. Ibid., 260.
9. Gilles Deleuze and Claire Parnet, *l'Abécédaire de Gilles Deleuze* (Paris: Editions Montparnasse, 2004), DVD, Style.
10. Giles Deleuze, *Le Plis* (Paris: Les Editions de Minuit, 1988), 248.
11. Deleuze, op. cit., 124, citing Cocteau, *La Difficulté d'Être*.
12. Jean-Luc Nancy, *The Inoperative Community* (Minneapolis and Oxford: University of Minnesota Press, 1991).
13. For example, 'the *platt* and fabrick of our purpose', 'the captain did *plat out* and describe the situation of all the ilands', see W.W. Skeat, *An Etymological Dictionary of the English Language* (Oxford: Oxford University Press, 1979), 459.
14. Bailly, op. cit., 228.
15. Ibid., 225.
16. The first city builder is the metalworker Tubalcain (Latin: Vulcan), whose father, the sedentary Cain, kills his nomadic brother Abel. This myth is read by René Guénon as a metaphor for the destruction of time (nomadism) by space (sedentarism) – and by implication, of the uncivilized by the civilized, of the earth by the city, of the organic by the crystalline and of Nature by Culture. See chapters 21 'Cain and Abel' and 'Time Changed into Space' in René Guénon, *The Reign of Quantity and the Signs of the Times* (Hillsdale, NY: Sophia Perennis, 2001), 144–51; 159–64.
17. Bailly, op. cit., 176–7.
18. GK: *ruthmos* = measured motion, flowing metre; *RT: rhythm as arrested, enchained, bound and formally directed or significant movement; fixation, punctuation; *RTH = arrested, retarded, enchained movement. HB: *RD = an iterative movement which returns to itself; replicate, render, restitution, articulate.
19. *Articulation* is from the Latin: *ars-* = to connect, join – hence connected, joined. Its correlate is *dispositio*. In both cases, the terminology refers less to formal characteristics than to a *dispositif* – a device, equipment or armature which affords or produces certain outcomes.
20. Bailly, *Champ Mimétique*: 101–2.

Limits of Fluxion

21 Ibid., 142, citing Pliny on the suppleness and ductility of contour attained by the sculptor Parrhasios.
22 Ibid., 108–10.
23 Plato, *Laws*, 728e; Emile Benveniste, 'La notion de "rythme" dans son expression linguistique' in *Problèmes de Linguistique Générale II* (Paris: Gallimard, 1966): 327–35.
24 *Ruthmos* is decomposed by Benveniste as *ru* = flow and *th)mos* = modality of accomplishment (332). According to René Guénon, the basis of all arts is the application of the science of rhythm in its various forms; a science tied to the science of number: 'For the plastic arts, the productions of which develop themselves through extension into space . . . rhythm is, as it were, fixed in simultaneity, instead of unrolling itself in succession [as in the case of music] . . . the typical and fundamental art being architecture . . . [in which] rhythm is directly expressed by the proportions existing between the various parts of the whole, and also by geometric forms, which are . . . the spatial translation of numbers and their relationships.' See his *Mélanges* (Paris: Gallimard, 1976), 106.
25 Bailly reads this as a conjunction of form (*schema*) and flux (*rheo*), inscription and headlong flight (*fuite en avant*), demeanor (*tenue*), holding (*tenir*) and flowing (*ecoulement*). See his *Champ Mimetique*, 173.
26 Michel de Certeau, *The Practices of Everyday Life*, trans. Steven Randall (Berkeley, CA: University of California Press, 1986), 117.
27 Gilles Deleuze, *Cinema 1. The Movement Image*, trans. Hugh Tomlinson and Barbara Habberjam (Minneapolis: University of Minnesota Press, 2001), 11: 'Now we are equipped to understand the profound thesis of the first chapter of *Matter and Memory*: 1) there are not only instantaneous images, that is, immobile sections of movement; 2) there are movement-images which are mobile sections of duration; 3) there are, finally, time-images, that is, duration-images, change-images . . . which are beyond movement itself.'
28 'We do not desire something or someone, but an assemblage (*agencement*) of things, of states of things, of modes and modalities of things, by which is operated a reorganisation of one's being in the world, which inspires, stimulates, incites.' Deleuze and Parnet, *l'Abécédaire,* D pour Désir.
29 Plato, *Laws*, 665. It is also, according to Aristoxenus, *taxis chronon*: the 'order of movement', which amounts to the same thing since the order or statute of a being is also its stature.
30 Plato, *Parmenides*, 402a–b,426e.
31 Plato, *Banquet*, 187b; Laws, 665a.
32 In Platonic cosmogony the demiurge 'judged uniformity [the "same": *auto* = self-sameness] to be immeasurably better [= more beautiful] than its opposite': *Timaeus*, 33b, 35a, 37c; cf. *Theatetus*, 185c, 186a; Sophist, 254e. The Same is *homoios tauton*: the self in itself and belonging to itself; the Different is *tauton heteron*: the self other than itself and belonging to the 'other'. Hence all motion (*kinesis*) has its origin in the self-motion of the World Soul (*Laws* 896a) whilst arising from a state of heterogeneity (*anomaloteta*) whose nature is the inequality (*anisotes au tes anomalou phycheos*) between the World Soul in its unmanifest self-sameness and its manifest self-difference (*Timaeus*, 58a).
33 St Augustine, *The Confessions*, Book 11, Chapter 15, at http://www.leaderu.com/cyber/books/augconfessions/bk11.html (sourced 22 June 2007).
34 Michael Tawa, 'Limit and *leimma*. What remains for architecture' in *Limits, Proceedings of the 21st Annual Conference of the Society of Architectural Historians Australia and New Zealand, 2004* (Melbourne: SAHANZ/RMIT, 2004), 455–60.
35 Bailly, *Champ Mimétique*, 61–2
36 Ibid., 211–12.
37 Lars Spuybroek, 'La structure du flou' in Frédéric Migayrou, *Architectures Non Standard* (Paris: Centre Georges Pompidou, 2003), 127: 'What is most surprising in this system is that it is

structured by holes; it is in their assembly (*agencement*) that resides the directing force of their formation; in opposition to the common apprenticeship of architects, taught to think the system by the elimination of voids.'
38 Spuybroek, op. cit., 126.
39 Giorgio Agamben, transl. Liz Heron, *Infancy and History: Essays on the Destruction of Experience* (New York: Verso, 1993), 135–40.

Index

In this index photographs are indicated in bold type. Notes are indicated by n.; footnotes by f.

1:1 Architects Build Small Spaces 94–5
30th February group 191

Acceptera 90–1
accumulation 130
action, and potential 200, 204–8, 211–12
activism: cyber 180, 181, 183–5, 187, 189, 190; Egypt 186–7; media 184; political 181, 188, 191–2
activists, flaneur 183, 190–4
actor network theory 179
actualization 205
affective fact 212
Agamben, Giorgio 205, 217–18, 231
Air 108
Altvater, Elmar 130
Ambience 108
ambient 49
amplification 21–4
anti-capitalist movement 184
anti-globalization movement 184, 186, 190
Anti-Oedipus 15, 20
apparatus: architecture as 222; of language 217–19
April 6th general strike 193–4
Arata Isozaki 68
Arcades project 102–3
architects 8, 35, 141, 142
architectural discourse 67, 169
architectural experience 87–8
Architectural Pieces 96
architectural praxis 64
architecture 63, 64, 141; as apparatus 222; of events 139; fluxional approach to 229–32; landscape 67; and light 107, 108, 109, 113; modern 2; and nature 103–5, 106, 111–13; as space of flows 207; as time-based field 66–7
Architecture from the Outside 67

Architecture Non-Standard 231
Architectures of Time 66–7
architecture-world 8
Arizona Corridor 121
Arizona Market 120–3
artificial flood 48
artificial intelligence 17
artists impression 49
Asakura Choso Museum 90, **91**
Asakuri Fumio 90
Asplund, Erik Gunnar 92, 94
asymmetry 84
Austin, Mike 69, 70
ava 68
Avalon 109

Bachelard, Gaston 81, 84, 88
Badovici, Jean 2, 3
Bailly, Jean-Christophe 218, 221
Banana Yoshimoto 94
Barthes, Roland 19, 89–90
Bartleby 9–10
Beetle House 95
behaviour: learned 5–6; patterns of 25
Beistegui, Miguel de 207
Belgian coastline 48–57
Bell, David and Jayne, Mark 101
Benjamin, Walter 101, 102–3, 105, 111–12, 113–14, 162
Bergson, Henri 63
Beskow, Elsa 81, 94
bloggers/blogs 180, 181–3, 187–90, 195n.16
blogosphere 195n.16; Egyptian 185–7, 194, 197n.52; in space of flows 181–3
blogosphere landscape 19, 180
Boh tea 25
Book of the Machines, The 20
borrowed scenery 84
Bosnia 120–3

235

Index

boundaries: architectural 77; London Thamesport 156; as political space 117
Branscombe Bay 147
Brčko 120–3
Broadbeach 108
Brunnberg & Forshed Arkitektkontor AB 94
building materials 31–4
buildings 35; preserved/protected 165, 170
built environments 161–2
Burleigh Heads 108
Butler, Samuel 4–6, 20

Cache, Bernard 66
Cairo 180, 191–3 see also Egypt
Camera Obscura, Interior Exterior 89
capitalism 123, 131, 153
capitalist economies, and democracy 123
capsular coast/entity 50
capsules 52–4
Castells, Manuel 30, 135, 148, 149
Chaosmosis 20
Chemical Basis of Morphogenesis, The 16
Cherkizovsky Market 127–8
chigaidana 84
Circle on Cavill 109–11
citizen journalism 190
city, the 228
civilian logistics 151
class, social 170
COASTOMIZE! 50, 55f.
co-creative world 51
collaborative webpages 185
colloquial architecture 142
commercial logistics 149–50, 157
commercial power 151
commodity flow 147
computer mediated communication (CMC) 181
'conditions of life' 6–7, 10
congestion, culture of 201
Congrexpo building 200
connection, light as 113
containerization 153, 159n.58
container movement 154, 156
contour 224
control, material realization of 153–6, 157
Coolangatta 106–7
Coromandel Peninsula 65–6, 67–8, 70–1, 74–8, 80n.35
Cowen, Deborah 155
creative cities 101
creative destruction 54

creative people 101, 114
Critical Art Ensemble (CAE) 185
crowds 18–20, 21
cultural identities 128
culture of congestion 201
Currumbin Wildlife Sanctuary 105
Curtain Wall House 95–6
cyber activism 180, 181, 183–5, 187, 189, 190

Darwin, Charles 6–7, 10, 13, 14, 37n.18
Davis, Mike 131
De Landa, Manuel 150, 151–2
Deleuze, Gilles 66, 162, 174, 208
Deleuze, Gilles, and Guattari, Félix 15, 18, 20, 24, 30, 99, 107, 113, 203–4, 209–10
democracy 123, 126
Derrida, Jacques 13–14
Descartes, René 17
designers in free association 51
desires 15, 18, 23, 111
desiring-production 99, 111
desperation 9, 12
determinism 211
deterritorialization 194, 199
deterritorialized flows 113
diasporic cultures 119
Dictyostelium discoideum 16–17
dispositifs 217, 232n.2, 232n.19
dissolution 20–1
distribution 150
distributive space 147
Drupal 186, 197n.55
durational flows 63, 66, 78

ecological functionalism 91
economic flows 117
economy, world 54–6
Egypt: activism 186–7; ancient 1–2
Egyptian, bloggers 180, 187–90
Egyptian blogosphere 185–7, 194, 197n.52
EGYPTIAN BLOG RING, THE 186
Egyptian Movement for Change 186, 188
Egyptian pyramids 1, 2
Eisenman, Peter 166
electronic communication 179
emergence 16
emergent order 28
emergent pattern 25
Emotion Machine, The 18
Engels, Friedrich 26–7
environment, and architecture 105–6

Index

Epicurus of Samos 13, 15
evolution 7
exfoliation 219–22

Fahmi, Wael 19
Fibonacci series 10
first move 4–9
flaneur activists 183, 190–4
flat 220
FLC 48, 51–2
flipmode era/society 53
flood, artificial 48
flood phenomenon 51–2
flow 221; stabilization of 222
flows 12, 66–7; of capital/economics 142; deterritorialized/multiple 113; light, air and vista 107; notion of 229; of power 201
flow-space, three layers of 149
fluxional approach, architecture 229–32
fluxions of sense 217–19
FOP 127–8
Fordism 152, 154
form-making 24
forms 224–5
Foucault, Michel 131, 167, 175
free associating designers 51
freedom 23
freeplay 13
free-trade zone 121
friction 151–2
friluftsrum 81, 85, 87, 88, 92, 94
Fru Ollon 81
fudo 88
Fujimori Terunobu 95
full 220
functionalism 82, 84; ecological 91
future conflicts 52
futureconflictzone 52

generic city 204, 205
gesture 231
glass-clad buildings 33
glass, plate 33
global capitalism 131, 153
global economy 117, 118
globalization 119, 130, 132
global network migration 132
global networks 183
Godts, Marc 24
Gold Coast 99–100, 102
Gothic era 165

Graham, Stephen 149, 155, 156
Gray, Eileen 2–3
grey customs clearance 129
grey trade 121
grid-bound hyper-economy 53
grid, hyper-economic 55–6
Grosz, Elizabeth 66, 67, 71
ground, as a fluid 69–70
Ground House 71–3
ground space 71–2
Guattari, Félix 20

habit 5–6
Hacking, Ian 173, 174
hacktivists 181, 183
Hak, Bregtje van der 202
Hamm, Marion 194
Hannah, Dorita 63, 66
Hansen, Mark 210
Harari, Josué and Bell, David 149
Harvard Project on the City 201
Hearn, Lafcadio 84
Hegel, G.W.F. 163
Heidegger, Martin 88, 217
Hellquist, Hanna 94
Herakleitos 1, 2, 6
Here Comes Everybody 21
heritage 166; agenda of 171
history/historicism 13, 162, 163–75
Hobbes, Thomas 172
Holocaust Memorial 166
Holy Cross Chapel 92
Hoppets Kapell 92
Hounshell, David 152
houses 174; role of 4; and social class 170
hubs of information exchange 184
human scale 12–13
humid grid 230
hylomorphic order 28
hyper-economic grid 55–6
hyper-economy 54, 55
hyper-flux 54
hypermobility 180

identity formation, urban 105–6
immigrants 128–9
Independent Media Centres (IMCs) 184, 194
individuation 210, 211, 214n.27
'industrialization of memory' 6
Indymedia 184, 185, 194
informal economy 125

237

Index

informal markets 117–19, 130, 131, 132–3
informal ordering 26
informal organization 131
informal trading areas 130
information technologies 179, 180
infrastructure, organisational 148–9
intelligence, artificial 17
intelligent community 16–17
interactice model 54
interlocking 154, 155–6, 157
internet, and activism 187
interstitial 54
In the House of my Father 84
IRC (Internet Relay Chat) 181
Isozaki, Arata 68
Istanbul Topkapi 123–6
ItalProject 121–2
Izmailovo market 126–30

Janssens, Nel 24
Japan 90
Japanese teahouse 87–8
Jewish Museum 166
Johansson, Bengt O.H. 92
Junichiro Tanizaki 83
junkspace 202

Kakuzo Okakura 88
Kant, Immanuel 163
Kefaya 186, 197n.56
Kinkabool 102
Kirra 108
Kirshenblatt-Gimblett, Barbara 67
Koolhaas, Rem 199–200, 201–3, 212, 213
Korniyenko, Sergei 127
Koyaanisqatsi 19
Kunsthal 200
Kwinter, Sanford 66–7

labyrinth 228
Laclau, Ernesto 125–6
Lagos 201–2, 212
La Mettrie, Julien O. de 14
landscape architecture 67
landscape, layers of 84, **85**
landscaping, Gold Coast 112–13
language, apparatus of 217–19
Law, John 149
learned behaviour 5–6
lebenswelt 165
Le Corbusier 2, 3

Lefebvre, Henri 103–4, 149
Leviathan 172
L'Homme Machine 14
Libeskind, Daniel 166
Life and Habit 5
light: and architecture 107, 108, 109, 113; Australian 99–100; and marketing 110
Linux 183
logistical flow: impediment 151–3; layering of 148–51
logistical time-space 153
logistics 149–50, 151, 152, 153, 156–7
logistics management 147–8
London Thamesport 153–6
loss 164

ma 68, 79
machinic 20
machinic phylum 30–1
Mae-Klong Market 136–42
magnification 56
Mahnkopf, Brigitte 130
Manchester 26–7; Town Hall 7–8
Mare Meum 48, 55
marketing 34; Gold Coast 109, 110
market mentality 130
Marvin, Simon 155, 156
Masaharu Anesaki 84
Massumi, Brian 63, 212
materials, metamorphic 31–4
Mattson, Helena 90
media activism 184
Media Alliance 185
Melville, Herman 9–10
mental time 83–4
Merleau-Ponty, Maurice 96
metamorphic materials 31–4
migrants 119, 128–9
migratory economies 132
military logistics 150, 151, 157
military power 151
Minsky, Marvin 17–18
Mitsuo Inoue 90
mixed reality continuum 55
mobile blogging 180 *see also* bloggers/blogs
mobile technology 183
moblogging 180 *see also* bloggers/blogs
Moonlight Shadow 94
Mooshammer, Helge 26
Mörtenböck, Peter 26
Moscow Izmailovo 126–30

movement, control of 151, 155
movement space 90
Mrs. Acorn 81
M.U.D. project 47–57
MUDs (multi-User Domains) 55, 181
multitudes 12–14
multitude, the 205–6, 207, 208–9, 211, 212
Multi User Domain/Multi User Dimension 55, 181

nature: and architecture 103–5, 106, 111–13; incontinent 221–3
nautilus, the 10–11
nearness 88
Negri, Antonio 205
networked social movements 183–5
network society 30
networks of alternative communication 183, 194
new media 180
news websites 190
New Zealand 69; Ground House 71–3; Sounds House 73–4; Tokatea 65–8, 70–1, 74–8, 80n.35
Nietzsche, Friedrich 162, 167, 174
Nigeria 201–2
Nile 1–2
Nirvana 108
nonconscious thinking 14–15
Notes on Gesture 231
Notopia 183

object-as-event 66
objectile 66
Oceanic architecture 69, 70, 73, 79
Oceanic region 64, 68–70
oceanscape 68–9
Ocean Skyhomes 107
Ocke, Nutta och Pillerill 81, **82**
Okakura, Kakuzo 88
On Present Day Architecture 102
On the Origin of Species 6–7, 10, 13, 14
ontology 207, 208, 211
open-air room *see friluftsrum*
openness, space of 69
Oracle, The 102
order 27–8
ordering, informal 26
ordering strategies 149
organisational infrastructure 148–9
'organisms of society' 7

Origin of Species, On the 6–7, 10, 13, 14
Östra Kvarnskogen 94
Otto, Frei 230

Pacific architecture 64, 70
Pacific region 68–70
Packwood, Nicholas 181
Palladio, Andrea 173
Pallasmaa, Juhani 87–8, 91, 94
Pamuk, Orhan 22
panoramas, and property value 105, 110
Parables for the Virtual 63
patterns, emergent 25
people in crowds 18–20
performance design 67, 125
peripheral perception 94
Perlstein, Jeff 185
Pirilä, Marja 89
place, dynamics of 135
place identity, and virtuality 181
plane of immanence 208, 209–10
Planet of Slums 131
plateau, a 24
plate glass 33
Plato 224–5
play 220–1
Pleasant Moment in Time: M.U.D. as Ambient Information and Cognition System, A **44–6, 59–61**
political activism 181, 188, 191–2 *see also* activism
politics, and blogging 188
polygons 224
Ponifasio, Lemi 68–9
Portugali, Nili 165
postmodernism 166
potential, and action 200, 204–8, 211–12
power: constituted/constituent 204, 213; desire for 172; flows of 131; military/commercial 151; State 205; virtual 209
praxis, term 64
Present Day Architecture, On 102
preserved sites 170
Prigogine, Ilya 153
property value, and panoramas 105
protected buildings 165, 170
provocative instrument 56
public impression 49
publishing, new methods of 182
Pugin, Augustus W.N. 164–5
Pure War 152–3

Index

PXL 56
pyramids, Egyptian 1, 2

Q1 102, 106, **107**, 111, 113
Queensland 99–100

real estate, Gold Coast 105, 109
Reclaim the Streets (RTS) 191
reduction 56
Refiti, Albert 68–9
Reflection 106–7, 108
Renaissance 167
repetition 149, 170
resistance, and architecture 199, 200, 213, 231–2
resistant networks 183
reterritorializing 194
reverie 88
revivalism 164
rhythm 223–5, 233n.24
Right to the City charter 190
Robbe-Grillet, Alain 83–4
Rom-Hoob Market 136–42
routinization 149
RSS (Really Simple Syndication) 182
rua kai 69, 71
Ruskin, John 13
Russian State University of Physical Education (RGUFK) 127, 129
ruthmos 224, 232n.18, 233n.24

Santayana, George 167
Sassen, Saskia 131
Sauvanet, Pierre 223
scale, human 12–13
scales 28–30
schema 224–5
Scherman, Georg 82, 92, 95, 96
Schopenhauer, Arthur 163
sea changers 100, 101
sea, ownership of 48
sea squirt 11–12
Sea world 105
second nature 103–4
security, Thamesport 154
segmentation 204
self organization 130, 202
Semper, Gottfried 7, 8
sense flows 219
shakkei 84, 91
shell, the 3, 7, 8, 10–11
Shigeru Ban 95–6

Shirky, Clay 21
signs, marketing 34
Simondon, Gilbert 210, 211
Simone, AbdouMaliq 132
Siva Nataraja 227
Skogskyrkogården 92, 94
Skygarden 113
slime mould 16–17
slow-flow 94
smart mobs' 179, 195n.8
smooth flow 203, 206
smoothness: of flow of power 201; in space of flows 212
smooth space, and space of flows 203–4
social centres 183
social class, and houses 170
social movements, networked 183–5, 191, 194
social networks, in blogosphere 182
social organism 8, 9, 10
social thought 17–18
Society of Mind, The 17
Some Assembly Required 199
Sorkin, Michael 199
Sounds House 73–4
space: of common sense 139; of the in-between 71; of openness 69; production of 142; as temporal zone 63; of total flow 182
space of flows 78–9, 135, 148, 149, 157, 219, 228–32; architecture as 207; efficiency of 155; smoothness in 212; and smooth space 203–4
Spaces of Freedom 180, 192–3, 194–5
spaces of resistance 183, 194
spatial flow 63–4
spatial practices, Oceanic 69
Speed and Politics 151
Spinoza, Baruch 15, 23
stability 153
stabilization of flow 222
Stalder, Felix 212
standstill 226–28
steel 32
steel frames 31–2, 33
Stiegler, Bernard 6
stone 32
street blogging 180 *see also* bloggers/blogs
subjectivity 20
subjugated knowledges 167–8
sukiya-architecture 90

Index

summer cottage, Sweden 81–6, 88–94, 96, **97**, 98n.26
Sunland Group 112
supply chain management 149, 150
Surfers Paradise 109
Swedish summer cottage 81–6, 88–94, 96, **97**, 98n.26
Swedish Welfare State standard 94

tactility 84
Tadashi Ogawa 96
Tanizaki, Junichiro 83
teahouse, Japanese 87–8, 91
tea plantation, Boh 25
temporal discontinuity 166
temporal flows 63, 66, 161
temporal modulations 66
temporal zone, space as 63
tent poetics 94
Terunobu, Fujimori 95
Tetsuro Watsuji 88
thinking 24
Thoreau, Henry 3–4
Thousand Plateaus, The 209–10
time 161, 162, 163, 165, 166, 226–28
time-space relationship 63, 153, 155, 157
Tokatea 65–8, 70–1, 74–8, 80n.35
Topkapi bazaar 123–6
total flow 180
Total Logistics Concept (TLC) 150, 154
trading areas, informal 130
Très Grande Bibliothèque 200
Tschumi, Bernard 67
tunnel effects 156
turbo architecture 122–3
Turing, Alan 16

Universal Review 5
urban identity formation 105–6
urbanism, and flow 201–3
Urban Network Coast 52
urban planning 50–1f.

va 68, 79, 80n.21
Van Creveld, Martin 150
van der Hak, Bregtje 202
Villa Hill 82
Virilio, Paul 150, 152, 157
virtual community 182
virtual crowd 21
virtual identities 181
virtuality, and place identity 181
virtual power 209
virtual public spheres 19, 180
visual blogs 183
Vitruvius Britannicus 170

wa 64, 68, 71, 79, 80n.21
wabi sabi 91
Wallenstein, Sven-Olov 90
Ware, Isaac 170
War in the Age of Intelligent Machines 150
Waterhouse, Alfred 7
Watkin, David 163
Watsuji, Tetsuro 88
Wave, The 108
weave 219
weblogs 182
Weiss, Srdjan Jovanović 122
whare 70, 71
When Furniture is Talking, How Can You Sleep? 22
Wild Girl of Chalons 14–15
Woodland Cemetery 92
Woody, Hazel and Little Pip 81, **82**
word fold 219
World Congress of Architecture 123
world economy 54–6

Yoko Ono 96
Yoshimoto, Banana 94
youth activists 192, 193

zone of indiscernibility 107
Zui-Ki-Tei 87